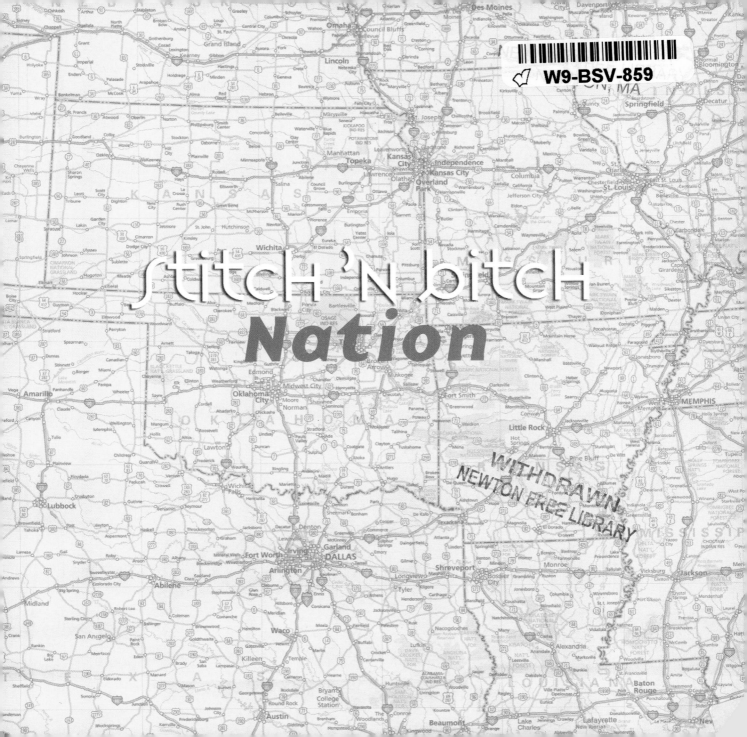

stitch 'n bitch
Nation

stitch 'N bitch
Nation

BY DEBBIE STOLLER

Fashion Photography by Karen Pearson   *Illustrations by Adrienne Yan*

WORKMAN PUBLISHING · NEW YORK

Dedication

For Shadow, my little bear

Art direction and design: Janet Vicario

Cover photography: Karen Pearson

Workman books are available at special discounts when purchased in bulk for premiums and sales promotions as well as for fund-raising or educational use. Special editions or book excerpts can also be created to specification. For details, contact the Special Sales Director at the address below.

Workman Publishing Company, Inc.
708 Broadway
New York, NY 10003-9555
www.workman.com

Printed in the United States of America

First printing: October 2004

10 9 8 7 6 5 4 3 2 1

Acknowledgments

More than a hundred people were involved in the production of this book—from those who reviewed their favorite yarn stores, to the folks who contributed their favorite knitting tips, to the Stitch 'n Bitch members who sent in profiles of their groups—and I am deeply indebted to them all. But I owe my greatest appreciation to the amazing knitters whose innovative designs are included here, and who deserve the most credit for making this book what it is.

The past six months have been a whirlwind of late nights and working weekends as I raced to meet a series of tight deadlines. I never would have survived it, and this book wouldn't have come together, if it hadn't been for the hard work, support, and love of the following people and one dog.

At Workman Publishing, I'd like to thank Ruth Sullivan, my meticulous and tireless editor, and designer Janet Vicario, for putting so much time and care into this book, and, of course, Peter Workman, for giving me the opportunity to continue stitchin' and bitchin'.

I am grateful to Leora Kahn for organizing such a fabulous photo shoot, as well as Ellen Silverstein for picking such stylin' clothes and Amy Schiappa for creating such purty hair and makeup, as well as photographer Karen Pearson for taking the beautiful shots. The super-cute models—Kelly Alpin, Melinda Ball, Kate Edwards, Brian McCormack, Joy Merrifield, and Aja Spears—also played a big part in making these projects look their best. I am so glad that Adrienne Yan was available to make such awesome illustrations for the book once again. If you ever want to know what Adrienne looks like, just look at the girls she draws: most of them look just like her!

I'd like to thank technical editors Kate Watson and Kiki Wolfson for plodding through the jungle of numbers in these patterns and weeding out errors. Their fastidious attention to detail on these patterns was remarkable. Many thanks go out to production editor Anne Cherry, to copyeditor Judit Bodnar, and to Jarrod Dyer, Michael Fusco, and Philip Hoffhines for technical support. I am very thankful for the great job that Colleen Kane did on editing the Stitch 'n Bitch group descriptions and Local Yarn Store reviews, and I also want to give a shout-out to my brother, Peter

Stoller, the Linus to my Lucy, who helped me in the early stages of this book by sending out contracts and contacting yarn companies on my behalf.

I am, once again, so very appreciative of the members of the NYC Stitch 'n Bitch who were willing to lend a helping hand to get some of these projects knit, including Jill Astmann, Jackie Broner, Kimberli MacKay, Claudine Monique, Katy Moore, Diana Parrington, Karola Wright, and especially my speed-knitters, Eileene Coscolluela and Marney Andersen. Y'all's willingness to help out a knitting sister in need is so moving to me.

Big sloppy kisses go out to the lovely ladies of *BUST* magazine for cutting me some slack when this book pulled me away from my responsibilities at the mag, and especially to my co-publisher, Laurie Henzel, for being the best business partner a girl could ever hope for.

I want to thank Johanna and Bernard Stoller for their unwavering confidence in me, and especially Michael Uman for always helping me to step away from the cliff, even when the knit hits the fan. His love and support have kept me sane for the past nine years and three books, and I am grateful.

Finally, I wish to thank my seventeen-year-old blind dog, Shadow, one of the sweetest creatures ever to walk the planet, for teaching me more about unconditional love and trust than I ever thought possible. He's brought so much joy to my life in the twelve years while he's been my roommate and companion, and there hasn't been a thing I've knit that didn't have a little bit of him woven into it. As he battles cancer and nears his final days, I know I'll miss him forever.

CONTENTS

PART I
I Knit It My Way /1
HOW TO MAKE ANY KNITTING PATTERN WORK WITH YOUR YARN,
YOUR GAUGE, YOUR BODY, AND YOUR STYLE

PART II
The Patterns /31

SCARVES, HATS, AND MITTENS

Scarf It Up
 Yo, Drop It! /34
 Wavy Gravy /36
 Mom's Sophisticated Scarf /37
 Warm Fuzzies /39

Butterflies
Are Free /40

Bzzz Hat for
Queen Bees /44

Russian Winter /50

Valentine's Hat and
Mittens /54

Head Huggers: Neckwarmer
and Earwarmer /58

Headline News:
Cabled Newsboy Cap /66

Later 'Gator Mitts /70

Basic Cable /74

SWEATERS AND PONCHOS

Jesse's Flames /78

Fairly Easy Fair Isle /82

Razor's Edge /86

London Calling /92

Flower Power /96

Lucky: Clover Lace Wrap /102

Spiderweb Capelet
/110

That Seventies
Poncho /114

Bam 13 /118

SEXY SUMMER KNITS

Ultra Femme /122

Sexie /126

Mud Flap Girl Tank Top /132

Quick and Dirty: 2-Needle
Fishnet Stockings /136

Itsy-Bitsy Teeny-Weeny Purple
Polka-Dot Tankini /140

Accidentally On Purpose:
Drop Stitch Vest /144

Totally Tubular:
Miniskirt/Boob
 Tube /148

The Patterns (CONTINUED)

LEGS, BAGS, AND BEYOND

Candy Stripers: Messenger
and Laptop Bags /152

Letter Have It /158

Poster Boy /164

Om Yoga Mat Bag /168

Saucy Tote /174

Going Out with a Bag /178

The Bead Goes On: Beaded
Wrist Cuffs /182

Roller Girl Legwarmers /186

Felted Furry Foot Warmers /192

Hurry Up Spring
Armwarmers /196

Belt de Jour /200

BABIES, DOGS, AND CATS

Li'l Devil Pants /204

Baby's First Tattoo /208

Bunny Hat /212

One-Hour Baby Booties /216

Casey's Coat /222

Catwarming Set /226

GIFTS AND MORE

Mobile Monsters /230

Knit Your Own Rock Star /234

Knit My Ride: Fuzzy Dice and
Steering Wheel Cover /240

Chill Pillows /246

Two for Tea /250

PART III
The Knitty-Gritty
A REFRESHER COURSE /253

PART IV
Resources
YARN STORE NATION /270
YARN SUPPLIERS /282
INDEX /283
KNITTING NOTES /290

I Knit It My Way

HOW TO MAKE ANY KNITTING PATTERN WORK WITH YOUR YARN, YOUR GAUGE, YOUR BODY, AND YOUR STYLE

W hen *Stitch 'n Bitch: The Knitter's Handbook* was published last year, I was both proud and relieved. I and so many others had put so much work into it, and now, finally, it was out there in the world. Seeing it displayed in bookstores across the country was exhilarating, but it was even more exciting the first time I saw a project made from the book posted on the Internet. Soon I began spotting all sorts of projects from *Stitch 'n Bitch*: knit wrist cuffs, baby hats, baby blankets, kitty hats, and Skully sweaters. People were even showing up at my book signings wearing items they'd made from the book. It was amazing!

Of course, many of these knitters chose their own colors for their projects, and others used entirely different yarn than the pattern called for. Still other brave souls made more extensive alterations to the patterns—from replacing the star motif on the wrist cuffs with little Pacman figures to lengthening the Under the Hoodie sweater so that it was less cropped, making a mini version of Meema's Felted Marsupial Tote for a toddler, shortening the extra-long sleeves on To Dye For, and adding shaping to the loose, oversized Skully sweater.

It was clear that at least a few knitters were ready to look at patterns, not as a be-all and end-all to their knitting projects, but rather as a starting point from which to make their knitting dreams come true. And from the questions and enthusiastic comments about these revised SnB projects that were being posted on knitters' blogs, it seemed that many other Stitch 'n Bitchers were hungry to do the same, if only they knew how.

I also found, unfortunately, that some folks who had completed projects from that first book were less than pleased with their results. One knitter discovered that the Skully sweater was much too loose and oversized for her to wear; yet another, posing in her newly completed Skully, proved that the sweater fit her just fine. So why did one knitter get such unhappy results, while another knitter didn't? I realized that if knitters could figure out from a pattern how a sweater might fit them before they made it, they'd encounter less frustration. Better yet, they'd know how to pick the right size to knit from the list of available sizes.

In fact, it seemed that all across the country, a nation of knitters—both brand new and more seasoned—were beginning to get restless. They were crying out for knowledge. They wanted to have the power to really understand what it was they were making, so that they could take their knitting to the next level, and make changes if they wanted to. They yearned to be free to use a yarn of their own choosing, whether or not it matched the gauge stipulated in the pattern. They longed to be able to make simple alterations to patterns—lengthening a body here, shortening a sleeve there. And they were itching to make projects that would fit and flatter their bodies. They didn't want to spend countless hours working on sweaters only to have them be more appropriate for an elephant or an Olson twin than themselves.

In this chapter I'll try to arm you with some of that knowledge. I'll help you understand the secret language of knitting patterns and tell you a few things you need to think about when you're choosing a different yarn for a project. I'll show you how—with the miracle of math—you can rewrite a pattern to use thicker or thinner yarn than the pattern calls for or make simple alterations so that it will fit you better. I'll even explain the mystery of pattern fit and sizing, so that you can choose the correct size to knit from the get-go. Finally, I'll teach you how to change particular details of a sweater—like switch a turtleneck to a V-neck or replace a ribbed edge with a rolled one. Eventually, you'll be changing so many things about a pattern—using thicker yarn, shortening the sleeves, popping on a crew neck, lengthening the body, adding a different edging, replacing a picture of a rock star with a picture of your doggie—that it may become an entirely different project altogether. In fact, you may have changed it so much that you will have practically designed your *own* sweater. With a bit more practice, and a bit more willingness to take the leap and depart from following patterns to the letter, you'll be ready to do just that.

Very few of the patterns in this book were made by folks who are knitwear designers by trade. Most of them were contributed by knitters who were just brave (or stubborn) enough to get an idea into their head for a project and not let go until they had figured out how to make it. Soon you'll be one of them too, or maybe you already are. And perhaps it will be one of your patterns that will appear in a future *Stitch 'n Bitch* book, for others to knit, and, of course, change completely to suit their whim and fantasy.

So what are you waiting for? It's time to get your knit on.

Decode the Code

HOW TO UNDERSTAND A KNITTING PATTERN

When you first start knitting, a pattern can seem a lot like a pirate's map pointing the way to buried treasure. It promises to give you every bit of information you need—from the brand, color, and quantity of yarn to buy to specific step-by-step knitting directions, which, if followed exactly, will lead you to the treasure: that sweater you've been drooling over in the book or magazine. And it may also seem that unless you follow the directions exactly, you run the risk of landing in quicksand or at least winding up with something other than that longed-for garment.

But after you've knit enough patterns, you discover something else: Following the directions doesn't always take you to the treasure. You may very well end up with the same sweater the model is wearing, but you didn't realize it would look baggy on you. Or you may decide that the fitted cropped sweater which made the model look so cute and sassy makes you look short and dumpy. How much nicer would it be to foresee these problems and knit the sweater into the exact, flattering shape you actually want?

Alternately, maybe you really like the shape of the mohair hoodie the model is wearing, but you already have a large bag of ribbony rayon you'd like to use. Or perhaps you're a vegan, and would prefer to knit something out of acrylic instead of wool. Finally, suppose you just bought a giant load of gorgeous sport-weight cashmere blend yarn on eBay, and you want to use it to knit up a sweater that calls for worsted-weight yarn. What you really want to do is change the pattern so it will work with *your* yarn. Is that so wrong?

I'm here to tell you that any and all of these things can be done. That's because a pattern is not at all like a cryptic pirate's map. Instead, in every pattern the designers have laid bare, for all to see, exactly how the fabric for the sweater is to be made. They have included explicit details about every tiny curve and inch-by-inch information about the exact size it will turn out to be. And they won't mind a bit if you use their instructions as a guideline for working out a sweater that will fit you a bit better, or be a bit longer, or narrower, or in an entirely different gauge yarn than they call for. In fact, they would probably be thrilled to have you do that. Once you understand how to read all the clues that are written out for you in each and every pattern, you'll realize that it's much more than just a way to get to the buried treasure: It offers you the keys to the entire friggin' city!

In order to make changes to a pattern, you need to really understand it—not just the stitches or the instructions, but what makes it tick. Every pattern is jam-packed with numbers: measurements in inches, numbers of stitches to cast on and decrease or increase, and how many rows to knit. But why are those numbers there? What do they mean? How does the jumble of numbers in your pattern relate to the finely detailed pullover in the photo? In this next section, I'm going to walk you through a few simple patterns so that you can get to know them from the inside out. Before we begin, though, you might want to put on your propeller beanie: There's lots of math involved here. It's simple math, for the most part, but there's plenty of it. I believe it was talking Barbie who so famously said, "Math is hard," but pay her no mind. Women have been relying on math in their knitting for centuries, and these days, knitting is even used in certain elementary school programs to help kids understand arithmetic. If you were born with the math gene, have fun with the next section. And if you were born without it, just remember that math is your friend. It's the secret code of all knitting, and it is the shared language that all knitters speak. In fact, math is as powerful and magical as any kind of witchcraft.

CONTESTANT NUMBER ONE
A Simple Scarf

Let's take a look at the pattern below for a knit scarf. How can you know what this scarf will look like before you go ahead and knit it? Is it a skinny, '80s-style scarf, or is it wide? Will it be long enough to wrap around your neck twice or does it fit like an ascot? You can tell it has stripes—the name gives that away—but are they narrow or wide? The answers to all these questions lie in the pattern itself.

The key piece of information in any knitting pattern is the **gauge**. Most patterns will give a gauge over 4 inches. The first thing you want to do when reading a pattern is to calculate the gauge of stitches and rows per *inch*. This information can work like a decoder ring to help you understand everything else that's going on in a pattern. Here's how:

STITCHES PER INCH = NUMBER OF STITCHES
DIVIDED BY SWATCH WIDTH

For example, in this scarf pattern, the designer tells me she has to knit 28 stitches in the pattern to get a swatch of fabric 4" wide.

WHITE STRIPES SCARF

Materials

Cuddly Wuddly Cotton (100% cotton)

Color A: 3 skeins Rock Red

Color B: 3 skeins "Meg White"

US 9 (5.5 mm) straight needles

Gauge

28 sts and 15 rows = 4" in st patt

STITCH PATTERN
K3, p3.

DIRECTIONS

With color A, CO 36 sts.

*K with color A in st pattern for 18 rows.

K with color B in st pattern for 18 rows*.

Rep from * to * 5 times more.

List of abbreviations appears on page 32.

I pull out my handy-dandy calculator (no old-school long division for me), divide 28 by 4, and get 7. Okay, so that's my stitches-per-inch gauge: 7.

Next, I figure out my row gauge.

ROWS PER INCH = NUMBER OF ROWS DIVIDED BY SWATCH LENGTH

Here, the designer tells me she has to knit 15 rows to get 4" of fabric.

So, I divide 15 by 4 and get 3.75. I like to keep only one digit after the decimal, so I'll round this up to 3.8. Okay, so 3.8 is my row gauge.

Now, back to that pattern. The designer tells me to start by casting on 36 stitches. I already know that every 7 stitches equals an inch, but just how many inches does that number 36 represent? In other words, how many times does 7 (the stitches per single inch) go into 36? That's easy: just divide 36 by 7, and you get 5.1428571429. This is a bit unwieldy, so let's just say the scarf is gonna be about 5" wide—a nice size for a scarf.

Next, the pattern says to work 18 rows of color A. How long is that? Easy, peasy: Take 18 and divide it by the row gauge, which was 3.8. 18 ÷ 3.8 = 4.73. So each stripe is about 5" long. The pattern tells me to make this two-stripe color pattern once, and then 5 times more; in other words, I have to do it 6 times altogether. One stripe is 5", so two stripes are 10". Knitting those two stripes 6 times would result in a scarf that's 60" (or 5 feet) long. I will definitely be able to wrap this cute stripy scarf around my neck and have both ends hanging down to keep me warm.

We've used our decoder ring—the stitches per inch and rows per inch—and figured out what's going on in this pattern. It's all a bit like dissecting a frog: kinda gross, kinda nauseating, but extremely informative. It's super important to understand how things are put together if you ever want to change them.

CONTESTANT NUMBER 2
A Straightforward Sweater

If you want to add a room to a house or remodel the kitchen, you need to be able to understand the blueprints. It's the same thing with altering a sweater: To lengthen a sleeve, change a neckline, or shorten the body, you need to understand the pattern. Sweater patterns often include what's called a "schematic"—a blueprint-like line drawing that gives you the exact measurements, in inches, of the completed pieces of knit fabric. So, unlike with the "White Stripes Scarf," you don't need the stitch and row gauge to picture what you're making: It's all laid out for you. But you'll still need your decoder ring—that business about the stitches and rows per inch that you just learned—to help you understand what's really going on in each of those pieces, and it will be the key to changing anything in the pattern.

Let's take a quick stroll through a typical sweater pattern just to see how this works. But I have to warn you: The following section contains plenty of twists and turns, so hang on tight. When we come out on the other side, you might be a bit dizzy, but you'll be a changed knitter. Never again will you blindly increase, decrease, and cast on stitches just because someone told you to; you'll actually understand why you're doing those things, and that knowledge will allow you to do things differently. May the force be with you.

Here is a pattern for a baby sweater:

DIRECTIONS

BACK

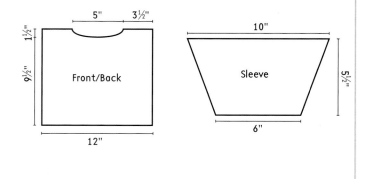

Ⓐ CO 42 sts.

K 2 rows in seed st.

K in St st until piece measures 9½" from beg, ending with a WS row.

Ⓑ Next row: K16, BO 10 sts, k16.

Working both sides at the same time, BO 1 st each neck edge EOR 4 times.

BO remaining 12 sts.

FRONT

Work same as for back.

Ⓒ #### SLEEVES (MAKE 2)

CO 21 sts.

K 2 rows in seed st.

Cont in St st, inc1 st each side EOR 2 times, then every 4th row 5 times (35 sts).

Cont in St st until sleeve measures 5½".

FINISHING

Sew shoulder seams.

Sew sleeves to front and back, beg and ending 5" down from shoulder seam on each side.

Sew side and sleeve seam.

Size

12 months

Finished chest = 24"

Materials

3 skeins Funky Monkey Chunky Yarn (80% merino wool/20% acrylic; 1.75 oz/137 yds)

US 9 (5.5 mm) straight needles

Gauge

14 sts and 20 rows = 4" in St st

List of abbreviations appears on page 32.

According to the pattern, the gauge for the sweater is 14 stitches and 20 rows per 4".

Before we do anything else, we need to get out that decoder ring. In this case, the stitches per inch = 3.5 (14 stitches ÷ 4" swatch). And the rows per inch = 5 (20 rows ÷ 4" swatch).

Now, let's take on this sweater piece by piece.

Ⓐ THE BACK

The pattern says that to knit the back of this sweater, you start by casting on 42 stitches. If you take that and divide it by your stitches per inch, you should get the width of half of the sweater. Sure enough, 42 ÷ 3.5 = 12.

Next, the pattern says to knit 2 rows in seed stitch, and then to continue in stockinette stitch until the back measures 9½" from the beginning. It does not tell you how many rows to knit to get there, and that's one of the truths about most patterns: row gauge is not as important as stitch gauge.

Ⓑ THE NECK

After you have a 9½"-long piece of fabric, the pattern tells you to knit 16 stitches, bind off the center 10 stitches, and then knit another 16 stitches. Next, you have to bind off 1 stitch at each neck edge on every other row 4 times—that eliminates 8 stitches altogether. Thus, the neck, which you created by binding off 10 stitches and then decreasing another 8 stitches, is 18 stitches wide. According to the stitch gauge, that makes it 18 ÷ 3.5, or 5.14" wide. Sounds kinda like 5" to me.

In fact, all those numbers check out with the schematic. It's right, we're right, and all's right with the world (or at least with the pattern).

The back of the sweater is done. For the front, knit another piece just like it.

Ⓒ THE SLEEVES

Now that we're at the sleeves, things are about to diverge from the straight and narrow. I just said that row gauge was less important than stitch gauge in most patterns, but that's not to say that row gauge doesn't matter to the pattern designer—especially when it comes to sleeves or other areas with a good number of increases or decreases. She cares about row gauge truly, madly, and deeply, and she's very carefully worked out just how many stitches you need to increase, and over how many rows, so those sleeves don't wind up so long that you can't find the baby's hands. These numbers have been calculated with the beady-eyed precision of a child who is being forced to share half her candy with her brother.

You can see from the schematic that this sleeve gets quite a bit wider between the wrist, where it begins, and the shoulder, where it will be attached to the body of the sweater. Let's see how this is done.

The instructions for the sleeves say "CO 21 stitches."

Okay, that's easy: 21 stitches ÷ 3.5 stitches per inch = 6". The bottom of the sleeve is going to be 6" wide, and that checks out with the schematic.

Next, the directions say to knit 2 rows in seed stitch, and then to continue in stockinette stitch, increasing 1 stitch at each side every other row 2 times, and every 4th row 5 times (35 sts)—so you'll end up with 35 stitches. Then it says to continue in stockinette until the piece measures 5½".

So what's going on with those increases? Why is it written so enigmatically, with all the "every other row

2 times and every 4th row 5 times"? If I keep saying "there's no place like home" while I'm doing them, will I end up in Kansas?

Well, actually, there is something a bit like magic going on there, and I'll explain. First off, the designer wants a sleeve that starts off 6" (21 stitches) wide, and ends up 10" (35 stitches) wide. She also wants that sleeve to be exactly 5½" long, so it can fit that tiny arm correctly. But how does she get from the 21 stitches, at the wrist, to the 35 stitches, at the shoulder, in only 5"? (Remember she doesn't start increasing the sleeves until after about ½ inch of seed stitch rows.) Since we know the row gauge, we know she has only 25 rows over which to add on those 14 stitches (5" × 5 rows per inch = 25 rows). And, if she is a nice designer, she probably wants to make the increases symmetrically: 1 on each side of the sleeve. She also wants to place them so all the increases are made on the right-side rows, because it's easier to make them on knitted stitches than on purled stitches.

This is where the "every other row 2 times and every 4th row 5 times" mumbo-jumbo comes in. The designer has done some fancy-ass math, and figured out that this is the prettiest way to make those increases work out evenly along the sleeve. She may have used trial and error till she got to these numbers, working out the sleeves on graph paper till the numbers worked. She may have used something called "the magic formula" to work out the nice increases (there is such a thing, really, see page 18). Hell, she may have just punched the numbers into some knitting software she had. Whatever the case, she's sharing the fruits of her calculations with you in her pattern.

I'm just pointing out the fancy footwork that goes into placing increases or decreases in a knitting pattern, because this is one of the places where altering a pattern can get a little hairy. In the next few sections I'll show you a number of ways to deal with this when making changes, and if you can keep your eyes on the prize and your finger on the calculator, you'll be sure to get through it.

The Li'l Dumplin' Baby Sweater is simpler than many patterns you may knit, but not by much. All patterns are based on this business of gauge, from the cast-on to the bind-off and all the increasing and decreasing in between. And now that you understand the real knitty-gritty of all knitting patterns, the power is yours. You can change the gauge. You can change the shape. You can do whatever you want.

The Gauge of Reason
REPLACING ONE YARN WITH ANOTHER OF THE SAME GAUGE

the most common alteration to any pattern, and one you may already have done, is to replace the yarn the pattern calls for with a yarn of your own choosing. Now that you know how absolutely dependent each line of a pattern is on that decoder ring—the gauge—you can also understand why replacing yarn with another *of the same gauge* means that you'll be able to follow the pattern exactly as written. But figuring out what yarn to use as a replacement can be a little tricky.

The first challenge is to find yourself some yarn that knits up to the same gauge as called for in the pattern. But where do you begin? There are thousands of yarns out there; do you just choose one willy-nilly and start swatching like mad?

Well, of course not. The first thing to do is figure out what weight the yarn in the pattern is, then try replacing it with a *yarn of the same weight*. The problem is, most patterns don't tell you what weight yarn was used. They do give you the gauge, though, from which you can probably figure this out.

For instance, a pattern may state at the top:

Materials

Loonyland Quikstuff (70% wool, 30% acrylic; 3 oz/135 yds)

8 skeins Flamin' Flamingo

Gauge

12 sts and 17 rows = 4" in St st using size 10½ needles

Just look up that gauge on the Craft Yarn Council's table on the next page, which gives yarn weight standards and categorizes yarn into six weights.

As you can see, there is quite a bit of variety here. "Superfine," for instance, is any yarn whose recommended gauge is between 27 and 32 stitches per 4", knit on size 1, 2, or 3 needles. Although it's awfully nice of the Craft Yarn Council to have come up with these categories, it doesn't do us much good if the yarn companies don't label their stuff with this information—and most of them don't.

Still, with a bit of detective work, you can figure out the weight of the yarn in the pattern. We'll start by look-

ing at our gauge again. In this case, the gauge is 12 stitches per 4", which would place this yarn right into category 5: bulky-weight yarn. We're lucky that this gauge is given over stockinette stitch; if it had been given over a pattern stitch—especially ribbing, which pulls the stitches closer together—the gauge would not be so useful. The bulky yarn in this pattern might very well knit up to 16 stitches over 4" when it's knit in a k1, p1 rib, but that certainly doesn't mean that it's suddenly transformed itself into a category 4, medium-weight yarn.

But all is not lost. If the gauge is given over a pattern stitch, just look at the needle sizes suggested in the pattern to get a sense of the yarn's weight. In this case, the needle is 10½, which is again consistent with this yarn falling into category 5, bulky.

When determining a yarn's weight by looking at gauge and needle size, you also need to be aware of the texture of the finished piece. Take a close look at the completed project, or as good a look as you can get from a photo. Does the yarn seem like it's been knit to the recommended gauge, yielding a nice, solid fabric that you can't see through? Or does it look almost netlike, similar to a mesh, so that if the model hadn't worn a T-shirt under that sweater you'd see her bra? If it's loose, then the yarn was likely knit at a larger gauge than is recommended for that yarn, meaning that the designer used needles quite a bit thicker than would normally be used with this weight of yarn so that she could achieve an open, airy texture. Thus, neither the gauge nor the needle size given will help you in your quest to figure out this yarn's weight. What's a knitter to do?

Well, you could head over to your LYS, find the yarn in question (assuming that they carry it), and read the

Standard Yarn Weight System

Yarn Weight Symbol & Category Names	⓵ SUPER FINE	⓶ FINE	⓷ LIGHT	⓸ MEDIUM	⓹ BULKY	⓺ SUPER BULKY
Type of Yarns in Category	Sock, Fingering, Baby	Sport, Baby	DK, Light Worsted	Worsted, Afghan, Aran	Chunky, Craft, Rug	Bulky, Roving
Knit Gauge Range in Stockinette Stitch to 4 inches	27–32 sts	23–26 sts	21–24 sts	16–20 sts	12–15 sts	6–11 sts
Recommended Needle in Metric Size Range	2.25–3.25mm	3.25–3.75mm	3.75–4.5mm	4.5–5.5mm	5.5–8mm	8mm and larger
Recommended Needle U.S. Size Range	1 to 3	3 to 5	5 to 7	7 to 9	9 to 11	11 and larger

ball band to find the recommended gauge and needle size, and thereby figure out its weight. But, of course, you don't have to actually leave the house to find info about a ball of yarn. Today we have the Internet, and if you can track down information about old classmates and ex-boyfriends on the Web, you can certainly get the lowdown on some yarn. Just enter the full name of the yarn you want to know about in your favorite search engine. Yarn stores that carry the yarn will pop up (possibly even the company that makes the yarn), and at least one of them will list the recommended gauge and needle size. With that info in hand, you can finally figure out the weight of that darn yarn.

SWATCH WATCH
What a Gauge Swatch Can Tell You About Your Yarn (Besides Its Gauge)

Of course, the main way to figure out what's going on with your yarn, and whether it will make a good replacement, is to really get to know it. And you do that by making a swatch. After all, yarn can look just so cute in its balled-up state, but you really don't know what it can grow up to be unless you knit up a bit of it and find out. Some yarn shops even have sample skeins of the yarn they carry so you can swatch some up in a corner of the store and get an idea of what the yarn does before you take it home and marry it.

To make a nice swatch, begin with the needle size suggested on the ball band and cast on one and a half times the number of stitches suggested for a 4" swatch. You need to make a sizable swatch at least 6" wide if you really want to get a sense of the yarn. Knit a couple of rows in garter stitch, then continue in stockinette till you have about 3" of fabric. Stop. Count how many stitches are in a 2"-wide area smack in the center of the swatch. If all you get is one leg of the stitch at the end, count it as half a stitch. Measure another 2" spot; count again. If you keep getting different numbers, take an average. Then double that to get the gauge for 4". If you have fewer stitches in that 4" swatch than the pattern requires, go up a needle size and swatch some more. If you have too many stitches, go down a size. Work another row of garter stitch before you start the new section, so you can keep them separated. Knit another 3" of stockinette and measure again.

Now you can begin learning about your yarn's personality. What is its "hand"? Meaning, how does it feel in your hand? Lay it over your fist or a can of soda. How does it drape? Will a sweater made out of it hang nicely on your body or is it so stiff that it will stand away from you like a cardboard box? Feel up your swatch. Does it have some "body" or is it completely spineless and loose? How much elasticity does it seem to have? Is the yarn so slippery and drapey that the lovely poncho you want to make will hang on you like so much wet hair? If it's very colorful or slubby or furry, you may realize that the busyness of the colors will obscure all those interesting (and time-consuming) knit-and-purl patterns or cables that are the coolest thing about the sweater, and you may decide to save this yarn for something knit in plain stockinette. Or maybe, hopefully, you'll think, Hot damn, I love this yarn and I can't wait to make this sweater out of it—it's perfect.

GOODNESS GRACIOUS, GREAT BALLS OF FIBER
How Much Yarn Do You Need?

Once you've decided on your replacement yarn, it's time to figure out how much of the stuff you'll need to make the sweater (or, if it's yarn you already have on hand, whether you have enough of it). This is super easy to do. Just look at the number of yards of yarn the original pattern calls for, and figure out how many balls of your replacement yarn would be required to yield that many yards of yarn. In the Loonyland example, every 3-ounce ball of Quikstuff contains 135 yards, and for your size, the pattern says you'll need 8 balls of it. That means you need at least 1,080 yards of Quikstuff to make this sweater (135 yards per ball × 8 balls = 1,080 yards).

Now let's say the yarn you want to use, Marvelous Munchkin, is sold in 50-gram balls that contain only 60 yards of yarn apiece. If you're in a car traveling at 60 miles an hour on your way to your LYS, how many balls of Marvelous Munchkin will you need to buy when you get there? Well, this math problem is no problem at all: You just divide the total number of yards of yarn needed by the yards per ball of the replacement yarn. In this case, that's 1,080 ÷ 60 = 18. So, you whip out your credit card, take home 18 balls of the Munchkin yarn, and get down to the business of making your new dream sweater.

Gauging a Reaction
KNITTING A PATTERN USING A DIFFERENT GAUGE YARN

Knitting a sweater out of a different yarn of the same gauge is easy because you can use the pattern exactly as written. But sometimes you really want to use a yarn that's just not going to work at that gauge. You may have chosen a yarn that you thought would knit up to the same gauge as the one called for in the pattern, but it turns out that in order to get that gauge, you have to knit it on such small needles, it makes the fabric really tight. You quickly realize that if you knit the sweater at this gauge, you'll end up with a garment that could stand up by itself. You've tried larger needles and found that this gives you a much nicer, drapier fabric, but, of course, that also gives you an entirely different gauge.

Or maybe there's a sweater you want to knit that calls for such lightweight yarn you just know it will take too long for you to knit it. You want to knit it in a bit heavier yarn, say a worsted rather than a sport-weight, and you've already swatched up the yarn and know that your sweater would hang just as nicely using this yarn.

Since you know how important gauge is to any pattern, you already know that changing the gauge is gonna require a good number of changes to the pattern. You also know you can do it. With some time, and a calculator, you can knit whatever you want in whichever yarn you want.

Let's start with a simple alteration, by considering a super easy scarf pattern:

SCARF FACE

Materials

3 skeins Free Woolly (100% wool; 4 oz/350 yds)

Gauge

24 sts and 28 rows = 4" in garter st

DIRECTIONS

CO 42 st, k in garter st till piece measures 50", BO.

Like most scarf patterns, this one doesn't give you a schematic, but you can tell that this pattern is going to make a scarf that's exactly 7" wide by 50". (You know it's 7" because the designer tells you she gets 4" to every 24 stitches, which is a gauge of 6 stitches to the inch; since she's casting on 42 stitches, and 42 ÷ 6 = 7".)

Now, let's say you want to knit this in some yarn that's got a different gauge—say, an acrylic yarn that gives you 18 stitches and 24 rows per 4" in garter stitch.

First you need to get your decoder ring: In this case, for the acrylic yarn, that's 4.5 stitches per inch (18 ÷ 4 = 4.5) and 6 rows per inch (24 ÷ 4 = 6). Since you want a scarf that's 7" wide, you just multiply your stitches per inch by the number of inches for the width of the scarf: 4.5 × 7 = 31.5. Since you can't cast on 31.5 stitches, you'll round it up to 32 stitches and call it a day.

For the next part, the pattern tells you to knit in garter stitch till the scarf measures 50". Well, guess what? That's just what you're gonna do. There's no decreasing, no increasing, nothing special that happens in this pattern on any special row, so you can just knit the light fantastic and put your dang calculator away for the time being. That's that: You've recalculated your first pattern. Good times.

THE GAUGE OF CONSENT
Dealing with Pattern Repeats

Now let's take a look at that White Stripes ribbed scarf pattern we dissected awhile ago (p. 6). This scarf was knit in a k3, p3 rib that had a gauge of 28 stitches and 15 rows per 4". Once we decoded the pattern, we discovered that the scarf was 5" wide and 60" long, with 5" stripes of alternating colors.

Let's say you want to do it in a thinner yarn that gives you 32 stitches and 24 rows to 4". Your decoder ring tells you that means you get 8 stitches to the inch and 6 rows per inch. You might think you just multiply 8 (the stitches per inch) by 5 (the width of the scarf), get the answer 40, and cast on 40 stitches and start knitting.

But you'd run into a problem, because that ribbing pattern (k3, p3) is based on a 6-stitch repeat, and that's why the pattern designer so thoughtfully told you to cast on 36 stitches—36 is a multiple of 6.

If you cast on 40, you'll innocently knit and purl along 6 times, and then, after knitting 36 stitches, you'll go knit, knit, knit, purl, OH NO! You'll have run out of stitches, and you won't have finished off your purty ribbing pattern!

Don't panic. You have options. One of them is to say, "Screw the ribbing pattern." So what if you have one lone stitch at the end that doesn't get to make a whole rib? Don't worry about it, just knit away.

Another option is to split the difference: Instead of leaving those 4 stitches at the end of your row, where they'll be hanging out possibly looking all kinds of wrong, why don't you stick 2 of them at the beginning of your row and 2 at the end?

Or you could just add another 2 stitches to your cast-on, making it 42, then do your k3, p3 rib according to the pattern. The scarf may be a bit wider than the one the designer envisioned, but what the hey.

Of course, which options you choose will depend on your own taste and on what it is you're knitting. Adding or subtracting a couple of stitches on a scarf might not matter so much, but doing it on a snug-fitting hat may mean you'll have to give it to your friend's small-headed baby, or, if it's too big, to someone with a Charlie Brown head. In sweater knitting, things can also get sketchy if you're adding extra stitches or taking them away willy-nilly. In those instances, evaluate your options and do what you think is best. It might not matter if your sweater is ½" wider in the front and the back, making it 1" wider all around. On the other hand, you might prefer to have some stitches on either side of your work that don't quite make up an entire pattern repeat, but at least the thing fits right.

GAUGE AGAINST THE MACHINE
Knitting a Sweater in a Different Gauge

Of course, you can also rewrite a pattern for something more complicated than a scarf, using a different gauge. Let's try the baby sweater (p. 8). It was designed using yarn that has a gauge of 14 stitches and 20 rows per 4". But say you've got something really lovely and soft you'd like to use for it that's a bit thinner, and it knits up at 18 stitches and 26 rows per 4".

Now, there are two ways to go about this. One would be to take all the measurements from the schematic—the width of the bottom of the sweater, the length of the sweater, the width and length of the sleeves, the width of the neck—and calculate the number of stitches and rows you'll need in order to knit all those dimensions and shapes. Luckily, there is an easier way to do this: You can just take the numbers in the existing pattern and resize them up or down in the same proportion that your yarn's gauge differs from the pattern's gauge.

The first thing to do is to get your stitch ratio; meaning, the ratio of the stitches per inch of your yarn to the stitches per inch of the pattern's yarn. Here's the formula:

STITCH RATIO = YOUR STITCH GAUGE DIVIDED BY THE PATTERN'S STITCH GAUGE

In this case, the stitch ratio is $18 \div 14 = 1.29$, which you'll round up to 1.3.

One nice thing about the above formula is that it doesn't matter if you're plugging in your gauge per 4" or per 1" or per $6\frac{1}{2}$", as long as the pattern gauge is for the same measurement.

There are a couple of things to notice about the number 1.3. For one thing, it's greater than 1, meaning that you will have to knit all the stitches PLUS MORE to get the same measurement your pattern is calling for. Actually, you already know that, because you had to knit 18 whole tiresome stitches just to get the same 4" that the pattern designer whipped out in a mere 14 stitches.

Seeing what the ratio turns out to be, and whether it makes sense to you, is one way to remember how to calculate this figure. But if you ever have a hard time remembering the order of the numbers, just remember this: As in everything else in life, YOU COME FIRST! It's always YOUR number on the top of the division line, and the pattern designer's gauge at the bottom. YOU COME FIRST, she comes last. You're on top, she's on the bottom. (I mean, who the hell is she, anyway?)

Once you have your stitch ratio, you'll also need to figure out your row ratio. You're a pro at this by now, so I bet you already figured out that:

ROW RATIO = YOUR ROW GAUGE DIVIDED
BY THE PATTERN'S ROW GAUGE

Once again, you come first!

In the example above, the original Li'l Dumplin' pattern called for 20 rows per 4", and your lighter-weight yarn is giving you 30 rows per 4".

So what's your row ratio? It's 30 (your row gauge) divided by 20 (the pattern's row gauge). And here ya go: it's 1.5.

Now, to really get down to modifying that pattern for this new yarn, all you need to do is take your stitch ratio and multiply all the stitches in the pattern to get the new stitch numbers, and take your row ratio and multiply all the rows in the pattern to get the new row numbers. Basically, you're adjusting the horizontal measurements on the pattern using your stitch ratio, and the vertical measurements using your row ratio.

Ⓐ FRONT AND BACK

For the front and back, where it says to CO 42 stitches, multiply that by your stitch ratio. So, you'll cast on $42 \times 1.3 = 54.6$ stitches, which you'll round up to 55 stitches.

Next, you'll knit for $9\frac{1}{2}$", just as the pattern says, in however many rows it takes you to get there, and you'll end on a wrong-side row.

Ⓑ THE NECK

Next, the pattern says to knit 16 stitches, bind off 10 stitches, and knit 16 stitches.

You'll multiply each number by the stitch ratio:
$16 \times 1.3 = 20.8$, round up to 21
$10 \times 1.3 = 13$
$16 \times 1.3 = 20.8$, round up to 21

This means you should knit 21 stitches, BO 13, then knit another 21. Just to check your math, these numbers should add up to all the stitches you have on the needle. And, indeed, $21 + 13 + 21 = 55$, which is how many stitches you cast on to begin with.

Now things get a bit tricky. The pattern says to BO 1 stitch each neck edge every other row 4 times.

We already figured out that this means you have to knit 8 rows, over which you'll be decreasing 8 stitches. Now, let's multiply both of these by your row and stitch ratios:

8 rows (for decreasing) × 1.5 (row ratio) = 12 rows
and
8 stitches (to be decreased) × 1.3 (stitch ratio) = 10.4, round down to 10.

So where the original pattern told you to decrease 8 stitches over 8 rows, you'll need to decrease 10 stitches over 12 rows. How can you do that? Again, it's easy: You'll just bind off 1 stitch each side every other row 5 times, which will use up 10 of those rows, and then knit 2 more rows plain. Done deal.

ⓒ THE SLEEVES

The pattern says to cast on 21 sleeve stitches. Multiplying that by your stitch ratio gives you 21 × 1.3 = 27.3, so you'll cast on 27 stitches.

Then you'll knit 2 rows in seed stitch before continuing with stockinette stitch.

Now, you need to end up with 35 stitches × 1.3, or 45.5, which you can round *down* to 45 (you'll see why in a second). This means you need to go from 21 stitches to 45 stitches—giving you 18

stitches to increase. Since this is an even number, you can make these increases in pairs. (Now you know why we rounded down, instead of up.) But how? You can increase 2 stitches at a time, 9 times.

To figure out how many rows you need to make those increases over, let's go back to the original pattern. It says to increase every other row 2 times, and every 4th row 5 times. In other words, increase 7 times altogether, adding 2 stitches each time, for a total of 14 stitches increased. And it says to make them over 24 rows $(2 \times 2) + (4 \times 5)$.

Multiplying that 24 by your row ratio (24×1.5) gives you 36. Next, take these rows (36) and divide them by the number of increase rows you need to make (9). Or $36 \div 9 = 4$. So, you'll increase 1 stitch on each side of the sleeve every 4 rows, and you'll do it 9 times total.

Unfortunately, many times the division won't work out so neatly. When that happens, just tuck those increase rows here and there as evenly as you can. I told you there was magic involved in getting those numbers in the first place—and if we're gonna muck with magic, we need to use a little fudge. So, let's say you had 10 decrease rows instead of 9 to fit into those 36 rows above. 3 divided by 10 gives you 3.6. Why not just make half of those decreases—5 of them—every 4th row, to use up 20 rows,

Hocus-Pocus

USING THE MAGIC FORMULA TO SPACE INCREASES AND DECREASES EVENLY ALONG A DIAGONAL

A long time ago, during the time of the Greeks, some mathematician with a lot of time on his hands came up with a formula that, thousands of years later, is frequently used by knitters to calculate nice increases and decreases along a diagonal.

I've seen this formula explained in a number of ways, but the one I like best is Maggie Righetti's version, in her wonderful book, *Sweater Design in Plain English*.

Here's my variation on her theme:

Say you have to increase 28 stitches over 91 rows for a sleeve. First, reduce the rows you're working with to the next even number down. So, here we'll make that 91 into 90 rows. Next, realize that since you'll be making one increase at each side of the sleeve, you really only need 14 spaces in the sleeve to make your 28 increases (28 ÷ 2 = 14). Now, divide the number of increases you need to make by the number of rows you have available to you: 90 ÷ 14 = 6.42

Obviously, you can't make those increases every 6.42 rows. You probably would, however, like to make your increases only on your right-side rows, or on the knit side in stockinette stitch. To make that happen, you need to find the first even number that's less than your result, and the first even number that's greater.

In this case, that's 6 and 8. These two numbers are now the number of rows between your increases.

Next, pretend you were going to make all the increases using the lower of these two numbers, and figure out how many rows that would use up. In our case, that would be 6 (the lower even number) × 14 (the number of increase rows we need to make), and the result is 84.

Now, figure out how many rows are left, divide that number by 2, and you'll get the number of times you need to do the larger increase. So, 90 rows − 84 = 6, and 6 divided by 2 is 3. You'll have to increase every 8 rows 3 times.

The number of increases you have left to make is how many times you'll need to increase by the lower number: So, we had 14 increases altogether, and we're doing 3 increases every 8 rows, which leaves us 11 more increases left to do. We'll be doing those 11 increases every 6th row.

Does it all check out? Indeed it does: 11 increases every 6th row = 66 rows, 3 increases every 8th row = 24 rows. That's 14 increases over 90 rows.

I told you it was magic!

and then make the other 5 every 3 rows, to use up another 15. Sure, it only adds up to 35 rows instead of 36, but that's what makes fudge so delicious: You don't need to worry about it. Or, if you have a really strong stomach, you can take a spin on the Magic Formula (above) to figure out the perfect spacing of increases over the rows you have.

Having a Knit Fit

HOW TO GET GREAT-FITTING KNITTING

few things are more frustrating than spending weeks or months on a sweater only to discover, once it's done, that it pulls too tightly across your chest or that the sleeves are so long you have to roll them back just to find your fingers. In this next section, I'm going to show you how you can figure out how well a pattern for a sweater is going to fit *before* you make it, and then alter it, if necessary, so it fits you the way you want it to.

First you need to understand some basics about how knitwear is sized. Designers work up their sweaters around certain well-proportioned body standards, and, for the most part, they think of you as nothing more than a pair of boobs. (Or, for gents, a set of pecs). You may be tall, you may be thin, you may be short, you may be chubby. But if you have a 38" bust, as far as the designer is concerned, you're gonna wear a sweater sized for that 38" chest. Based on that one measurement, she's gonna make assumptions about your arm length, your shoulder width—hell, even your hip size. She's going to get this information, not by coming over to your house and measuring you, but by looking up your measurements on a table.

For a long time there were no real knitting size standards, so designers were free to refer to their own standard sizing charts, but now the Craft Yarn Council has come up with a set of measurements that's based on figures averaged from a whole lot of people (see the chart on page 20). Designers are supposed to refer to these when they are making their sweaters for a variety of sizes of imaginary people (we used them for the sizes in this book). In the real world, however, we know that people don't come in standard sizes. I mean, Pam Anderson and Kathy Bates may very well measure the same size around the chest (I'm just guessing here), but I don't think they're going to be sharing clothing anytime soon, least of all sweaters.

EASE ON DOWN THE ROAD
Understanding Ease

even if you're built exactly like a store mannequin, deciding which size sweater to make can be less than simple. That's because, for one thing, many patterns don't tell you what size person they're made for; they just give you the finished measurements, and usually only the finished circumference at the bust. But just take a look at any book of patterns, and you'll see that a woman's medium-size sweater can have a finished bust measurement anywhere from 30" to 42". So, what's going on here? Certainly the designers aren't so far out of synch that one considers medium to be a 30" pair of knockers while another thinks medium is a 42" rack?

No, that's not the problem. The difference in the bust measurements here has to do with the amount of ease that's added to the sweater. Ease is simply the additional number of inches the designer added (or subtracted) from the wearer's bust measurement to design a sweater that would fit in a certain way. Lana Turner and Kurt Cobain were both known to be sweater wearers, but the way Lana wore hers definitely differed from how Kurt wore his. Whereas Lana's sweaters were stretched taut across her bosom to achieve that much-coveted "sweater girl" look, Kurt's mohair cardigans were baggy and slouchy, hiding the outlines of his body and giving him the quintessential grunge silhouette. These variations in sweater styles are due to variations in the amount of ease in their sweaters: Lana's were probably about 1" to 2" narrower than her actual body size (a 36" sweater stretched across a 38" chest), whereas Kurt's were probably 4" to 6" wider than his body (a 44" sweater around a 38" chest).

Craft Yarn Council Standard Body Measurements*

Woman's Size	X-SMALL	SMALL	MEDIUM	LARGE	1X	2X	3X
Bust (inches)	28–30	32–34	36–38	40–42	44–46	48–50	52–54
Center Back (Neck to Cuff)	27–27½	28–28½	29–29½	30–30½	31–31½	31½–32	32½–33
Back Waist Length	16½	17	17¼	17½	17¾	18	18
Cross Back (Shoulder to Shoulder)	14–14½	14½–15	16–16½	17–17½	17½	18	18
Sleeve Length to Underarm	16	17	17	17½	17	18	18

*For more sizes, including men and children, go to www.yarnstandards.com.

In fact, designers usually design to one of the following **ease dimensions**:

- **Very close fitting:** 1"–2" narrower than your actual measurements. Hello, Lana Turner!

- **Close fitting:** Snug but not tight, your exact size. Works best with lighter-weight yarns. Knit summer tanks are often sized this way.

- **Standard-fitting:** 2"–4" more than your body measurements. You can easily wear this over a T-shirt or other top; it will still show your curves quite nicely. This is the basic fit of most pullover sweaters.

- **Loose fitting:** 4"–6" wider than your body. Nice, comfy, sweatshirty or almost baggy sweater; it will hang straight on your body rather than hug your curves. Cardigans that are meant to be worn over other shirts and sweaters are often made with this much ease.

- **Oversized:** 6" or more of ease. Something you want to cuddle up in. An oversized sweater is so loose, you could probably even fit something else—a cocker spaniel, a baby, your own folded-up legs—in the sweater along with you.

Armed with this knowledge, you can now begin to get a feel for how that size medium sweater with a finished bust measurement of 40" is going to fit your 38" bust.

SWEATIN' TO THE OLDIES
Getting Measurements from Your Fave Sweaters

Now that you understand fit, the real question is how you want your sweater to fit you. Perhaps you're the kind of gal on whom standard-fitting sweaters show not only the luscious curves of your bust but also those of your beer belly, and you really only like to wear much baggier sweaters. Alternately, maybe you are so petite that wearing anything but a close-fitting garment gives you such a shapeless form that you look like you left the house wearing your boyfriend's clothes. The best way to know how you'd like a sweater to fit is not to measure your own body and compare it to the pattern, but to measure one of your favorite sweaters. Simply lay the sweater down flat and measure it across the chest, right below the armpit. Double that, and you have the finished chest measurement you want to go for. Or try measuring a number of your favorite sweaters and comparing them to your own chest measurement (measured around your back and across the pointiest part of your bust, while you're wearing a bra. Boys don't have to wear a bra while measuring but should feel free to do so). Not only will this give you a good idea of the sweater sizes you should be knitting, but also how these variations in fit—very close fitting, close fitting, standard, and oversized—look and feel in relation to your body. And, hell, if you don't have a large enough sweater wardrobe to do this, pop into a store and take a stack of sweaters and your handy-dandy measuring tape into the dressing room. There's no law against it!

While you're trying them on, measure how long they are from the top of your shoulder to the bottom of the sweater. The length of a sweater also makes a big difference in how it fits and feels. A sweater may be just long enough to primly reach one woman's waist, but may give another an inadvertent Britney Spears, belly-baring look. And while most patterns won't give you a finished length measurement, you can usually see what that is from the pattern's schematic. Hip-length

sweaters are also nice; how long you want yours to be is another thing to check out during your sweater-measuring expedition.

Now you have a better idea of the right size sweater to knit for your size and your tastes. If you have a 36" chest and your very favorite sweater is 19" across when you measure it flat (38" around), then by all means choose the sweater that has a 38" finished measurement, no matter what size it's intended for. But be aware of something: A sweater that's designed to be big and boxy will never give you a sweater-girl shape even if you knit it 2" smaller than your bust size; that boxiness is in the shape of the sweater itself. So play with the ease and your selected size just a bit, but don't try to force a style or design to be a completely different one. If it's body hugging you want, choose a sweater that hugs the body of the model in the picture; if you like boxy, choose one that looks like that in the picture. Use the ease and size measurements here to help you select which size instructions you should follow. Finally, consider the material you're using in your sweater when determining the amount of ease you want. Close-fitting garments work best in knits made of thinner yarn. Thicker yarns are better suited to projects with more ease, because the width of the yarn itself will use up some of that ease.

THE SHAPE OF THINGS TO COME
Basic Sweater Shapes

there's one more thing that will affect how a sweater fits, and that's the shape of the sweater itself. At first glance, most sweaters seem to be pretty similar: They're basically a torso with sleeves. But take a closer look and you'll see that a sweater is really a body tube connected to two sleeve tubes. How those sleeve tubes connect to the body determines the three basic sweater shapes.

First, and simplest, is the **drop shoulder sweater.** The body is a straight rectangle, and the sleeves grow at an angle and then are bound off all at once, in a straight line, across the top. Those sleeves are knit shorter than a person's arms, because when you wear a sweater like this, the shoulders of the sweater hang down over your own shoulders, and cover part of your arms. The sleeves drop down from that. A drop shoulder sweater is the quintessential slouchy sweater shape—they were a huge hit in the '80s. Because this type of sweater will always hang over your shoulder, it will not work well for a sweater that you want to hug your body.

A raglan sweater has a body that angles inward toward the neck a bit below the armhole point, and the tops of the sleeves also angle toward each other. The very top of the sleeves becomes part of the shoulder and neckline. Raglan sweaters are shaped like baseball jerseys; they have a nice, classic fit, and while they should be rather roomy in the armpit area, the body can fit quite closely if you want it to.

A sweater with fitted sleeves has a little bite taken out of each side where the sleeves will go, and then the sleeve has a matching sleeve cap that fits perfectly into that hole on the sweater. A fitted sleeve is what most sewn shirts have: Blouses and T-shirts are fitted this way. As their name suggests, fitted sleeves are the nicest style to use if you want a sweater or tank that will really hug your body and arms, but this style of sleeve can easily be used on a roomier sweater as well.

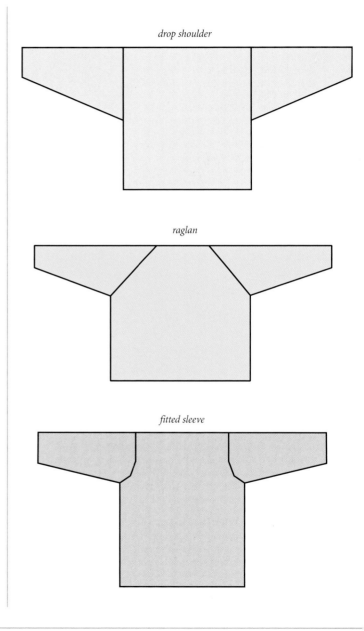

drop shoulder

raglan

fitted sleeve

MEASURING UP

Taking Your Own Measurements

If you want to guarantee a great-fitting garment, you should also quickly take your own (or the intended wearer's) measurements. Although these will not tell you how a sweater is likely to fit, they can tell you how much you follow or deviate from the standard measurements used by pattern designers. In other books and on some Web sites, I've read this procedure given in such intense and complicated detail that it makes taking your measurements sound only slightly less exacting and time-consuming than an MRI. It doesn't need to be. Just whip out a tape measure, and measure yourself this way:

CENTER BACK, NECK TO CUFF: Hold one arm straight out to your side, then measure from the bump at the top of your spine to the bump at the side of your wrist.

BACK WAIST LENGTH: Measure from the bump at the top of your spine down to your waist—the part where your body is most indented.

CROSS BACK, SHOULDER TO SHOULDER: Measure from the bump at the top of your shoulder across to the bump on your other shoulder.

SLEEVE LENGTH: Measure from your armpit, down your slightly bent arm, to the bump on the outside of your wrist.

BUST: Measure around those two bumps on your front. Hold the tape measure across the fullest part of your chest, right across your nipples, and if you're a 36L (long!), be sure to wear a bra when you're measuring.

You'll need someone to help you get your back-to-waist measurement and your shoulder-to-shoulder measurement, but as long as you don't mind said person seeing you in your bra, it could be just about anyone. Also, although the standard measurements don't call for it, measure your waist at its most indented place as well (useful with a pattern that has waist shaping or if you decide to add your own; see pages 25, 27).

Now, compare your measurements to those of the Craft Yarn Council's table on page 20. There's enough leeway in those measurements, so maybe you're lucky to fit pretty comfortably into a standard size. But you might not fit into them so well, because these standards assume that if one part of you is bigger, all the other parts will be bigger, too. Larger boobs go with longer arms, smaller boobs with shorter ones. Of course, a lady who gets breast implants and goes from a size 32B to a size 32D doesn't all of a sudden get longer arms, too. An extra-small sweater will pull tightly across her bodacious frame, while a large might give her sleeves that hang below her fingertips.

Let's say you're tall, slender, and somewhat flat-chested: A large sweater will bag across your chest, although the sleeves may fit you nicely, and a small one will fit your chest nicely, but the sleeves will always look pulled up. Or your boobs and arms may be a designer's dream and fit the chart exactly, but if you've got a long torso (your neck-to-waist measurement deviates from the standard), you're probably mighty tired of wearing sweaters that always ride up on you. All of you should choose the size that fits best across your chest, and then shorten or lengthen the sleeves to fit your arms, if necessary, and shorten or lengthen the sweater so that it lands in the right place on your torso. In the next section, I'll show you how to do that.

Ch-Ch-Ch-Changes

HOW TO MAKE ADJUSTMENTS TO A PATTERN TO FIT YOUR BODY AND YOUR STYLE

Here's where you'll learn to make adjustments to sweaters to accommodate your real-life body. But even if your measurements are a designer's dream, you may still want to alter a pattern. You may be drooling over a cropped sweater, but your belly hasn't seen the sun since 1975 and you don't want to reintroduce the two of them now; instead, you'd like to lengthen the sweater to hip length. Or the sleeves of a sweater you're interested in making are primly wrist length, and you'd like them to hang a bit over your hands for a nice punky or matchstick girl look. You might like to show off your neck by swapping a turtleneck with a scoop neck, or make the sweater more femme-y by replacing a roll bottom with a picot edge hem. Using your pattern as a guide, and a trusty little calculator, each of these things can be accomplished.

GET SHORTY
Making a Sweater Longer or Shorter

This one's the easiest to do. If you have a long torso and would prefer to add a few inches to your sweater, just go ahead and add them. To make it shorter, do the reverse: Subtract a couple of inches. Look for the beginning of the armhole shaping instructions—most often, they start with having you bind off about 1" worth of stitches on each side of your sweater—and make sure you add or subtract the extra stitches *before* that point, and *after* the bottom ribbing (or whatever the bottom edge is).

AT ARM'S LENGTH
Making Sleeves Longer (or Shorter)

Adding or subtracting length from sleeves is a bit more challenging, as they often get wider from the wrist to the shoulder, and thus there are increases involved. You want to try to make your length changes evenly between those increases. So, first get your row gauge, figure out how many inches of fabric you're adding and how many extra rows that means you are going to knit. To make things easy on yourself, round that up or down to the closest even number. Then take that number of rows and distribute them as evenly as possible among your increases, in sets of 2 rows at a time.

Let's try this out with our old pal, the Li'l Dumplin' sweater. Suppose you want to knit this for a baby who has exceptionally long arms (perhaps Mommy or Daddy hadn't quite finished evolving), and you now want to add 2 whole inches to each sleeve. Here are the original instructions for the sleeve:

SLEEVES

K 2 rows in seed st.

Cont in St st, inc1 st each side EOR 2 times, then every 4th row 5 times (35 sts).

Cont in St st until sleeve measures 5½".

The row gauge on that sweater is 5 per inch, so you'll have to add 10 rows to the sleeves.

Since you'll be adding those 10 rows 2 at a time, you'll need 5 places in the pattern where you can slip in your extra rows. This pattern has 7 places for increases already built in (every other row 2 times, every 4th row 5 times).

Waist Management

ADDING WAIST SHAPING TO A SWEATER

Most sweater patterns have a simple, straight shape that can be unflattering to many women. Waist shaping is easy to add, and this method will work well on a sweater that is hip length or below and has a raglan or set-in sleeve. Here's how.

When you knit a sweater, you typically work between 1" and 3" of edging (ribbing, seed, garter, etc.), followed by 10" to 14" of body before the armhole shaping. With this method, you'll decrease stitches between the ribbing and the waist, knit for about an inch, then increase till you reach about 3" before the armhole shaping. The beauty part is, you'll have the exact same number of stitches at this point as if you hadn't done any shaping at all. Waist not, want not!

Know your measurements and know your pattern: Take your bust and waist measurements, be honest with yourself, and write them down. You'll figure out the amount of decreasing you need to make at the waist by subtracting your waist from your bust measurement. You don't need a sweater to be waist-hugging in order to be flattering; often, decreasing about 4" at the waist is enough.

Next, measure yourself from your armpit to the most indented part of your side, where your waist is. Then look at your pattern and calculate how many inches you are supposed to knit before you get to the armhole shaping.

Finally, check your gauge. Figure out how many stitches per inch and how many rows per inch you're knitting.

Calculate: Start with the number of inches you are going to decrease; multiply that by your stitches per inch; divide that number by 4. This gives you your total number of decrease and increase rows (X). Take your length from armpit to waist (A) and

subtract 3½". Multiply your result by your rows-per-inch gauge. This is the number of rows over which you will be increasing after the waist (Y).

Take the length of the sweater from armpit to lower edge (B), subtract A, and subtract 3½". Multiply the result by your rows-per-inch gauge. This is the number of rows over which you will be decreasing to the waist (Z).

Divide Y by X. This is the number of rows you will be making between increase rounds.

Divide Z by X. This is the number of rows you will be making between decrease rounds.

On your mark, get set, knit:

Begin by knitting 3" according to the pattern directions.

Next, decrease 1 stitch each edge every (Z ÷ X) rows. If you're knitting flat, that means decrease 1 stitch at each side of the front and back pieces. If you're knitting in the round, place a marker at the points that would be the left and right side edges; then decrease 1, knit 1 before marker and knit 1, decrease 1 after marker.

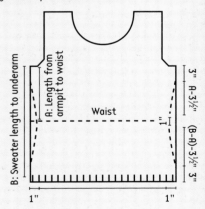

Knit straight for 1".

Next, increase 1 stitch each edge every (Y ÷ X) rows.

Knit straight for 3". You should now be at the correct length for the underarm shaping.

Christina McNamee, Arlington, VA

Lucky you, you can just slip the 2 extra rows between the last 5 increases every 4th row and be done with your 10 extra rows. So, after the ribbing, you'll increase 1 stitch each side every other row 2 times, and every 6th row 5 times, instead of every 2nd and every 4th row, as the pattern was written. And, of course, you continue in stockinette stitch until the sleeves for the baby with the monkey arms measure 7½". Obviously, if you're trying to shorten the sleeves, you do the same thing in reverse: you subtract pairs of rows from between your increases.

PRIMARY COLLARS

Choosing Your Own Neckline

I f you don't like the turtleneck called for on a sweater, and would prefer a roll neck, or you want to raise the scoop neck that's on a woman's sweater and add a nice

little crew neck when you knit it for a guy, you can. Here's how:

● For a **crew neck,** you want the neckline to be only about 2" deep. If you're working on a design with a neckline lower than that, you'll have to adjust where you start your neckline. Figure out how many stitches are cast off for the neckline in the original pattern, and don't start binding them off until you are about 2" from the top. You'll want to bind off at least half of the neckline stitches in that first step, then bind off 1 or 2 stitches at each end of every row till you get through them all. Figure out how many rows you have in that 2", and if you need to add a few more stitches to that first bind off, go ahead and do so.

Next, sew one or both of the shoulder seams. Then, using straight needles if you sewed up one shoulder, or

crew neck   turtleneck   roll neck   scoop neck   V-neck

circulars if you seamed them both, pick up one stitch for every stitch bound off, all around the front and the back of the neckline. Now just knit a k1, p1 rib for about an inch, then bind off *very loosely.* In fact, to make sure that the sweater will go over anyone's head, and not just a pinhead, you might want to bind off using needles one or two sizes larger.

- For a **turtleneck,** follow the directions for a crew neck but keep knitting for about 3" of rib, then switch to larger needles and knit another 3", then bind off. The last bit of ribbing knit on larger needles will fold nicely over the ribbing knit on smaller needles.

- For a **roll neck,** follow the directions for crew neck but instead of knitting ribbing on your picked-up stitches, just knit straight stockinette for about 1½". It will roll over onto itself, just as God intended stockinette stitch to do.

- For a **scoop neck,** make the neckline a bit deeper—at least 3" deep. The simplest way to finish off a scoop neck is to crochet the edge in crab stitch (see page 268).

- For a **V-neck,** things get a little more complicated. Begin shaping the V-neck at the same point as where the armhole shaping begins. You'll want to bind off the V-neck stitches on each side in a nice diagonal line from here to the shoulder. Use the Magic Formula (page 18), or trial and error, to calculate the diagonal decreases so that you can bind off all of the neckline stitches evenly—it should be

It's a Cinch

ADDING RIBBING TO MAKE A SWEATER MORE SHAPED

I love big, warm, bulky sweaters, but sometimes you need a sweater that shows off what you've got. Adding ribbing to the sides of a garment is a great way to make it form-fitting without the complication of increasing and decreasing. All you need are two measurements: how much narrower you'd like the sweater to be (in inches), and the number of stitches per inch of your gauge. The first measurement tells you how much ribbing you want on each side of the sweater, and the second tells you approximately how many stitches to rib.

If the sweater circumference is 35" and you want it to fit your waist at 30", you will need to knit 5" of ribbing on each side of the sweater body, from bottom ribbing to armpit. That's because an equal rib (1 × 1, 2 × 2, 3 × 3, etc.) contracts to about half the width of even knitting, so 10" of ribbing (5" on each side) will pull the sweater in about 5". If your gauge is 4 stitches per inch, for example, that means you'll need to rib about 20 stitches on each side to get 5" less overall. If you're knitting the sweater flat in two pieces (back and front), divide that number in half and rib that number of stitches at each side of the front and the back. For the example above, you'll rib 10 stitches at the left and right sides of the front and do the same on the back. If you're knitting in the round, just rib 20 stitches on each side. If the sweater has a ribbed collar or cuffs, use that as a guide for your side ribbing. Fortunately, ribs are very forgiving, so the same stretch that allows them to hug your curves will also hide any mishaps while you experiment with this technique.
Susan Kelley,
Portland, OR

about a third of the stitches you have left after binding off for the armholes. Now sew both shoulder seams, and pick up stitches evenly around the back and front of the neckline, being sure to pick up one stitch right smack in the center of the lowest point of your V. Knit in k1, p1 rib till you get to two stitches before that middle stitch; ssk, then knit the center stitch, then k2 together, and carry on in the k1, p1 rib from before. Do that every row for about an inch, then bind off all stitches loosely.

EDGING OUT THE COMPETITION
Changing the Edging at the Bottom of Sweaters and Sleeves

Sweaters and tanks are almost always knit with some kind of edging at the bottom. That's either to make the sweater hold closer to the body at those points, which is what ribbing does very well, or just to keep the dang stockinette fabric from rolling up, which may be accomplished with a number of seed stitch or garter stitch rows.

What if you really hate the way ribbing at the bottom of a sweater looks, and you'd prefer to let it just all hang out? Ribbing pulls in at the bottom of a sweater, while a garter-edge border hangs straight. Beware, though, that while ribbing is narrower than stockinette, garter stitch is wider (and also stiffer), so if you don't want your sweater to look like a hoop skirt, you'll want to knit your garter-stitch border using needles one or two sizes smaller than the needles you use for the rest of the sweater. Also, you'll only need to knit a few rows of garter stitch—about 1/2" worth—to make a nice straight edge.

You might like the look of a rolled stockinette stitch edge, and if so, more power to you! This is a very cool look. Just be sure to add a good number of extra rows at the bottom of your piece, so that it can roll up and still be the right length. Otherwise, you might look like someone accidentally yanked on the shade-pull of your sweater: it could roll up and let your belly stick out.

If you like ribbing at the bottom of your sweater but don't want it to pull in so much, just make the ribbing shorter: say, 1" or 1/2" ribbing. You could also try knitting the ribbing on needles a size or two larger than you plan on using for the rest of the pattern.

Last but not least, if you'd like an edge that's completely straight and hemmed (and this works best with thinner yarn) begin by knitting for about 1/2" to 1" in stockinette stitch. Then do one purl row, and continue in stockinette or whatever stitch pattern your sweater calls for. When the front and back pieces are done, fold the lower edge along that purl row—sometimes called a "turning row"—and sew the edge of the hem to the

SHOW ME YOUR TIPS! Earnestly Hemming Away
HOW TO KEEP A HEM FROM FLIPPING OUT

To keep stockinette stitch hems from rolling up or flipping out, try the following: Cast on with needles one size smaller than the rest of your work, then knit for the number of stockinette stitch rows you would like for your hem, usually at least 1/2" of knitting (this part will be folded under). Make one purl row, then switch to regular-size needles and knit two extra stockinette stitch rows before you start on the pattern. This will cause the hem to roll under slightly. Without those two extra stockinette stitch rows, my hems start to flip out after a couple of minutes. *Tina Hsu, Washington, D.C.*

inside. For an even fancier finish, make a picot edge, something my mom says they called "mouse teeth" in her day: Follow the directions above, but instead of knitting a purl row, you'll yarn over, knit 2 together, all the way across the row, then continue on in stockinette stitch. When you fold up the hem on this row, you'll have super-cute little "mouse teeth" across the bottom of your sweater.

Try making a swatch of your intended edging, followed by a couple of inches in stockinette stitch, just to see how it behaves with your yarn. If worse comes to worst and you hate the way your new edging experiment turned out, don't fret. It's not too hard to unravel the sweater from the bottom up, then knit back down using an edging that works better.

DIG IF YOU WILL, A PICTURE
Adding or Changing Color Designs

just because your pattern calls for stripes or features giant, corny reindeer heads doesn't mean you can't replace them with something else. If squirrels are your thing, knit an army of them along the yoke of a sweater, or add a tribal tattoo design around the sleeves. If you're into old-school video games, decorate the front of your piece with a realistic Space Invaders motif, or knit a Rubik's cube and be part of the '80s revival.

Start, as always, by working out your gauge, then sketch out how many stitches wide and how many rows tall your design should be. For a Fair Isle pattern, try not to let your color stitches be more than 4 or 5 stitches apart from each other, and for an intarsia design, remember that large blocks of color work best; if you have lots of little details in your image, you might want to add them on at the end with duplicate stitch.

The most important thing when working out a picture to knit into your work, however, is to remember to draw it on knitter's graph paper (see page 30). Unlike regular graph paper, where each box is a square, knitter's graph paper has boxes that are wider than they are tall. That's because knit stitches are not shaped like squares; in fact, each knit stitch is only about $2/3$ as tall as it is wide. If you use graph paper that is not made to these proportions, you'll end up with knit images that are squashed flat, and your squirrels may look like they've been run over by a car. And that would be very sad.

Looks Like You Made It
TAKING THE PLUNGE AND LEARNING FROM YOUR MISTAKES

If I had a Girl Scout–type badge to give you for making it through this chapter I would—you've certainly earned it. Once you peel back the skin of a knitting pattern, you see that the guts can be pretty gnarly. Still, it's the only way to really get a handle on what you're knitting and, best of all, knit things the way you truly want them to be. And, as you may have guessed by now, once you master making major and minor alterations to knitting patterns, you're just a hop, knit, and a purl away from designing your own.

There is one cautionary word I want to leave you with, and that is to expect failure. You may add a crew neck to a sweater, thinking it will look great, and decide that you hate it when it's done. You may try shortening the sleeves and find that you made too many decreases and the thing now makes your arms look like sausages. You may have changed the gauge of a sweater successfully, and even checked your little swatch, but now that it's all done you decide that the bulky cotton you used doesn't wear nicely after all.

What I want you to know is that in knitting, as in life, sometimes making mistakes is the best way to learn something. It's like when you were first learning to knit: It wasn't until you made a ribbing that went all wrong that you figured out what needed to be done for it to go right, and now you'll never make a ribbing the wrong way again. It's the same with mucking about with sweater patterns. I've learned the very most when things have gone wrong as I tried to execute an idea.

The good news is, you can afford to make mistakes in knitting. Unlike in woodworking—where the rule is to measure twice, cut once, because once the wood is cut you can't put it back together—in knitting, if you don't like the way something has turned out, you can always unravel it and do it over. In fact, I'm willing to venture a guess that there isn't a single thing you'll try from this chapter that *will* go according to plan the first time. It may take a second or even a third attempt. But then, once you get it, you *really* get it, in a way that no book or class alone can ever teach you.

So go out there. Get some yarn and some needles, and a pattern. Make some changes. Small ones at first, then bigger ones. Make mistakes. Unravel your work. Do it again. The exhilaration you'll get out of completing a project that is really and truly as unique as you are will give you the kind of pride known only to first-time mothers. And if that's not worth a few late nights and curse words, what is?

Graphic Design

MAKING YOUR OWN KNITTING GRIDS

I have made my own patterns from day one, but I'm a perfectionist and always want the flexibility to try a few different ideas. Instead of using grid paper, a pencil, and a *large* eraser, I use Excel to create custom knitting-stitch-size graph paper on my computer. I format the cells into squares and use the background color to fill them in. Then I put a P in the square to indicate a purl, etc. I used this format to make a chart from an illustration of a piece of sushi that will some day be knitted into the side of a purse. It works great for any intarsia-type color combo. Then I thicken the left border on every 5th cell, and those lines are where I place my stitch markers. Makes it easy to keep track of complicated designs. *Sharon Silverman, Portland, OR*

● To make knitting graph paper in Excel, open a new worksheet and select the entire sheet (click in the box that's to the left of column A and above row 1). Format all your rows to have a height of 10, and the columns to have a width of 1.2. Finally, with all the cells selected, apply borders around each cell by choosing the All Borders option from the borders pull-down button.

To make knitting graph paper in Word, open a new document. From the menu bar at top, choose Table and then Insert Table. Create a table with 31 columns and 67 rows. Then select the entire table by choosing Select All in the Edit menu. With the table selected, go to Table and then Cell Height and Width. Set the width of the columns to be .2", then click on the Rows tab. Here, set the width to be "Exactly" and enter the number 9.6. Click OK. *DS*

The Patterns

SCARVES, HATS, AND MITTENS
34

SWEATERS AND PONCHOS
78

SEXY SUMMER KNITS
122

LEGS, BAGS, AND BEYOND
152

BABIES, DOGS, AND CATS
204

GIFTS AND MORE
230

Knit Happens
PATTERNS FROM THE EDGE

Welcome to the creamy chocolate filling of this book: the patterns. To find them, I put out a call for submissions to Stitch 'n Bitch groups all across the country and beyond. I was overwhelmed by the response; there was so much great stuff, it was really difficult to choose. In the end, I selected the fifty fun, fierce projects you see here. They were designed by knitters who hail from all corners of the country: from Philadelphia to Phoenix, San Diego to St. Paul, Los Angeles to Lexington, and everywhere in between. These ladies and gents vary in experience from impassioned newbie knitters to those who have knit their way around the block a few times. The one thing they share is the ability to think of something cool to knit, then work out an interesting way to make it. The energy, inspiration—and, of course, frustration—that went into designing these projects and writing up these patterns just about explode off these pages, and I hope you'll dig them all as much as I do. I am truly awestruck at the talent, creativity, and balls-out bravery of our nation of knitters.

ABBREVIATIONS

beg	begin(ning)(s)	dpn	double-pointed needle	pm	place marker	ssk	slip next st knitwise twice, k sts tog tbl
BO	bind off	EOR	every other row	psso	pass slipped stitch over		
C4B	sl 2 sts to cn and hold to back, k 2, k 2 from cn	ER	every row	pu	pick up	ssp	slip 2 stitches from left needle to the right, then slide the left needle through them from the left to right through the back legs, and purl them
		est	established	pwise	purlwise: insert needle into the next stitch as if to purl		
C4F	same as above, but hold cn to front of work	f&b	front and back				
		foll	follow(ing)	rem	remain(s)(ing)		
		inc	increase	rep	repeat(ed)(ing)(s)		
C6B	sl 3 sts to cn and hold to back, k3, k3 from cn	k	knit	rev St st	reverse stockinette stitch	sssk	slip next st knitwise 3 times, k all sts tog tbl
		k2tog	insert needle through next 2 sts knitwise, knit them as one	RH	right hand		
C6F	same as above, but hold cn to front of work			rnd(s)	round(s)	st(s)	stitch(es)
		kwise	knitwise: insert needle into the next stitch as if to knit	RS	right side(s)	St st	stockinette stitch
CC	contrasting color			sc	single crochet	tbl	through back loop
ch	chain	LH	left hand	skp	slip 1 st, k next st, pass slipped st over k st	tog	together
cn	cable needle	M1	make 1 increase			yo	yarn over
CO	cast on	MC	main color			W&T	wrap and turn
cont	continu(e)(ed)(es)(ing)	meas	measures	sl	slip	WS	wrong side(s)
		p	purl	sm	slip marker	yd(s)	yard(s)
dec	decrease	patt	pattern				

In addition to the patterns, the next section contains profiles of a number of Stitch 'n Bitch groups (by region) that have sprung up all across America—as well as a few that have popped up beyond our borders. So many new SnB groups have been started in the years since I began one in New York City five years ago, and since the publication of *Stitch 'n Bitch: The Knitter's Handbook* that number has mushroomed. Today, thousands of knitterati are enjoying getting together to work on projects and to shoot the knit. Contact info for most of these groups is listed on Brenda Janish's amazing Web site: www.stitchnbitch.org. If you're looking to hook up with an SnB in your neighborhood, her site is the first place to go. If there doesn't seem to be a group in your area, do what I and everyone else in this book did: Start your own. The success stories on these pages prove how easy—and satisfying—that is to do.

I've also collected tried-and-true tips from knitters all across the land. You may already be familiar with some of these, but others are sure to be a useful surprise. One of the best things about having a Stitch 'n Bitch is the ability to share knitting knowledge with one another, just as women have done for centuries: handing down the craft from generation to generation. Now we have the chance to do the same. So slip one, knit one, pass slipped stitch over—and don't forget to pass along your knitting know-how to the next gal. Knitting is not a craft that belongs to an inner circle of people in the know—there's no room for elitism here. Share the joy, share your skills, and welcome every new knitter into the fold. Our Stitch 'n Bitch nation is always happy to have new citizens.

Some of the projects that follow are quite simple; others are more challenging. The directions to make each one are explained, step by step, in each pattern. On the opposite page is a glossary of all the abbreviations used in the book, in the sidebar, right, are reminders about how to read the patterns. If you can't remember how to make a certain stitch, be sure to check out the knitter's cheat sheets that appear at the end of the patterns section, page 253.

Pattern Recognition

HOW TO FOLLOW A KNITTING PATTERN

*M*ost patterns are written the way we present them here. First, the pattern will give you the finished measurements of the garment, followed by the materials you'll need to make the project, including the brand and amount of yarn; the size and type of needles; and any additional notions or tools.

Next, and perhaps most crucial, is the gauge information. Here's an example: 15 sts and 17 rows to 4"/10cm over k2, p2 rib using size 11 needles. This means with your size 11 needles you knit up a swatch that's a little bigger than the 15 stitches—say, 20 stitches—in the stitch pattern requested (here it's knit 2, purl 2 ribbing). Knit a piece a little longer than 4", then bind off, lay the swatch down flat, and measure it to see if 15 stitches do in fact make up 4". If your swatch comes out bigger, reknit another swatch using knitting needles one size smaller. (If it comes out smaller, go up one needle size and reknit.)

Then come the instructions. When knitting patterns give directions for more than one size, the first number given refers to the smallest size, and the instructions for the remaining sizes are presented, from smallest to largest, in parentheses, separated by commas. For example, if a pattern says: S (M, L), the first line of that pattern might read: CO 24 (30, 38) st.

Last, but not least, is the shorthand of asterisks for repeating something in a pattern. For example, "K2, *k2, p1; rep from * 6 times, k4" translates as: Start your row by knitting 2 stitches (k2). Then repeat what comes between the asterisks the number of times given. In this case, you'd knit 2 and purl 1 six times. Then you finish the row with 4 knit stitches. Finally, patterns that involve knitting pieces into somewhat complicated shapes will often give you schematics, or diagrams, of all the pieces you'll be making, which can help you visualize what it is that you're doing.

Scarf It Up

You can never make too many scarves. Yet scarves are deceptively demanding: They have to be made in a stitch that will lie flat, they should look good from both sides (since both sides show when folks wear them) and they should be simple to make, as you often find yourself cranking out a whole bunch of them come the holidays. Here, then, are four scarf patterns that meet all these criteria and more: They're complicated-looking but easy to do, they're cool and a bit different, and they're ready, willing, and able to decorate the necks of all your friends and family.

ELLEN R. MARGULIES

Yo, Drop It!

I've made several scarves from ribbon, but never felt that the ribbon's texture was properly highlighted. Every stitch combination fell short, until I discovered the magic of drop stitches, which expose the ribbon's character. I love the "danger" of drop-

ping the stitches off the needle. Usually drop stitch causes knitters grief, but in this case it's a fun way to make a cool design.

Size

Finished length: 88"

Finished width: 3½"

Materials

Trendsetter Aquarius (78% polyester, 22% cotton; 50g/96 yds), 2 skeins #810 Abalone

US 11 (8 mm) straight needles, or size needed to obtain gauge

Gauge

16 sts and 20 rows = 4" in garter st

STITCH PATTERN
DROP STITCH PATTERN

Row 1: *K1, yo; rep from * to last st, k1.

Row 2: *K1, drop the yo by slipping it off the needle; rep from * to last st, k1.

Rows 3 & 4: K.

DIRECTIONS

CO 17 sts.

Work 6 rows in garter st.

Work in drop st patt until piece measures 86½" from beg, ending with a Row 2.

Work 6 rows in garter st.

BO.

RACHAEL RUSS
Wavy Gravy

the idea for this pattern came to me while flying on an airplane. As I was looking out the window at the amazing patterns in the landscape, I started playing around with knitting wavy shapes and ended up with one of my favorite scarves. It's pretty simple, and it's a great way to practice increasing and decreasing stitches. You can have lots of fun playing around with color combinations and different sizes of "waves."

About Ellen

When I was a teenager, I found a miraculous little book in the library that was illustrated with fluid line drawings of yarn looping and twisting over itself. I kept renewing it, reading it again and again, mentally rehearsing the process, until all of a sudden it clicked—and I was knitting. Although I'm originally from Sheepshead Bay, Brooklyn, I now live with my husband and daughter in the beach community of Pacific Palisades, California.

Size

Finished length: 58"

Finished width: 5"

Materials

Brown Sheep Lamb's Pride Worsted
(85% wool, 15% mohair; 113g/190 yds)

A: 1 skein #M51 Winter Blue

B: 1 skein #M16 Sea Foam

US 11 (8mm) straight needles,
or size needed to obtain gauge

Gauge

14 sts and 21 rows = 4" in garter st

DIRECTIONS

With one strand of A and B held tog, CO 6 sts.

**K 1 row even.

Next row: K1, inc 1, k to last st, inc 1, k1.** Pm at end of row to mark RS.

Rep from ** to ** until there are 16 sts.

Work 3 rows in garter st.

**K1, k2tog, k to last 3 sts, k2tog, k1.

Next row: K.**

Rep from ** to ** until there are 8 sts.

Work 3 rows in garter st.

Rep from ** until piece measures 58" from beg, ending with 8 sts after decs. K 1 row even.

Next row: K1, k2tog, k2, k2tog, k1.

BO and weave in ends.

NICHOLAS CARATZAS

Mom's Sophisticated Scarf

I made the mistake of letting my mother know about my new hobby about three weeks after I'd started knitting. That's when she conscripted me: "That's great! I want a scarf for my birthday to go with my new red jacket." You don't say no to my mother, so I got to work. This scarf is made in a merino yarn that's soft on the skin but twisted more tightly than most wool, which helped to keep my clumsy

About Rachael

My childhood was filled with all kinds of crafty projects inspired by my mom—everything from bags made out of old blue jeans to the many uses for the Be–Dazzler! My love of crafts took me all the way to an M.F.A. in metalsmithing, and now I work in sculpture and installation using various kinds of materials. I'm part of a small crafts circle here in Chicago called the Crafty Beavers (they rock!), and I especially love knitting booties for my new nephew, Zev.

Size

Finished length: 70"

Finished width: 7½"

Materials

Karabella Aurora 8
(100% merino wool; 50g/98 yds),
5 skeins #22 Charcoal

US 8 (5mm) straight needles,
or size needed to obtain gauge

Gauge

20 sts and 28 rows = 4" in basketweave patt

beginner's fingers from splitting loops. The basketweave stitch is so easy to knit up, it almost seems like cheating to be making such an interesting pattern using nothing more than knits and purls. Now Mom wants me to teach her to knit.

STITCH PATTERNS

SEED STITCH

Row 1: *K1, p1; rep from * to end.

Row 2: *P1, k1; rep from * to end.

BASKETWEAVE PATTERN

Rows 1, 3, 6, 8: K1, p1, k1, *k2, p4; rep from * to last 5 sts, k3, p1, k1.

Rows 2, 4, 7, 9: K1, p1, k1, *p2, k4; rep from * to last 5 sts, p2, k1, p1, k1.

Row 5: K1, p1, k1, p to last 3 sts, k1, p1, k1.

Row 10: K1, p1, k to last 2 sts, p1, k1.

DIRECTIONS

CO 38 sts.

Work 6 rows in seed st.

Work in basketweave patt until scarf measures 68" from beg, ending with a patt row 9.

Work 6 rows in seed st.

BO and weave in ends.

About Nick

*B*esides being a financial analyst I'm a nerd with a natural interest in technology, so when my girlfriend, Karen, bought the first *Stitch 'n Bitch* book I absolutely had to learn the theory behind her mysterious new hobby. She got me started right after Christmas 2003, and by the time New Year's rolled around I was hooked. My approach to knitting is heavily influenced by my analytical background; I use Excel, experiments, and equations as much as pencil and paper when planning a piece. Since then, Karen has organized a Stitch 'n Bitch that meets weekly in New Haven, Connecticut, and our mutual hobby has become an excuse to go on weekend yarn-store road trips.

AILEEN ARRIETA

Warm Fuzzies

nitially I designed this remarkably soft and fuzzy scarf for my niece, who loves all things pink. But when I finished, I couldn't bear to part with it. It's a perfect project for anyone just beginning to learn about cables—you don't even need to use a cable needle. When you're done, one side of the scarf will show the cable pattern; the other side will be ribbing.

STITCH PATTERN

MOCK-CABLE RIB PATTERN

Row 1: *P1, k the second st on the left needle, leave this st on the needle and k the first st on the left needle; drop both sts off needle; rep from * to last st, p1.

Row 2: *K1, p2; rep from * to last st, k1.

DIRECTIONS

With one strand of each yarn held tog, CO 22 sts.

Work in mock-cable rib pattern until piece measures 54" from beg.

BO and weave in ends.

Size

Finished length: 54"

Finished width: 4½"

Materials

Anny Blatt Angora Super
(70% angora, 30% wool; 25g/116 yds)

2 skeins #164 Dragee

2 skeins #50 Blanc

US 11 (8mm) straight needles,
or size needed to obtain gauge

Gauge

19 sts and 15 rows = 4" in mock-cable rib patt

About Aileen

When I was seven, a neighbor from Germany taught my mother, sister, and me to knit. I picked it up again when living in Sweden as a foreign exchange student (the coldest winter in Sweden since 1898). My best friends at school sat in the back row so that they could knit sweaters during class—without looking and without patterns! I let my knitting drop when I became a securities litigation partner in a large law firm. When I was forced into early retirement, I turned to knitting again. Now I knit for relaxation—and to enjoy the finished product. When I'm not knitting, I'm busy remodeling my 1907 San Francisco Victorian, which I share with my two standard poodles, Fiona and Gracie.

ADINA ALEXANDER

Butterflies Are Free

With all the floral embellishments around, I'd never seen a knitted butterfly, so I invented one. Butterflies fascinated me long before they became part of the current fashion trend, and this was a fun way to combine that interest with my knitting. The loop underneath the butterfly keeps the scarf from slipping out of place while you wear it and requires no sewing—you just pick up stitches from the scarf and bind them back to the scarf after a few rows. Since the butterfly is attached to the loop, it's always sitting in the right spot, no matter how you adjust the fit. I've based the colors of my butterflies on actual species, but of course you're free to make them whatever color you like.

DIRECTIONS

SCARF

With MC and straight needles, CO 12 sts.

Work in 1 × 1 rib until piece measures 48" from beg.

BO.

SCARF LOOP

Pu 7 sts from the center of the scarf 14" from the CO edge.

Size

Finished length: 48"

Finished width: 2"

Materials

Crystal Palace Cotton Chenille (100% mercerized cotton; 50g/98 yds)

MONARCH BUTTERFLY

MC: 1 skein #4043 Cypress

CC1: 1 skein #2230 Mango

CC2: 1 skein #3433 Rosewood

MORPHO BUTTERFLY

MC: 1 skein #1015 Natural

CC1: 1 skein #2214 Bluebell

CC2: 1 skein #9292 Charcoal

US 6 (4mm) straight needles, or size needed to obtain gauge

US 6 (4mm) double-pointed needles (set of 2)

US G (4.25mm) crochet hook

Stitch holder

Gauge

16 sts and 20 rows = 4" in St st

Special Skill

SINGLE CROCHET

Work in garter st until loop measures 3" from beg.

BO and secure loop 17" from the CO edge.

BUTTERFLY
WING SET 1 (MONARCH)

With CC1 and straight needles, CO 7 sts.

Row 1: K4, turn, placing rem 3 sts on holder.

Row 2: P2, m1, p2.

Row 3: K.

Row 4: P.

Row 5: K2, m1, k1, m1, k2.

Row 6: P.

Row 7: K.

Row 8: P.

Row 9: K2tog, k3, k2tog.

Row 10: P2tog, p1, p2tog.

BO and, with RS facing, rejoin CC1 to sts on holder.

Row 1: K.

Row 2: P.

Row 3: K1, inc1, k1.

Row 4: P.

Row 5: K2, m1, k2.

Row 6: P.

BO.

WING SET 2 (MORPHO)

With CC1 and straight needles, CO 7 sts.

Row 1: K3, turn, placing rem 4 sts on holder.

Row 2: P.

Row 3: K1, inc1, k1.

Row 4: P.

Row 5: K2, m1, k2.

Row 6: P.

BO and, with RS facing, rejoin CC1 to sts on holder.

Row 1: K.

Row 2: P2, m1, p2.

Row 3: K.

Row 4: P.

Row 5: K2, m1, k1, m1, k2.

Row 6: P.

Row 7: K.

Row 8: P.

Row 9: K2tog, k3, k2tog.

Row 10: P2tog, p1, p2tog.

BO.

BODY

With CC2 and dpns, CO 5 sts. Work in I-cord for 2½".

Next row: K2, ssk, k1, turn; place
last 2 sts on holder.

Work in garter st for 4 rows.

BO and rejoin CC2 to sts on holder.

Work in garter st for 4 rows.

BO.

FINISHING

With crochet hook and CC2, beg between forewing and hind-wing, SC around outer edges of both sets of wings. Break yarn, leaving a 12" tail.

Using the 12" tail from one of the wings, sew both wings to body.

Using the 12" tail from the other wing, sew butterfly to center of scarf loop.

Weave in ends.

About Adina

I was born and raised in Hamden, Connecticut, and I am a Web designer, photographer, sewer, costumer, and theatrical swordfighter. At age fifteen I was taught to knit by my mother, who had learned from *her* mother, but my interest didn't resurface for almost another decade. My primary reinspiration was my great-aunt Adele, who was an extremely talented and experienced knitter. As a "picker" rather than a "thrower," I am a firm believer that there is no wrong way to knit as long as you get the results you want.

Organizing Principles

KEEPING YOUR YARN, NEEDLES, AND PATTERNS IN ORDER

*I*f you want a nice holder for your beautiful bamboo needles, check out an art supply store for the pretty roll-up cases that are designed to carry calligraphy brushes. These look like sushi mats on the outside and are lined with canvas and have multiple pockets. They tie with a canvas strip and match your wooden needles perfectly. *Christina Berdoulay, San Mateo, CA*

● Keeping my patterns organized was becoming overwhelming until I bought some large three-ring binders, dividers, and sheet protectors. Now I keep each pattern in its own sleeve in the appropriate binder for babies, kids, men, and women. I use the dividers to organize each binder by type of project. For instance, in my Babies binder I have sections for blankets, booties, hats, cardigans, pullovers, and other. This keeps me from going bonkers trying to find a particular pattern. *CB*

● Removing one of the inside dividers from a laptop computer bag turns it into a great carry-all for knitting supplies. It has a lot of pockets for small stuff and zipper compartments for patterns. *Lou Simon, Atlanta, GA*

● The best bags to hold your stitch markers, tape, notebook, and other knitting accessories are the ones you get at bonus time from Clinique. Everyone in my Stitch 'n Bitch group seems to be using one. They come in great colors, are made of sturdy plastic, and are just the right size. *Sara Daily, Chapel Hill, NC*

● Here's a good way to keep your circular needles organized: Simply write both the gauge and length on the needle with a fine permanent marker, then cover with a thin layer of clear nail polish to keep it from rubbing off. *Mary Goodman, New Canaan, CT*

ANNE WOLFE

Bzzz Hat for Queen Bees

M y roommate likes homemade presents, and before Christmas she was debating taking a class in beekeeping, so I had bees on the brain while trying to come up with a present for her. I'd never even knit a hat before, so getting my first one published is amazing. A friend of mine said, "Your beehive hat is inspired!" to which I replied, "No, I just copied a beehive." The hat has since turned into a group effort. I had help from my friend Lora Power, whose synesthesia dictated the final number of buttons (to her, seven is the same color as the hat). Joe Blair suggested doing the hats in different "funky" colors and getting more stylized buttons so that men would wear them too instead of just buying them for their girlfriends. And Catherine Chang (age four) gave them the name "Bzzz."

DIRECTIONS

With circular needle, CO 100 sts. Pm, join, and K 1 rnd tbl.

Work in rev St st for 4 rnds. Work in St st for 2 rnds. Rep from * to * 6 times.

Work in rev St st for 4 rnds.

Next rnd: *K8, k2tog; rep from * to end.

K 1 rnd.

Work in rev St st for 4 rnds.

Next rnd: *K7, k2tog; rep from * to end.

K 1 rnd.

Size

Finished circumference: 20"

Materials

Harrisville New England Highland (100% wool; 100g/200 yds), 1 skein #4 Gold or #22 Plum

US 8 (5mm) 16" circular needle, or size needed to obtain gauge

US 8 (5mm) double-pointed needles (set of 5)

7 bee buttons from Incomparable Buttons, www.buttonmad.com

Tapestry needle

Gauge

20 sts and 36 rows = 4" in patt st on larger needles

Change to dpns.

Cont as est, alternating 4 rnds of rev St st with 2 rnds of St st and working 1 st less between decs per dec row until 40 sts rem.

Work 4 rnds in rev St st.

Break yarn, leaving a 12" tail. Draw tail through rem sts and secure on the inside of the hat.

FINISHING
Sew on bee buttons to correspond with picture.

Weave in ends.

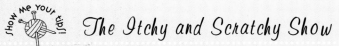

The Itchy and Scratchy Show

TESTING ITCHY YARN AND DEALING WITH A SCRATCHY HAT

To find out if a yarn is itchy and whether it will fuzz or pill under agitation, try the following: Thread a couple of strands of the yarn you want to test through a pendant and wear it around your neck for a few days. Move it around your neck often. Then you can decide if you want to use it.

If you don't have a chance to do this and end up knitting a hat that's too scratchy, here's how to fix it: Pick up all the stitches at the bottom edge of the hat, using a smaller needle than you used for the original hat, and knit a hat liner out of a yarn that doesn't make you itch.

Michelle Ciccariello, Yermo, CA

About Anne

After my third law degree, I ran away for a year to travel the world. To be practical, I learned to knit to while away hours on buses and trains. On the eve of a three-week trip on the Trans-Mongolian Express, I bought a lot of yarn in China, then knit my way across Asia and Europe. Much to my surprise, it turned into a big bonding experience, with everyone—the older women in my group and even Russian soldiers—working on my project. Now I'm back in the United States and knitting on my lunch hour from work, and to avoid doing my homework for an L.L.M. in global technology law. In my nonknitting time, I row, cycle, and blog at www.goannego.com.

STITCH 'N BITCH ACROSS THE NATION
New England

BOSTON, MASSACHUSETTS, SNB

I founded Stitch 'n Bitch Boston in the spring of 2002, when I was a newly-wed who knew few young knitters. After asking around my office to see if anyone wanted to learn to knit, I ended up teaching a packed class of twenty eager young women on their lunch hour. When the class was over, a large group wanted to continue getting together to knit. So when a friend told me about the Stitch 'n Bitch phenomenon, I started a group here through flyers left at a local yarn shop and word of mouth. When I moved that fall, I passed on my leadership role to Martha Spizziri.

Fueled by items in local papers, including the *Boston Globe*'s November 2003 story on knitting, which featured our group, SnB Boston's membership sky-rocketed, expanding from a single weekly meeting in Cambridge to about a dozen in greater Boston and beyond. The Yahoo group has snowballed to around 900 members, and today you can go to a Stitch 'n Bitch somewhere around Boston pretty much any day of the week.

We've also organized charity knit-ting and held group dinners and parties, and were involved in Boston's Knit-Out & Crochet, where we came out to teach people to knit on the Boston Common.

*Laura Erickson and
Martha Spizziri*

HARTFORD, CONNECTICUT, SNB

Here in Hartford, the knit-ting craze hit in Christmas 2003—suddenly, the scarf was the new black. That's what prompted a bunch of us to learn to knit last winter. Being the punk rock, crafty fashion-ista that I am, I was drawn to the Stitch 'n Bitch phenomenon as some-thing that would allow me to let my inner grandma out. It was a loophole for cool people to do something ol' fogie and be damn proud of it! Before I set up the Yahoo group for Hartford, I took a trip to the New Haven SnB and learned the magic combination: coffee, talk, and knit. Pretty simple!

By the second Hartford SnB meeting, twelve people were squished around a few tables at the local Borders. Since then, about eight regulars meet every Wednesday

Hartford, Connecticut

Boston, Massachusetts

evening, and it's a fight to find table space. We'll often sit like vultures around a little square table until we see someone leaving another table. Then we'll spring up and grab it and drag it across the café. We look a little crazy and territorial, but hey, we love it.

This summer we've been working on bags and beach totes, bikinis, tanks, baby clothes . . . and did someone mention strippers' tassels?

Erica Chandler

NEW HAVEN, CONNECTICUT, SnB

I started knitting back in December 2003, after I bought myself a knitting kit and the *Stitch 'n Bitch* book. My mom (who died 10 years ago) had taught me to knit and purl when I was little, but I hadn't touched a needle in almost 25 years.

After reading the book, I sought in vain for a local SnB. So I made a New Year's resolution to start my own group, and in January a friend and I began meeting at a local coffeehouse. Now we have close to seventy members, thanks to my pimping the group on the SnB site, in the *New Haven Advocate,* in the Yale bulletin and calendar, and on various Web sites. Among our members are undergrads at Yale and Southern Connecticut State College, grad students and their spouses, and Yale employees and townies. Ages range from freshmen to "ladies of a certain age," and there are two guys. Knit, crochet, embroider, or sew; we're open to men and women of all ages and skill levels who like to partake of portable crafts.

Karen Unger

New Haven, Connecticut

PEAKS ISLAND, MAINE, CHICKS WITH STICKS

We are a tight-knit group of women who live on beautiful Peaks Island, Maine, about two miles out to sea. Our group emerged one evening in the fall of 2003 as we gathered at the community center to watch a movie, and several women brought their knitting, which piqued the interest of others.

We now get together one afternoon a week to knit a little, eat a little, laugh a lot, and spin a few yarns. Sometimes we gather in front of a fire, sometimes on a deck, sometimes on the rocks, but wherever we choose to click our sticks, the ocean is always our backdrop and inspiration. We also draw inspiration from the artists who live and work on Peaks Island, some of whom have joined our group, bringing their color and design savvy to original fabric creations. Watching them has inspired many of us to "stitch outside the lines" by changing a pattern to make it our own.

Our group shrinks in winter as summer residents depart for warmer climes. One of them, Claire, had become so obsessed that when she went back to South Carolina for the winter, she started her own group there. We call her our knito-maniac; we got her started knitting, and now we can't get her to stop.

Knitting together has itself become a pattern for us, as much a part of the rhythm of our days as the tides and the ferry schedule. Yes, we take great collective satisfaction in the completion of each project. But the greatest boon of our weekly group is that it gives good friends another good reason to get together.

Roxanne Marks

PORTLAND, MAINE, KNITTERS OUT ON THE TOWN

It started simply enough—just a few friends getting together at my house for a night of knitting, snacking, and a little reality TV. My dog was happy to have the extra company, and I enjoyed getting to share my passion with some wonderful women friends. But as the knitting wave rose, I thought, "This isn't just a stay-at-home kind of craft anymore." So in January of 2004 we decided to scout out a place and take our knitting "out on the town." Since then, about seventeen of us have gotten together to knit in Portland's coffee shops, bookstores, wine bars, and an Irish

Portland, Maine

Peaks Island, Maine

pub. We've recruited interested comrades through friends, at work, and through the Maine Stitch 'n Bitch online group.

We've got a great mix of styles—one knitter has been working on the same afghan for months; another only does scarves, but never uses a pattern, coming up with her own fabulous combinations of yarns and beads. She even makes up her own stitches. And for three members, Knitters Out on the Town has become an extension of their divorced women's support group.

As our first official summer together approaches, we look forward to really taking our knitting outdoors—to patios, the beach, maybe even a boat.

Tina Curcuru

Size
Adult

Materials
A: GGH Lara
(90% wool, 10% nylon; 50g/55 yds)

Plain: 3 skeins #2 White

Bear: 3 skeins #12 Coffee

B: GGH Davos (60% merino wool,
40% acrylic; 50g/95 yds)

Plain: 1 skein #9 White

Bear: 1 skein #6 Dark Brown

CC (Bear only): GGH Maxima
(100% merino wool; 50g/120 yds),
1 skein #34 Rose

US 8 (5mm) straight needles

US 10½ (6.5mm) straight needles,
or size needed to obtain gauge

US 10½ (6.5mm) 24" circular needle

US 15 (10mm) 24" circular needle,
or size needed to obtain gauge

Tapestry needle

4 safety pins

2" pom-pom maker or template

Gauge
10 sts and 14 rows = 4" in St st with
2 strands of MC held tog and larger
needles

KATHY BATEMAN
Russian Winter

've always loved hats. Even as a kid, when I helped my mom cook, I wore a metal colander upside down on my head as a "cooking hat." My fashion sense has improved since then, but I still enjoy unique hats. These bonnets, as with many of the hats I make, were inspired by the vast array of lovely eyelash yarn available these days. I'm amazed by how similar to real animal fur the knit yarn looks. Using circular needles for this pattern isn't strictly necessary, but it will make it significantly easier to knit, because of the tight curve of the bonnet shape. And because they're made of wool, these hats will actually keep your head warm, even in Siberia.

DIRECTIONS
BONNET
With 2 strands of A held tog, using size 10½ circular needle, CO 8 sts.

Row 1: K.

Row 2: P.

Row 3: K2, inc L, k to last 2 sts, inc R, k2.

Row 4: P.

Rep these 4 rows 3 times more—16 sts.

Rows 17, 21, and 23: K.

Rows 18 and 20: P.

Row 19: K1, ssk, k to last 3 sts, k2tog, k1.

Rows 22 and 24: P1, p2tog, p to last 3 sts, ssp, p1.

Row 25: Rep Row 19—8 sts.

Abbreviations
Inc R: Insert right needle into top of the loop below the next st. K the loop.

Inc L: Insert left needle into top of the loop below the st. K into front of loop.

Break yarn, leaving sts on needle.

With RS facing, pu 20 sts between right side of CO edge and sts on needle. K sts from needle. Pu 20 sts down left side to CO edge—48 sts.

Beg with a WS row, work in St st until piece measures 7" from picked up sts.

Using size 15 needle, BO very loosely.

EARS (BEAR ONLY; MAKE 2)

Back side:

With 2 strands of A held tog and size 10½ straight needles, CO 10 sts, leaving a 24" tail.

Rows 1, 3, and 5: P.

Rows 2 and 6: K.

Row 4: K2tog, k6, ssk.

Row 7: Ssp, p4, p2tog.

Row 8: K2tog, k2, ssk—4 sts.

Break yarn, leaving a 48" tail. Leave sts on needle.

Front side:

With CC and size 8 needles, CO 12 sts, leaving a 24" tail.

Rows 1, 3, and 5: P.

Row 2: K.

Rows 4 and 6: K2tog, k to last 2 sts, ssk.

Row 7: Ssp, p4, p2tog.

Row 8: K2tog, k2, ssk—4 sts.

Break yarn, leaving an 8" tail. Leave sts on needle.

FINISHING

Ear assembly:

Holding front and back with WS tog, use top MC tail to whipstitch the live sts tog. Whipstitch from top down on both edges. Slip tapestry needle under whipstitches. Pull gently on the yarn until ear curves forward and arcs, resembling a D if turned. Weave in ends, leaving the 48" tails loose.

Make 2nd ear as first.

Ear placement:

With safety pins, arrange ears on hat 5" from the front edge of the bonnet. The inner corners should be placed 4" from each other. The outer corners should each be 6" from the lower edge of the bonnet.

Use corresponding tails to sew back and front of ears to bonnet.

TIES (MAKE 2)

With B, size 8 needles, and a double CO, CO 50 sts.

BO.

Attach one end of each tie to front corners of bonnet.

Use A to make two 2" pom-poms.

Attach one pom-pom to end of each tie.

Weave in ends.

Optional finishing:

Gently brush bonnet with a cat slicker brush to bring more of the fur to the outside.

About Kathy

As a child I was taught how to knit using sharpened pencils. After finishing a few inches I put it away and forgot it. Years later, after a friend reintroduced me to knitting, I quickly became caught up and absorbed in it. Now, whenever I'm not doing something technical or artsy on my computer, I spend my time knitting. I enjoy the meditative quality of it and the challenge of developing new patterns. Many of my hats can be seen on my Web site, www.PlatypusDreams.com, along with the various knitwear creations I sell through my company, Platypus Dreams. I live in Austin, Texas, in a house full of people, rabbits, and yarn.

It All Adds Up

COUNTING YOUR STITCHES

When casting on a large number of stitches, I usually put a plastic ring every 25 or 30 stitches. It saves on counting and recounting! *Debbie Brown, Evanston, IL*

● When I picked up knitting again, I remembered one thing my grandma Mitchell had taught me: When counting your stitches, count by twos and then by threes. So count 2 stitches, then 5, then 7, then 10, then 12, then 15, and so on. It takes a little bit of time to get the flow, but once you do it's quick and I find that I lose count less often. *Sue Mitchell, Raleigh, NC*

HEATHER DIXON

Valentine's Hat & Mittens

My city is frigid in February, so when Valentine's Day rolls around I don't want to be left out in the cold—not without something bright and cheerful to snuggle up in. That was the impetus behind this hat and mitten set, and I've loved it ever since! The hat keeps my ears from freezing and the flip-top mittens solve the problem of swiping my subway card without having to take them off.

You can change the colors and motif if pink hearts aren't your thing. Customize by adding tassels or pom-poms to the hat or a long I-cord to the mittens for times when just flipping the tops off isn't enough.

Enjoy, and stay warm!

STITCH PATTERN
STRIPE SEQUENCE FOR HAT
7 rnds CC, 2 rnds MC, 2 rnds CC, 2 rnds MC, 2 rnds CC, 2 rnds MC, 2 rnds CC, cont even in MC.

DIRECTIONS
MITTENS
With MC, CO 20 sts. Divide sts among 4 dpns, 5 sts on each.

Join and, working in k2, p2 rib, work 2 rnds in MC, then 2 rnds in CC. Rep these 4 rnds twice. Change to MC and work 1 rnd even in rib.

Next rnd: K2, p2, inc1, k1, p2, k1, inc1, p2, k2, inc1, p1, k2, p1, inc1—24 sts.

Work even in St st for 2".

Size

Women's M

MITTENS

Finished length: 10½"

Finished circumference: 7½"

HAT

Finished circumference: 19½"

Materials

Brown Sheep Lamb's Pride Bulky (85% wool, 15% mohair; 113g/125 yds)

MC: 2 skeins #M81 Red Baron

CC: 1 skein #M105 RPM Pink

US 10½ (6.5mm) double-pointed needles, or size needed to obtain gauge (set of 5)

Stitch holder

Tapestry needle

Gauge

13 sts and 20 rows = 4" in St st

Special Skill

DUPLICATE STITCH

Next rnd:

Right mitten: K12, place 4 sts on st holder, k8.

Left mitten: K8, place 4 sts on st holder, k12.

Next rnd:

Right mitten: K12, CO 4, k8.

Left mitten: K8, CO 4, k12.

Next rnd:

Right mitten: K5, k1 pm through this st, k14.

Left mitten: K14, k1 pm through this st, k5.

Work even in St st for 2".

Change to CC and BO tightly.

THUMB

With CC, k 4 sts from holder. Pu 4 sts over those that were CO over the held sts.

Divide sts among dpns and work in St st for 2".

Next rnd: K3tog twice, k2tog.

Next rnd: K3tog.

Break yarn and draw tail through rem st to secure.

FLIP TOP

With MC, tightly CO 12 sts.

Beg with a RS row, work in St st for 5 rows. Place sts on holder.

With MC, RS of mitten facing and working 5 rows down from mitten BO, pu 12 sts. K 12 sts from holder.

Divide sts among dpns and work in St st for 2".

Change to CC.

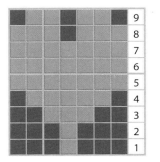

					9
					8
					7
					6
					5
					4
					3
					2
					1

◼ MC

◻ CC

About Heather

*B*orn and bred near Nottingham, England, I needed more excitement in my life, so I headed for the bright lights and high rents of New York City. There I fulfilled my dreams of becoming a successful fashion designer and underground rock 'n' roll goddess. I taught myself to knit at age six and haven't put my needles down since. I also design the contemporary ladies' sweater line called Relais. The small amount of spare time I have is spent enjoying my crazy adopted city and dreaming of travels to faraway places—taking my knitting with me, of course! My latest creations can be seen on my Web site, www.armyofknitters.com.

Next rnd: K2tog, k8, k2tog tbl, k2tog, k8, k2tog tbl.

Work 1 rnd even.

Next rnd: K2tog, k6, k2tog tbl, k2tog, k6, k2tog tbl.

Work 1 rnd even.

Next rnd: K2tog, k4, k2tog tbl, k2tog, k4, k2tog tbl.

Work 1 rnd even.

Next rnd: K2tog, k2, k2tog tbl, k2tog, k2, k2tog tbl—8 sts.

Break yarn, leaving a 6" tail. Draw tail through rem sts, pull tightly to the inside, and secure.

FINISHING
With CC, duplicate stitch motif from chart to top of each mitten, beg with marked st as the bottom point of the heart.

Weave in ends.

HAT
With CC, CO 9 sts. Divide sts among dpns, 2 sts on the first 3 and 3 sts on the fourth. Join and work 3 rnds in St st.

Working in stripe sequence, inc as follows:

Next row: Inc1, k1, (inc1, inc1, k1) twice, inc1—15 sts.

Work 2 rnds even.

Next row: Inc1, k3, (inc1, inc1, k3) twice, inc1—21 sts.

Work 2 rnds even.

Cont as est, working 2 extra sts per rnd between incs and 2 rows even between inc rnds, to 63 sts.

Work 13 rnds even.

Next row: With MC, k24; with CC, BO 15; with MC, k48 (24 sts past beg of rnd).

EAR FLAPS
Turn work and, beg with a P row, work 7 rows back and forth in St st.

Change to CC. K15 and place these sts on a holder, BO 18, k15.

Next row: P2tog, p11, p2tog.

Alternating 2 rows of MC and 2 rows of CC, dec 1 st from each edge on every row to 5 sts.

Work rem 5 sts in I-cord, cont to alternate colors as est, until cord measures 9½".

Break yarn and draw tail through sts to secure.

Rep for second flap with holder sts.

FINISHING
With CC, duplicate stitch motif from chart, centering bottom st of heart over center front, 7 rows up from CC BO.

Weave in ends.

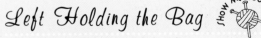

Left Holding the Bag
A NEW USE FOR BAG SEALERS

Use the sealers that come on plastic bread or potato bags to hold the leftover yarn from a long-tail cast on, or as smaller bobbins for intarsia work. *Lindsay Woodel, Providence, RI*

M. K. CARROLL

Head Huggers

NECKWARMER & EARWARMER

Size

Finished measurements, neckwarmer:
11" long (+ ties), 1½" wide

Finished measurements, earwarmer:
17" long (+ ties), 3¼" wide

Materials

MC: Debbie Bliss Cashmerino Aran
(55% merino wool, 33% microfiber,
12% cashmere; 50g/98 yds)

Neckwarmer: 1 skein #101 Ivory

Earwarmer: 1 skein #300 Black

CC1: Debbie Bliss Merino Chunky
(100% merino wool; 50g/55 yds),
1 skein 700 Red

CC2: Debbie Bliss Merino DK
(100% merino wool; 50g/102 yds),
1 skein 501 Lime

Flowers: DMC embroidery floss,
turquoise 3845, 1 skein

Optional: beads, bead needle, thread
to match flower

US 8 (5mm) straight needles (optional)

US 8 (5mm) double-pointed needles, or
size needed to obtain gauge (set of 2)

Stitch markers

Tapestry needle

Gauge

20 sts and 28 rows = 4" in St st

I was growing out a pixie cut and having a bad hair year. That autumn, I knit a little hair band to help keep it in check and, when the weather got colder, a wider one that would cover my ears, too. This project uses a single skein of a luscious yarn, making it a small, luxurious gift or a nice treat for yourself. The shorter band doubles as a neckwarmer, a sweet addition on days when you need a sweater but don't want a long, bulky scarf. The entire piece can be worked on double-pointed needles, especially if you use point protectors to convert them temporarily to straights (thereby giving the work only one end to leap off), or use straight needles if you prefer.

DIRECTIONS

NECKWARMER

With MC and dpns, CO 2 sts. Work in I-cord for 9".

Change to straight needles, or place point protectors at the ends of the dpns to convert them to straights.

Inc row 1: K1, m1, k1.

Row 2: Sl1, p to end.

Row 3: Sl1, m1f, k1, m1b, k1.

Row 4: Sl1, p to end.

Row 5: K1, m1f, k3, m1b, k1.

Row 6: Sl1, work in 1 × 1 rib to last 2 sts, p2.

Abbreviations

M1f: Make 1, front (left slanting). Pick up as for m1 from front to back. Knit the strand through the back loop.

M1b: Make 1, back (right slanting). Pick up as for m1 from back to front. Knit the strand through the front loop.

Row 7: Sl1, m1f, rib to last 2 sts, k1, m1b, k1.

Row 8: Sl1, p2, rib to last 2 sts, p2.

Row 9: Sl1, m1f, rib to last st, m1b, k1.

Row 10: Sl1, rib to end.

Row 11: Sl1, m1f, rib to last st, m1b, k1.

Pm on RS of work. Work in 1 × 1 rib, slipping first st of every row pwise, until piece measures 9½" from beg, ending with RS facing.

Dec row 1: Sl1, k2tog tbl, rib to last 3 sts, k2tog, k1.

Row 2: Sl1, rib to last 2 sts, p2.

Row 3: Sl1, k2tog tbl, rib to last 3 sts, k2tog, k1.

Row 4: Sl1, p2, rib to end.

Row 5: Sl1, k2tog tbl, p1, k1, p1, k2tog, k1.

Row 6: Sl1, rib to last 2 sts, p2.

Row 7: Sl1, k2tog tbl, k1, k2tog, k1.

Row 8: Sl1, p to end.

Row 9: Sl1, k2tog tbl, k2tog.

Row 10: Sl1, p2tog.

Row 11: K.

Change to dpns.

With RS facing, work in I-cord on rem 2 sts for 9".

Next row: K2tog, break yarn, and draw tail through st to secure.

EARWARMER
Using dpns, CO 2 sts. Work in I-cord for 11".

Change to straight needles.

Inc row 1: K1, m1, k1.

Row 2: Sl1, p to end.

Row 3: Sl1, m1f, k1, m1b, k1.

Row 4: Sl1, work in 1 × 1 rib to end.

Row 5: Sl1, m1f, rib to last st, m1b, k1.

Row 6: Sl1, rib to last 2 sts, p2.

Row 7: Sl1, m1f, rib to last st, m1b, k1.

Row 8: Sl1, p2, rib to last 2 sts, p2.

Rep rows 5 to 8 four times more.

Rep rows 5 to 6 once more.

Pm on RS of work. Work in 1 × 1 rib, slipping first st of every row pwise, until piece measures 13" from beg, ending with RS facing.

Dec row 1: Sl1, k2tog tbl, rib to last 4 sts, k1, k2tog, p1.

Row 2: Sl1, p2, rib to end.

Row 3: Sl1, k2tog tbl, rib to last 4 sts, p1, k2tog, p1.

Tie one on: Earwarmer may be fastened beneath chin or under hair.

Row 4: Sl1, rib to end.

Rep dec rows 1 to 4 four times.

Row 21: Sl1, k2tog tbl, k1, k2tog, p1.

Row 22: Sl1, p to end.

Row 23: Sl1, k2tog tbl, k2tog.

Row 24: Sl1, p2tog.

Row 25: K.

Change to dpns. With WS facing, work in I-cord on rem 2 sts for 11".

Next row: K2tog, break yarn, and draw tail through st to secure.

5-PETAL FLOWER
(MAKE 1 FOR EARWARMER)
With CC1 and straight needles, CO 42 sts.

Row 1: K.

Row 2: K2, *k1, slip st to left needle, lift next 5 sts over and off end of needle, k slipped st again, k2; rep from * to end.

Rows 3 and 5: P

Rows 4 and 6: K1, *k2tog; rep from * to end.

Break yarn and thread tail through rem sts.

6-PETAL FLOWER (MAKE 1 EACH FOR NECKWARMER
AND EARWARMER)
With CC1 and straight needles, CO 50 sts.

Row 1: K.

Row 2: K2, *k1, slip st to left needle, lift next 5 sts over and off end of needle, k slipped st again, k2; rep from * to end.

Row 3: K.

Row 4: *P2tog; rep from * to end.

Row 5: *K2tog, rep from * to end.

Break yarn and thread tail through rem sts.

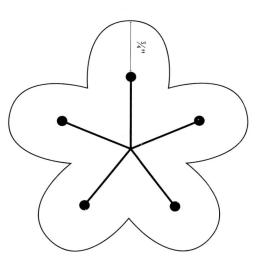

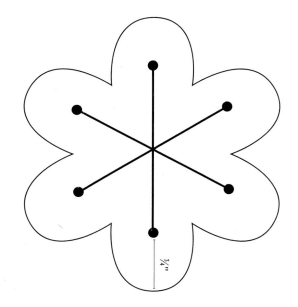

SMALL LEAF (MAKE 1 EACH FOR NECKWARMER AND EARWARMER)

With straight needles, CO 3 sts.

Row 1: P.

Row 2: (K1, m1) twice, k1.

WS rows 3 to 11: P.

Row 4: (K1, m1) to last st, k1.

Row 6: K.

Row 8: (K2, m1) twice, k1 (m1, k2) twice, k2.

Row 10: Sl1, *k2tog; rep from * to end.

Row 12: Sl1, *k2tog; rep from * to end.

Row 13: (Sl1, p1, psso) twice.

Row 14: K.

Change to dpns. With RS facing, work I-cord to desired length.

Next row: K2tog.

Break yarn, leaving a 6" tail, and draw tail through rem sts.

LARGE LEAF (MAKE 1 EACH FOR NECKWARMER AND EARWARMER)

Work as for small leaf to row 9. Work rows 6–7 twice. Work as for small leaf from row 10 to end.

FINISHING

Block all pieces. Whipstitch flower ends tog. Use a double strand of embroidery thread to make stamens in the center of the flowers with either beads or French knots. Attach flowers and leaves to warmers to correspond with picture. Weave in all ends.

Neckwarmer doubles as a vintage-style hairband!

About M. K.

My mother says that I insisted I knew how to sew at the age of four and that I demanded she teach me to knit when I was five. After learning to purl, I chucked knitting for crocheting and started telling grown-ups the same thing I tell people today when they ask me what I'm making: "I don't know." It took nearly twenty years for me to get back to it, but I haven't traveled without needles and yarn since. I've recently moved back to my hometown in Hawaii, where I'm exploring the knitting possibilities for subtropical conditions. When I'm not roaming around the United States, I'm working in natural-food cooperatives.

STITCH 'N BITCH ACROSS THE NATION
New York

Bushwick, Brooklyn

ALBANY, NEW YORK, KNITWITS

Albany's KnitWits was born when two chicks—Renee McAllister and Melissa Mansfield—met at a party and decided to get together for a knit. Renee had worked at most of the cafes in town and didn't care to return, and Melissa had enough energy that she didn't need a caffeine boost, so they decided to go the bar route. Dozens of knitters were invited to knit at Albany's infamous dive bar, the Palais Royale. Unfortunately, no one showed, so Renee and Melissa sat there alone. Renee taught Melissa how to purl and Melissa encouraged Renee to finish that pesky scarf, and they decided to keep meeting.

As they knit their way through trendy Center Square neighborhood watering-holes, the two became five, and they now have a rotating group of around twenty who meet regularly at the Wine Bar. Among their members is craftivist Cat Mazza, who knits corporate logos to raise sweatshop awareness and is responsible for the group's blog at www.microrevolt.org.

The Albany KnitWits are dedicated to teaching strangers and each other fiber arts while talking about needle preferences, boyfriends, and feminist porn within a bar scene. And it's working.

Melissa Mansfield

BUSHWICK, BROOKLYN, NEW YORK, HARBOR SCHOOL KNITTING CLUB

I'm a guidance counselor at the New York Harbor School, a themed high school in an impoverished section of Brooklyn where many students are recent immigrants and many have special needs. The intention behind the theme is to keep kids interested, and the after-school programs, such as the rowing team and the boat-building club, generally tie into it.

And then there's Stitch 'n Bitch. It started when a few students wandered into my office while I was knitting, asked me what I was doing, and said they wanted to learn how. I couldn't believe they wanted to learn to knit—I was so excited. I got donations of fifteen beginner knitting kits, and the Harbor School Knitting Club (aka Stitch 'n Bitch) was officially formed. The fifteen spots were filled before I could finish stapling the sign-up sheet to the bulletin board. When I looked at the names on the list, I did a double take: Ten of the fifteen kids who signed up were boys.

The first meeting was spent teaching the students the basics of casting on and knitting. The next day, I spotted my proud new knitters in the cafeteria finishing their lunch in a hurry so they could get back to their knitting! Soon enough, word spread and SnB Bushwick now has thirty new knitters (in a school of only 125) and

Albany, New York

twenty-five more kids on a waiting list. Lunch has become a knitting clinic, and the SnB meets every morning before school. Everyone's knitting: boys, girls, popular kids, not-so-popular kids, jocks, and bookworms. Knitting is the hottest thing to hit the Harbor School since Timberland boots and do-rags!

Ali Newman

HARLEM, NEW YORK, HARLEM KNITTING CIRCLE

After a workplace accident left me disabled, financially compromised, and temporarily discouraged, I took a knitting class in the spring of 2003. As I struggled with the technique the teacher was forcing on me, I suddenly remembered knitting as my grandmother had taught me at age eight. I left the class

Harlem, New York

and began knitting like a demon.

My knitting jones drove me to create the Harlem Knitting Circle, where no one is excluded, regardless of identity or income. The NYC Parks Department granted us a space for a few weeks, but then asked that we pay membership fees. This went against my premise that everyone should be included, so we found a new home in January 2004 at the George Bruce Library. The auditorium is beautiful and elevator accessible, which is very important to me.

Our diverse multicultural group reflects the changing landscape of Harlem. In HKC's core of about thirty knitters, crocheters, crafters, designers, and artists, the youngest participant is five years old and the senior member is eighty.

We recently completed our first charity project of chemotherapy hats and lap covers for Harlem Hospital's cancer unit. We welcome everyone and hope to see you soon!

Anntoinette Njoya Angrum

ITHACA, NEW YORK, SNB

After completing our first knitting class in the fall of 2003 at Homespun, our LYS, my friend and I couldn't bear for it to be over and launched the Ithaca SnB at Wownet Digital Café.

Ithaca, New York

With about five core members, Ithaca SnB sees a lot of folks cycle in and out—the largest crew so far is ten people plus two dogs. We've got folks working on everything from the ever-popular scarves to children's sweaters to yoga pants, and we're considering starting a "sweater support group" to encourage folks to branch out a bit. Our conversation topics range from politics to drug culture to parenting (although few of us are parents). A male knitting genius once made a cameo appearance, and at some meetings three generations of the same family show up—they're a total blast! I'm glad we took the plunge and started the group. It's helped me develop my knitting skills, and most of all, it's given me the opportunity to meet some amazing people who share a passion for creating.

Natasha Ribeiro

LONG ISLAND CITY, NEW YORK, SNB

Our meetings are about more than knitting and companionship. They're a comforting, familiar highlight to a stressful week—a refuge and a support group. Since we first formed, at Café Ten63, our members devoutly show up every week, rain or shine, and whoever doesn't attend hears about it. Like when our boy knitter, Dave, passed up an evening of knitting to sit outside his school classroom to catch a glimpse of P. Diddy—that stuff just doesn't float. And trying to avoid knitting a gauge swatch doesn't sit well with our resident Gauge-Swatch Patrol Woman, Melissa.

In the time our group has been in existence, all of us have come to know one another, our creativity, and our individuality, which we spend three hours every week turning into knitted objects in each other's company. We get excited about hearing the reactions of a mom or a brother when one of us gives away something she or he has just finished knitting, something we were privileged to watch grow stitch by stitch. We are the audience and the orators of countless stories of the trials and tribula-

tions, pitfalls and triumphs of every waking hour that is our life. What more could I hope for? Well, maybe that P. Diddy could start knitting with us.

Anja Shutz

NEW YORK, NEW YORK, SNB

Back in 1999 I became obsessed (obsessed!) with knitting and soon didn't want to do much else. I'd go to rock concerts or bars or parties, only to find myself standing there bored, wishing I were at home making progress on one of my knitting projects. At the same time, more and more people were asking me to teach them to knit. So I decided to combine two activities—knitting and socializing—and started NYC Stitch 'n Bitch. I invited anyone who knew how to knit or wanted to learn, and we began meeting in a small coffeeshop in the East Village. Over the years, we've moved locales many times, sometimes being welcomed into our new homes; other times not, like at one cafe where disgruntled baristas tried to blast us out by playing the most annoying heavy metal music they could find. It didn't work.

Our membership, too, is ever-changing, with very few folks from the early years still attending meetings today. In fact, every year or

New York, New York

so there seems to be a complete turnover, as people move out of town, schedule something else for that weeknight, simply decide to give up knitting or suddenly take it up. Even I have barely had time to attend the group since I moved to Brooklyn. But that doesn't matter; the group doesn't need me, or any leader—it just needs a day of the week, a place to meet, and folks who want to knit. Though not many of us socialize outside our SnB meetings, our connection is significant. Knitting somehow frees up your mind to listen more intently to someone who's speaking. As a result, like the strands of yarn that we weave together with the click-click-click of our knitting needles, we can't help but become entwined in each other's lives as we meet for a few hours each week to share stories, share laughs, and share skills.

Debbie Stoller

Long Island City, New York

SHANNITA WILLIAMS-ALLEYNE

Headline News

CABLED NEWSBOY CAP

n my quest for the perfect Rasta hat for my dredlocked huz, I found that almost any hat I could buy looked great on him. But when *I* tried them on, they looked awful. I decided to take matters into my own hands and make a funky newsboy-styled cap that could double as a Rasta cap with a few minor tweaks. I wanted the hat to be both funky and feminine, and flatter everyone from conservative grrls to sisters with attitude.

STITCH PATTERN

CABLE PATTERN

Rnds 1–3: *P2, k9, p2, k6; rep from * to end.

Rnd 4: *P2, k9, p2, c6b; rep from * to end.

DIRECTIONS

With shorter, smaller circular needle, CO 76 sts. Pm, join in the rnd, and work in 1 × 1 rib for 1". (Optional: To make rib tighter, carry a thin strand of matching elastic along with yarn in ribbing.)

Change to larger circular needle.

Next rnd: *K2, m1; rep from * to end—114 sts.

Work 1 rnd even in St st.

Work cable patt 3 times or, to make hat larger to accommodate dredlocks, braids, or big hair, rep cable patt until piece is 5 to 7" long.

Size
Women's M

Materials
Blue Sky Worsted Hand Dyes (50% alpaca, 50% merino; 100g/ 100 yds), 2 skeins #2004 purple

US 8 (5mm) 16" circular needle

US 8 (5mm) 24" circular needle

US 10½ (6.5mm) 16" circular needle, or size needed to obtain gauge

US 10½ (6.5mm) double-pointed needles (set of 4)

Cable needle

Tapestry needle

1 sheet plastic mesh

Optional: 1 card Rainbow Elastic in color to match

Gauge
16 sts and 22 rows = 4" in St st on larger needles

Special Skill
CABLES

SHAPE TOP

(Change to dpns when necessary.)

Rnd 1: Working in St st, *P2, k2tog, k7, p2, k6; rep from * to end.

Rnd 2: *P2, k8, p2, k6; rep from * to end.

Rnd 3: *P2, k6, k2tog, p2, k6; rep from * to end.

Rnd 4: *P2, k7, p2, c6b; rep from * to end.

Cont as est, working 1 less st before/after decs and maintaining cable every 4th rnd to 72 sts, ending with a rnd 4.

Next rnd: *P2tog, k2tog, p2tog, k6; rep from * to end.

Next rnd: *K1, p2, k6; rep from * to end.

Next rnd: *P2tog, p1, c6b; rep from * to end.

Next rnd: *K2tog; rep from * to end.

Next rnd: *K2tog; rep from * to end.

Next rnd: *K2tog; rep from * to end—6 sts.

Break yarn, leaving a 6" tail. Draw tail through rem sts, pull to inside, and secure.

BRIM

With longer, smaller circular needle,
pu 7 sts before and 7 sts after hat CO join.

P 1 row.

Next row: K2, m1, pm, k10, pm, m1, k2. Pu 2 sts from hat CO edge.

Next row: P to end, pu 2 sts from hat CO edge.

Next row: K to marker, m1, sm, k10, sm, m1, k to end, pu 2 sts from hat CO edge.

Next row: P to end, pu 2 sts from hat CO edge.

Rep last 2 rows until brim measures 2" (measured from center), ending with RS facing.

Turning ridge (RS): P 1 row.

Brim Template
(actual size)

**Next row: BO2, slipping first st before binding off rather than purling it, p to end.

Next row: BO2, slipping first st before binding off rather than knitting it, k to 2 sts before marker, ssk, sm, k10, sm, k2tog, k to end.**

Rep from ** to ** to 14 sts, ending with RS facing.

BO.

Using brim template, cut plastic mesh for brim. Slip into brim pocket and stitch edge closed.

Optional: To make hat more "Rasta," stitch edge closed without plastic mesh.

About Shannita

Once a devout crocheter, I'm a former marketing executive who learned to knit in the aftermath of the Great Dot-com Crash of 2001. With a severance package and too much time on my hands, I picked up two sticks and some string and never looked back. I now work at the Los Angeles knit shop Jennifer Knits and sell my own designs through my company, Craftydiva Handmade Wears.

Purl Jams

MAKING TIGHTER PURL STITCHES

If the last knit stitch of your cable or wide rib tends to be loose, try this: On the wrong side of the fabric, when you come to purl the stitch that would otherwise be loose, instead of wrapping the yarn over the needle counterclockwise (from top right) to purl it, try wrapping it the other way (clockwise from bottom right). This takes less yarn, so it creates a tighter purl stitch (and thus a tighter knit stitch on the right side of your work). Then, when you come to knitting that stitch on the right side, you will have to *knit it through the back loop*. If you purl much looser than you knit, this could be a permanent way for you to deal with that problem. Or you could just use a size smaller needle on the purl rows in stockinette stitch. Or you could change your name to Elizabeth Zimmermann and work everything in the round and never purl again.

Darrow Wendoloski, Victoria, Australia

LAURA GRUTZECK

Later 'Gator Mitts

Sizes

Child's 2–6 (Child's 8–12, Women's S/M)

Finished length: 6½ (8, 10¼)"

Finished circumference: 4¾ (6¼, 8)"

Materials

Cascade 220 (100% wool; 100g/220 yds)

MC: 1 skein #7814 Chartreuse

CC1: 1 skein #8895 Christmas Red

CC2: 1 skein #8505 White

US 5 (3.75mm) double-pointed needles
(set of 5)

US 7 (4.5mm) double-pointed needles,
or size needed to obtain gauge
(set of 5)

Two pairs sew-on wiggly eyes,
12 (12, 15)mm

Tapestry needle

Stitch holder

Gauge

20 sts and 26 rows = 4" in St st on
larger needles

22 sts and 44 rows = 4" in garter st on
smaller needles

his design is dedicated to my coworker Erin, because without her I would never have realized that I needed a pair of alligator mittens. Erin came in to work one day with a pair of child-size alligator mittens that her great-grandmother had knit more than twenty years ago. The mittens were really cute, but so small that Erin couldn't wear them without stretching the heck out of them. Everyone at work wanted a pair, so I told them I would try to create my own version of the mittens, for children *and* adults. This pattern is the result. One warning: Wearing these mittens may lead to impromptu puppet shows!

DIRECTIONS
(MAKE 2)

With smaller needles and MC, CO 24 (30, 38) sts. Divide sts among dpns, 6 (7, 9) sts on first 3 needles and 6 (9, 11) sts on 4th.

Join and work in k1, p1 rib for 13 (16, 20) rnds.

Change to larger needles and work 10 (13, 16) rnds in St st.

Next rnd: Inc1, k12 (16, 18), inc1 into next 2 sts, k8 (14, 16), inc1—28 (34, 42) sts.

Remainder of mitt is worked flat, using 2 of the dpns.

BOTTOM

Next row: Turn (WS facing) and p12 (16, 20) sts onto 1 needle, placing rem sts on a holder.

Work even in St st for 4 (6, 10) rows.

Next row (RS): K1, ssk, k to last 3 sts, k2tog, k1.

Next row: P.

Rep these 2 rows 2 (3, 4) times more—6 (8, 10) sts.

P 1 row even. BO and break yarn.

TOP

With WS facing, using MC, p16 (18, 22) sts from holder onto 1 dpn.

Work even in St st for 9 (13, 19) rows.

Next row (RS): K1, ssk, k to last 3 sts, k2tog, k1.

Next row: P.

Rep these 2 rows 4 (4, 5) times more—6 (8, 10) sts.

P 1 row even. BO.

MOUTH

With 2 of the smaller needles and CC1, CO 4 (6, 8) sts.

*Row 1: K even.

Row 2: K1, inc1, k to last 2 sts, inc1, k1.

Rows 3–4: K.*

Rep from * to * 4 (4, 5) times—14 (16, 20) sts.

Work even in garter st for 30 (40, 50) rows.

Next row (WS): P1, p2tog, p to last 3 sts, p2tog, p1.

Next row: K1, ssk, k to last 3 sts, k2tog, k1—10 (12, 16) sts.

Work 9 (13, 19) rows even in garter st.

*Next row (RS): K1, ssk, k to last 3 sts, k2tog, k1.

Next 3 rows: K.*

Rep from * to * 2 (2, 3) times—
4 (6, 8) sts.

K 1 row even. BO.

About Laura

My mother taught me to knit when I was about ten, but, for reasons I can't remember, my lessons never progressed past the garter stitch strip. Many years later something inspired me to knit mittens for Christmas gifts, so I bought yarn and a how-to book and taught myself to knit on double-pointed needles. Although the mittens came out looking like giant misshapen potholders, that didn't discourage me, oddly enough, and I have been knitting ever since. For the past two years I have worked part-time at Rosie's Yarn Cellar in Philadelphia, which has given me the opportunity to mingle with many talented and creative knitters. I plan to retire someday to a large house in the country, where I will have room for all my dogs and my embarrassingly large yarn stash.

FINISHING

Steam-block all pieces.

Using French knots and CC2, embroider teeth inside top and bottom of mouth as follows: Thread a tapestry needle with a length of CC2. Attach the yarn to the WS of the mouth and bring the yarn through to the front of the work. Hold the needle close to your work and wrap the yarn around the needle 3 times. Put the needle half a st away from where you originally pulled the yarn through and pull it to the back of your work. Carefully pull the yarn through until it tightens into a knot, holding the wraps against your work while you pull the yarn through. Be careful not to pull too hard, or the knot could be pulled through to the back.

Holding the WSs of the work tog and matching the wider part of the mouth to the wider part of the head, use mattress st to sew the pieces tog. Weave in all ends and sew the eyes to the top of the wider part of the head.

Lift and Separate

SHOW ME YOUR TIPS!

MAKING YOUR OWN YARN BRAS

I'm sure you've seen those plastic-netting "yarn bras" used to keep yarn from unraveling. Recently, while working on a pair of particularly fine-gauge socks, I found my ball of yarn unraveling. I improvised with the red netting that baby gouda cheese comes in. (It looks just like the yarn bras you see in yarn stores and magazines!) You can find those plastic nets holding little cheeses, potatoes, garlic, and so on in the produce aisle. Simply cut off one end and you have an instant homemade yarn bra. *Jamie Henderson, Chicago, IL*

● At any given time, I usually have several pairs of stockings that are too holey to wear (I don't know why I keep them, other than that I'm a third-generation pack rat). I've started recycling them to contain unruly balls of yarn in my WIP bag. Cut the foot off about 3 inches above the heel and stuff your yarn in the foot. It will hold your ball together nicely, keep it from tangling with other balls, and make it easy to "spin out" twisted yarn—just hold the yarn at one end, let the ball of yarn in the stocking toe dangle freely, and allow it to untwist itself. Should you need to knit with yarn from the inside and outside of the ball, there's enough give in the nylon to allow for a double feed. Simply cut the toe off and pull the other end of the yarn from there. *Mindy Weisberger, Union City, NJ*

● I've found that I can reduce tangles coming from the center of large skeins of yarn if I remove the label, then place 2 or 3 rubber bands loosely around the outside of the skein. This seems to keep the tension constant as I pull yarn from the center, which is how I prefer to work. A few rubber bands work just as well as the "yarn bras" sold for this purpose. *Shauna Armstrong, Austin, TX*

CHRISTINE QUIRION

Basic Cable

Size
Finished circumference: 21½"

Materials

JELLYBEAN HAT
Brown Sheep Lamb's Pride Worsted
(85% wool, 15% mohair; 113g/190 yds)

A: 1 skein #M69 Old Sage

B: 1 skein #M105 RPM Pink

C: 1 skein #M155 Lemon Drop

D: 1 skein #M110 Orange You Glad

BLACK LICORICE HAT
Brown Sheep Prairie Silk (72% wool,
18% mohair, 10% silk; 50g/88 yds),
2 skeins #PS150 Obsidian

US 7 (4.5mm) 16" circular needle

US 8 (5mm) 16" circular needle,
or size needed to obtain gauge

US 8 (5mm) double-pointed needles
(set of 4)

Cable needle

1 stitch marker

Jellybean hat only: 3" pom-pom maker
or template

Gauge
18 sts and 24 rows = 4" in 2 × 2 rib on
larger needles

Special Skill
CABLES

In the dead of winter, I had trekked north from Boston to Vermont, armed with a cable needle and some really wonderful yarn. Mittens were the original plan, but things weren't working out. My inner Girl Scout encouraged me to be experimental and try something else with my circular needles. I'd seen a few smartly cabled hats on the morning T train, and I thought I might be able to come up with a design of my own. I wanted a hat that would fit me snugly, without riding up my hair to the top of my head or stretching out to the size of a purse. Even on my very round head, this hat has stayed true to its shape, thanks to the cables and ribbing. The pattern is very versatile and with a change of colors looks great on both sexes.

STITCH PATTERN
JELLYBEAN COLOR SEQUENCE
*4 rnds A, 4 rnds B, 4 rnds C, 4 rnds D; rep from *.

DIRECTIONS
With smaller circular needle, CO 96 sts.

(For Jellybean colorway, follow stripe sequence for entire hat.)

Join and work in k1, p2 ribbing for 6 rnds.

Change to larger circular needle.

**Rnds 1, 2, 3, 4, and 5: *K2, p2, k6, p2; rep from * to end of round.

Rnd 6: *K2, p2, c6f, p2; rep from * to end of round.**

Rep from ** to ** 3 times.

Rep rnds 1 and 2 again.

Divide sts between 3 dpns, 32 sts on each.

Dec rnd 1: *K2, p2, k1, k2tog, k2tog, k1, p2; rep from * to end of rnd—80 sts.

Rnds 2, 3, and 5: *K2, p2, k4, p2; rep from * to end of rnd.

Rnd 4: *K2, p2, c4f, p2; rep from * to end of rnd.

Rnd 6: *K2, p2, k1, k2tog, k1, p2; rep from * to end of rnd—72 sts.

Rnd 7: *K2, p2, k3, p2; rep from * to end of rnd.

Rnd 8: *K2tog, p2tog, ssk, k1, p2tog; rep from * to end of rnd—40 sts.

Rnd 9: *K1, p1, k2tog, p1; rep from * to end of rnd—32 sts.

Rnd 10: *K1, p1, k1, p1; rep from * to end of rnd.

Rnd 11: *K2tog; rep from * to end of rnd—16 sts.

Rnd 12: K.

Rnd 13: *K2tog; rep from * to end of rnd—8sts.

Break yarn, leaving a 12" tail. Draw tail through rem sts to the inside and secure.

FINISHING

For Jellybean hat: Make pom-pom from colors A, B, C, D and attach to center top of hat.

Weave in ends.

Licorice basic cable

About Christine

I started knitting while I was finishing up grad school for library science. I bartered a lesson in computer graphics for a knitting lesson from a classmate. Since learning to knit, it's been the "knitting with others" experience that inspires me to take on new projects and try out new yarns. Each week, I look forward to seeing my knitting cohorts at Peet's in Harvard Square. Knitting and crafting have added a dimension to my life that I didn't even know was missing, and introduced me to intelligent, creative, and quirky people. I work as a librarian at an academic library in Boston, and when I'm not knitting or searching out new craft ideas on the Web, I spend time singing badly at karaoke, watching bad TV, going bowling, or hanging out with my favorite people and animals.

Pick Your Nostepinne

TWO WAYS TO MAKE YOUR OWN YARN WINDING TOOL

A nostepinne is an old Swedish knitting tool used to wind yarn into a beautiful center-pull ball by hand. To use one, begin by wrapping the end of your yarn a few times around the neck of the nostepinne, a few inches up from the bottom of it. Hold the nostepinne with your left hand, and, with your right, begin winding the yarn a few inches down from the top, laying each wrap of yarn next to another until you have about a 1½" width of wraps. Wind your yarn diagonally across these wraps while turning the nostepinne slowly with your left hand until all of the yarn is wound. When you're done, slip the ball of yarn off the nostepinne, and begin knitting with the yarn end that is hanging out of the center. *DS*

● Empty M & M tubes can be used as nostepinnes. I know people use empty medicine bottles and toilet paper tubes, but I find the large M & M tubes easier to hold on to. Plus, since it's about an inch wide, if the ball is wound tightly, there is usually enough give once the tube is removed from the ball that the ball will soften up and be perfect to knit from. *Helen Keier, Bronx, NY*

● You know those beautiful nostepinnes you see at craft sales? The ones for $25 and more? They look like they've been handmade on Grandfather's lathe. I come from a long line of women who see something they want (a dress, a sweater, a nostepinne) and decide that they can make it cheaper. So, I went to Lowes and bought an unfinished ash table leg (12" long). One end has a screw for attaching the leg to a table. The other is rounded. I sawed off the rounded end, drilled a hole in it, and screwed it into the other end, so it would have a narrow end for sliding off the finished ball and a nice pattern of grooves for anchoring the inside strand of yarn. I sanded and then finished it with Danish oil. Tada! A nostepinne for around $6.00! *Pamela Potter, Seattle, WA*

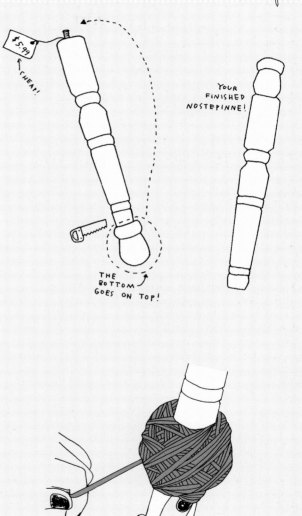

APRIL FISCHER

Jesse's Flames

Size

Men's S (M, L, XL)

Finished chest: 36 (41, 44, 47)"

Finished length: 25$\frac{1}{2}$ (26$\frac{1}{2}$, 27, 27$\frac{1}{2}$)"

Materials

Lion Brand Wool-Ease
(80% acrylic, 20% wool; 85g/197 yds)

MC: 7 (7, 8, 9) skeins #153 Black

CC1: 1 skein #102 Ranch

CC2: 1 skein #158 Buttercup

US 8 (5mm) straight needles,
or size needed to obtain gauge

US 7 (4.5mm) straight needles

Gauge

18 sts and 24 rows = 4" in St st

Special Skills

Intarsia/Duplicate stitch

the idea for this sweater came to me one night from an episode of *Monster Garage.* I was knitting a sweater for one of my kids and watching the show when Jesse James made a comment about projects and designs, saying, "everything looks cooler with flames." And a sweater pattern was born. Of course, Jesse was referring to the detailed, freestyle flames that adorn his Monster Garage projects and custom motorcycles, but I spent many nights trying to come up with a flame design that would look cool, be fun to knit, *and* stand out in a crowd. I think this sweater does just that.

DIRECTIONS

FRONT

**With MC and larger needles, CO 85 (92, 99, 106) sts.

Row 1: P1, *K6, p1; rep from * to end.

Next row: P.

Rep these 2 rows until work measures 15$\frac{1}{2}$ (16, 16, 16$\frac{1}{2}$)" from beg, ending with RS facing.

Shape raglan:

Change to CC1.

Dec row: K1, ssk, k to last 3 sts, k2tog, k1.

Next row: P.

Rep these 2 rows once.**

Change to MC and work dec row, then EOR 18 (19, 20, 20) times more— 43 (48, 53, 60) sts.

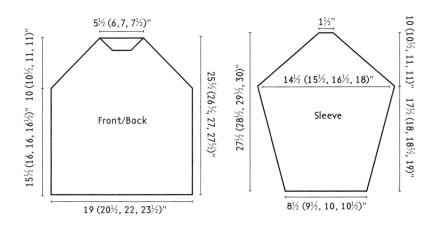

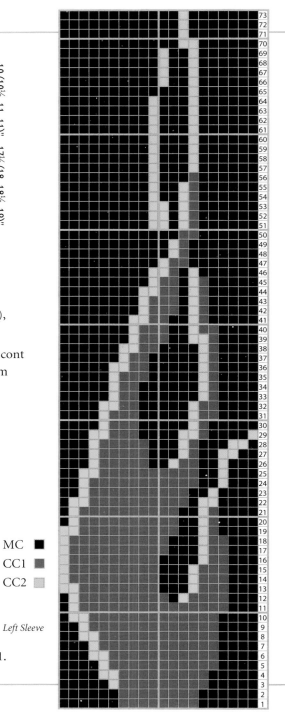

Work 1 row even.

Next row (RS): K1, ssk, k13 (14, 16, 18), BO 11 (14, 15, 18), k13 (14, 16, 18), k2tog, k1—30 (32, 36, 40) sts.

Joining a new ball of MC to left front, work both sides of neck at once and cont to dec one st at each shoulder edge EOR and, at the same time, BO 1 st from each neck edge EOR until there is 1 st on each side.

Break yarn. Draw tail through rem st to secure.

BACK

Work as for front from ** to **.

Change to MC.

Rep dec row as est 28 (30, 32, 34) times—25 (28, 31, 34) sts.

Next row (WS): P.

BO.

SLEEVES

With CC1 and smaller needles, CO 38 (42, 44, 48) sts.

Work 3 rows in garter st.

Change to MC and larger needles.

Next row (RS): K1, m1, k8 (10, 11, 13), pm, k20, pm, k8 (10, 11, 13), m1, k1.

MC ■
CC1 ■
CC2 ■

Left Sleeve

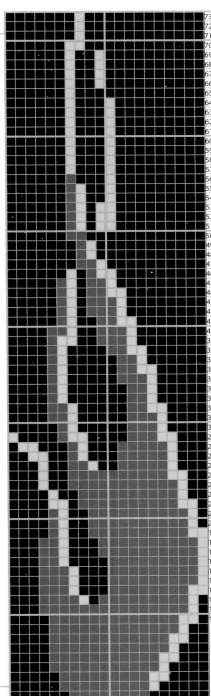

Right Sleeve

Working in St st, inc 1 st at each edge of every foll 7th row to 66 (70, 74, 80) sts.

At the same time, when work measures 1" from beg, foll chart between markers, working all CC2 sts in MC. (These will be duplicate-stitched on at end.)

When chart and all incs have been worked, work even until piece measures 17½ (18, 18½, 19)" from beg.

Shape caps:

Next row: K1, ssk, k to last 3 sts, k2tog, k1.

Next row: P.

Rep these 2 rows 28 (30, 32, 34) times—8 (8, 8, 10) sts.

BO.

FINISHING

Duplicate st CC2 between markers, beg 1" from CO edge on sleeves, following chart.

Mattress st both sleeves to front of body and right sleeve to back of body.

COLLAR

With MC and larger needles, pu 68 (76, 80, 88) sts around neckline.

Work in 2 × 2 rib until collar measures 1½" from beg, ending with WS facing.

Change to CC1 and p 1 row.

BO in rib patt.

Mattress st left sleeve to back of body and stitch collar edges together.

Mattress st side and sleeve seams.

Weave in all ends.

About April

I began knitting three years ago, when I decided I wanted to make my own sweaters. I went to the local crafts store, bought some yarn, needles, and a how-to book, and slowly taught myself to knit. Within a few months, I completed my first sweater, joined the local knitting guild, and began improving my craft. I finally became confident enough to put my first sketches on my knitting Blog, www.knittingiscool.type-pad.com/knit_kitty, and the response was very positive. Those sketches eventually became the sweater in this book. I live in Cary, Illinois, with my husband, our three amazing kids, and a very mischievous Labrador retriever.

KATE WATSON
Fairly Easy Fair Isle

f rightened of Fair Isle? Why not cut your colorwork teeth on this super-simple cardigan? The basic motifs, flat construction, and bulky yarn combine into a sweater that's as easy to knit as a single-colored version would be.

DIRECTIONS

BODY

With MC and longer circular needle, CO 105 (116, 128, 140, 152) sts.

Beg with a WS row, work 3 rows in garter st.

Work in St st until piece measures 13 (14, 14, 15, 15)" from beg.

Place all sts on scrap yarn.

SLEEVES (MAKE 2)

With MC and straight needles, CO 27 (32, 32, 42, 42) sts.

K 1 row (WS).

Work 2 rows in St st.

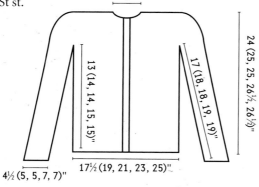

8"

13 (14, 14, 15, 15)"

17 (18, 18, 19, 19)"

24 (25, 25, 26½, 26½)"

4½ (5, 5, 7, 7)"

17½ (19, 21, 23, 25)"

Size

Women's XS (S, M, L, XL)

Finished bust: 35 (38, 42, 46, 50)"

Finished length: 24 (25, 25, 26½, 26½)"

Materials

Brown Sheep Lamb's Pride Bulky
(85% wool, 15% mohair; 113g/125 yds)

DARK

MC: 5 (5, 6, 6, 7) skeins #M05 Onyx

CC1: 1 skein #M83 Raspberry

CC2: 1 skein #M38 Lotus Pink

CC3: 1 skein #M34 Victorian Pink

FAIR

MC: 5 (5, 6, 6, 7) skeins #M10 Crème

CC1: 1 skein #M160 Dynamite Blue

CC2: 1 skein #M120 Limeade

CC3: 1 skein #M59 Periwinkle

US 10½ (6.5mm) straight needles (third needle optional), or size needed to obtain gauge

US 10½ (6.5mm) 30" circular needle, or size needed to obtain gauge

US 10½ (6.5mm) 16" circular needle

Six 1" buttons

Tapestry needle

Stitch holders

Gauge

12 sts and 16 rows = 4" in St st

Special Skill

FAIR ISLE

Work from sleeve chart for 11 rows.

Work 1 row in St st.

Next row (RS): Dec 6 (9, 7, 5, 5) sts evenly across—21 (23, 25, 37, 37) sts.

Work 1 row even.

Inc 1 st at each edge on next row, then every foll 6 (5, 4, 5, 4)th row 8 (10, 12, 9, 12) times more—39 (45, 51, 57, 63) sts.

Work even until piece measures 17 (18, 18, 19, 19)" from beg.

Place all sts on scrap yarn.

Join:

With RS facing and MC, using longer circular needle and beg at right front of body, work across 20 (23, 26, 28, 31) sts.

**Place 9 (11, 12, 13, 14) sts on holder.

Place 4 (5, 6, 6, 7) sleeve sts on holder.

Work across 30 (34, 39, 44, 49) sts from sleeve.

Place rem 5 (6, 6, 7, 7) sleeve sts on holder.**

Work across 42 (48, 52, 58, 62) sts from body back.

Rep from ** to ** once.

Work across 20 (23, 26, 28, 31) sts from left front—142 (162, 182, 202, 222) sts on needle.

YOKE

Work 3 rows even in MC.

Work from yoke chart for 4 rows.

Next row (chart row 5): K6 (11, 0, 11, 6), *k7 (5, 5, 4, 4), k2tog; rep from * 14 (19, 24, 29, 34) times, k6 (11, 7, 11, 6)—127 (142, 157, 172, 187) sts.

Work from yoke chart for 9 rows.

Next row (chart row 15): K6 (11, 0, 11, 6), *k6 (4, 4, 3, 3), k2tog; rep from * 14 (19, 24, 29, 34) times, k6 (11, 7, 11, 6)—112 (122, 132, 142, 152) sts.

Work from yoke chart for 5 rows.

Next row (chart row 21): K6 (11, 0, 11, 6), *k5 (3, 3, 2, 2), k2tog; rep from * 14 (19, 24, 29, 34) times, k6 (11, 7, 11, 6)—97 (102, 107, 112, 117) sts.

Work from yoke chart for 5 rows.

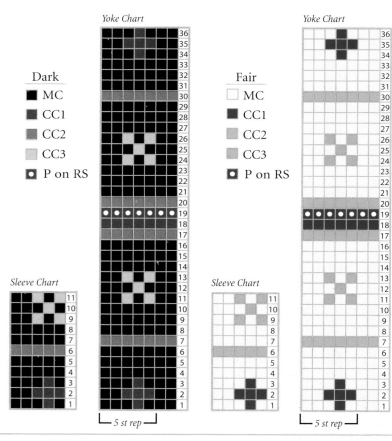

Yoke Chart

Dark
- ■ MC
- ■ CC1
- ■ CC2
- ■ CC3
- ◙ P on RS

Fair
- □ MC
- ■ CC1
- ■ CC2
- ■ CC3
- ◙ P on RS

Sleeve Chart

└ 5 st rep ┘

Next row (chart row 27): K6 (11, 0, 11, 6), *k4 (2, 2, 1, 1), k2tog; rep from * 14 (19, 24, 29, 34) times, k6 (11, 7, 11, 6)—82 sts.

Work from yoke chart for 5 rows.

Next row (chart row 33): K3, (K1, k2tog) 25 times, K4—57 sts.

Work remainder of yoke chart.

After all chart rows are complete, with MC only, work 2 (2, 2, 4, 4) rows in St st.

Work in garter st for 3 rows.

BO.

FINISHING
Button band:

Pu 56 (60, 60, 64, 64) sts from left side edge.

Work in garter st for 4 rows.

BO.

Buttonhole band:

Pu 56 (60, 60, 64, 64) sts from right side edge.

Row 1: K.

Row 2: K2 (4, 4, 6, 6), BO2, *k8, BO2; rep from * 5 times, k2 (4, 4, 6, 6).

Row 3: K2 (4, 4, 6, 6), CO2, *k8, CO2; rep from * 5 times, k2 (4, 4, 6, 6).

Row 4: K.

BO.

Transfer 11 holder sts from each armhole edge to straight needles. Use 3-needle BO or kitchener st to seam armholes.

Mattress st sleeve seams.

Attach buttons along button band to correspond with buttonholes.

Two's Company:

KNITTING TWO PIECES AT THE SAME TIME

When knitting two pieces that have to be even (sleeves or sweater fronts, for instance, as for a cardigan), knit them at the same time. Just cast them both onto the same needle, one after the other, using two separate balls of yarn. That way your pieces will always end up the same length, and your increases and decreases will be on the same row on each piece. The only tricky part is remembering which way you were going if you happen to stop with one piece on each needle. I always knit at least 2 or 3 stitches into the next piece before putting my project away. The other benefit to knitting two pieces at once is that when you're finished, you've got *both* sleeves or sweater fronts done! *Debbie Brown, Evanston, IL*

About Kate

Kate is fighting a losing battle in Toronto, Ontario, trying to maintain her sanity as a single mother of two boys. When not pulling out her hair (figuratively, since she shaves her head), she does technical editing for *Knitty.com* quarterly and writes sweater patterns on napkins, matchbooks, and anything else that doesn't move fast enough to get away.

NILDA MESA
Razor's Edge

I conceived this project because I wanted a hands-free shawl that I wouldn't have to clutch to keep from falling off (which is a drag when you're chasing after kids). In my art and in my knitting, I like working with light and shadow and using materials in unexpected ways, so I hit on the idea of making lace with bulky yarn. After a lot of swatching, the razor shell lace pattern rose to the top. The shape was inspired by a glorious cape worn by Donna Murphy in the Broadway show *Wonderful Town*. Even though the sides of this version don't sweep the floor, you can still fling it insouciantly when you enter a room, or just let it drape beguilingly.

STITCH PATTERN
MAIN LACE PATTERN
Row 1 (WS): P.

Row 2: K1, *yo, k2, sl1, k2tog, psso, k2, yo, k1, yo, k2; rep from * to last 7 sts, sl1, k2tog, psso, k2, yo, k2.

DIRECTIONS
With larger needles, CO 78 sts.

Work in garter st for 4 rows.

Work in main lace patt until piece measures 21" from beg, ending with WS facing.

Next row: P39, join 2nd skein of yarn and P to end. Cont in pattern as est, working both sides at same time with separate skeins of yarn for 10½", ending with WS facing.

Size
Finished width: 32"

Finished length: 53"

Materials
Brown Sheep Lamb's Pride Bulky (85% wool, 15% mohair; 113g/125 yds), 5 skeins #M05 Onyx

US 17 (12.75mm) 29" circular needle, or size needed to obtain gauge

US 15 (10mm) 16" circular needle

3" × 5" card stock

Crochet hook

Tapestry needle

Gauge
9 sts and 11 rows = 4" in St st on larger needles

Special Skill
LACE

With first skein of yarn, p across all sts. Break yarn from second skein, leaving a 6" tail.

Work in main lace patt until piece measures 53" from beg.

Work 4 rows in garter st.

BO.

FINISHING

Collar:

With smaller needle, pu 42 sts evenly around neck. Join and work in 1 × 1 rib for 3 rounds.

BO in rib.

Fringe:

Wrap yarn around 3" side of 3" × 5" card. Cut along one edge to make 6" lengths. Fold 6" lengths in half. Using 1 strand, pull loop through edge stitch with crochet hook and bring tail ends through loop to make fringe. Rep around bottom edge of poncho, working 1 fringe in each edge st. Trim ends to uniform length.

Weave in ends.

About Nilda

Cubans aren't supposed to need to knit, but here I am anyway. My Spanish grandmother taught me to knit and crochet when I was eight. It's always been part of my life. I knit a lot while at Harvard Law School, getting yarn in exchange for finishing friends' sweaters. I was an environmental policy wonk in the Clinton administration, then quit one week before Monicagate to go to art school. My husband, Rob, and I run an artists' residency program every summer in Brittany, where we are surrounded by sheep as well as other artists. Here at home I am teaching a new generation of knitters, including my daughter, at a New York City public school, in English and Spanish, just as my grandmother did. When I'm not knitting, teaching knitting, designing, or writing, I am an abstract painter and sculptor.

STITCH 'N BITCH ACROSS THE NATION
Mid-Atlantic

ARLINGTON, VIRGINIA, SNB

Our group attracted more than one hundred members in its first few months of existence this year, with about twenty terrific women showing up every week at Greenberry's, the neighborhood coffee place. At times, we have worried we would get kicked out for being too boisterous or scaring men away with our pointy objects! So far, though, we have been able to control ourselves.

We are lucky to have such a diverse group, with members of all different ages and levels of experience. At every meeting, there is lots of inspiration and support, knitting-related and otherwise. One of our recent hot topics was copyright as it applies to pattern design, and we gathered input from all sides, including straight from the U.S. Patent and Trademark Office. I look forward to our meetings every week; I absolutely love being around other people who "get it" and seeing what they're doing.

Brittany Martin

BALTIMORE, MARYLAND, CAST-OFF

Cast-Off is a continuation of a Stitch 'n Bitch that was started by Laura Cherry in 2001. It was held in the upstairs of a bar and was very popular—until the bar owners no longer wanted to be associated with something as feminine/feminist as a sewing circle, opting for Monday-night football instead.

Baltimore, Maryland, Cast-Off

In November of 2003, we began using the convenient, comfortable, and well-lit university lounges at Johns Hopkins to start a university-affiliated Stitch 'n Bitch for students, staff, and members of the community. Three weeks later, we were told that if we were to continue to use university Web space and claim affiliation, "bitch" was not allowed in the name. So we decided on "Cast-Off" to reflect the loss of the name, as well as the attitude of some university administrators toward the group. The controversy may have actually benefited us, since the graduate-student newspaper ran a conspicuous blurb with "bitch"

Arlington, Virginia

written 100 times next to an article intro-ducing Cast-Off.

Group attendance varies from five to twenty people and interest keeps growing. In March 2004 we organized a yarn swap and gave extra skeins of yarn to the Indiana Women's Prison knitting charity. We also plan to attend the Maryland Sheep and Wool Festival—a knitter's and spin-ner's dream/nightmare, depending on how much money and space you have for the amazing variety of beautiful yarns, wool, and fiber-art supplies sold there.

Sarah Carmichael

BALTIMORE, MARYLAND, SnB

Our group was founded in 1999 when knit-mistress Sarah Landon and some friends took a class at a local yarn shop. Their newfound passion for fiber led to countless questions, and they invited a friend and master knitter to join the group

to give lessons and soon found that they had created a new community of folks who just loved to bitch and knit.

Politics and education tend to dominate the conversations among our group of artists, professors, graduate students, moms, and pro-fessionals. We are unabashed liber-als who passionately debate topics that range from regime change in Washington, D.C., to giving our kids a progressive and rigorous educa-tion. An April 2004 knitting group was devoted to attending, with our children, the March for Women's Lives in D.C.

The most rewarding aspect of our Stitch 'n Bitch is the community we offer one another. The group is a place where we can complain, debate, and share ideas or problems without passing judgment. We look forward to meeting twice a month free from beckoning families, laundry, and dust balls in the house or weeds in the garden. We get to chat about whatever is bugging us as our needles click away in the comfort of one another's company.

Sarah Landon

JERSEY CITY, NEW JERSEY, SnB

Only one person showed up for the first Jersey City Stitch 'n Bitch meeting in the fall of 2003. Now more than

Jersey City, New Jersey

fifty people are on our e-mail list, and newcomers arrive at every session. Most of our members live in the neighborhood and walk over to Basic, the great local café where we get together. The group has all levels of knitters—from people who are just learning to those who've been knit-ting all their lives. There's always someone to help a person out when she is stuck, or who has a pattern for a project someone else wants to make. One of our members, a librarian, can always be counted on to bring the newest knitting books to check out. We do have a guy on our e-mail list, but so far only women have showed up to stitch and bitch. What do we usually end up talking about? Surprise—knitting!

It's always inspiring to see what other people are making, and we learn so much from one another. Last fall we took a trip upstate to Woodstock, N.Y., to check out

Baltimore, Maryland

its gorgeous knitting shop, and we're planning a trip this year to attend the Sheep and Wool festival. The group is a terrific way to meet people with whom you automatically have one thing in common—and often much more.

Christy Sayre and Barbara Landes

PITTSBURGH, PENNSYLVANIA, KNITTINESS

In December of 2002, when the owner of the Quiet Storm coffeehouse complained that people always mentioned using his space to do projects but never got around to doing them there, artist Jude Vachon grabbed a piece of paper and wrote up a contract to start Pittsburgh's Knittiness group. The former nuisance bar in a distressed neighborhood is now a welcoming coffeehouse and showcase for local artists, with great vegetarian food and comfy seating. A toy area and pinball machine keep children entertained while mamas knit, and one never knows what else might be going on in the shared space—shiatsu massage therapy, a band performance, or screenings of locally made films.

Jude (pictured right) recently demonstrated her new technique of knitting large,

Pittsburgh, Pennsylvania

webby fabric using her own arms as knitting needles and yarn she made of torn-up T-shirts.

"Age? What's that?" has become one of this multigenerational group's mottos. Being wacky, creative freethinkers, they know their different ages have nothing to do with the fun times, great conversation, and sharing of knitting tips that take place each week.

Kristilee Helmick

WASHINGTON, D.C., SnB

Our group began as just a few lonesome knitters at a Logan Circle coffee shop, but now we are part of nothing less than a Washington, D.C., knitting empire! When I moved to D.C. I was inspired by the SnB group I'd left behind in Chapel Hill, N.C., to begin a new group in my new town. We started out modestly, but when *Stitch 'n Bitch* was published, knitters and crocheters joined in droves, with membership in excess of 160 and three weekly meetings.

Sunday afternoon at Sparky's is our core knitting time. Here large groups of SnBers battle for seats with students and readers who are hoping

Washington, D.C.

for some peace and quiet to read (they soon leave). The more intimate Thursday night SnBers gather at a stitcher's house for cheap wine, cheese, and a wind-down from the week. These girls plan group events and craft nights. The talk gets a bit racy and they share the horror stories of the week as well as the triumphs. Popular demand for weeknight knitting has spawned Stitch 'n Belch, featuring half-off Belgian ales at a local bar in hopes of attracting more male knitters.

With the sheer creative force that comes with so many diverse talents and causes, SnB D.C. is a force to be reckoned with. Community is difficult to find in an urban setting of apartment buildings and inhabitants with long workdays, but Stitch 'n Bitch creates that community by bringing people who live close to each other into a place where they can meet, knit, and network.

Gwen Shlichta

Size

Women's S/M (L/XL)

Finished chest: 33 (41)" (see note)

Finished length: 23 (24)"

Materials

GGH Soft Kid (70% kid mohair, 25% nylon, 5% wool; 25g/154 yds)

MC: 7 (8) skeins #26 Blue

CC1: 2 skeins #2 White

CC2: 2 (3) skeins #30 Bright Red

US 10½ (6.5mm) straight needles

US 13 (9mm) straight needles

Optional: US I (5.5mm) crochet hook

Gauge

14 sts and 19 rows = 4" in St st

Special Skill

INTARSIA

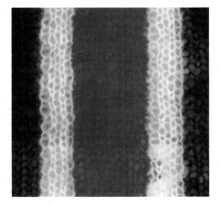

HANNAH HOWARD

London Calling

I grew up in Virginia Beach, Virginia, a town better known for its conservative leanings than its music scene. You could find a 7-Eleven and a church on any corner, making it the only place I know where you can self-medicate with Jesus and a Slurpee at any time of day. Nevertheless, my fondest memory is of moshing underage at the Boathouse. The musicians were gods to a suburban church girl turned punk rock acolyte, and salvation was a baptism in angry guitar riffs and cigarette smoke.

This sweater is inspired by all things punk rock and by my friend Christopher, closet rock star and Anglophile. **Note:** This very fine, almost diaphanous sweater is very stretchy. That's why the finished measurements are smaller than actual bust size, to achieve a nice fit.

DIRECTIONS

BACK

With MC, CO 66 (80) sts using larger needles.

Change to smaller needles and, beg with a RS row, work 4 (8) rows in St st.

Next (dec) row: K1, ssk, k to last 3 sts, k2tog, k1.

Rep dec row every 14th row 3 times—58 (72) sts.

Work even in St st until piece measures 14½ (15)" from beg.

Armhole shaping:

BO 2 sts at beg of next 2 rows.

BO 1 st at beg of next 4 rows 50 (64) sts.

Work even in St st until piece measures 21 (22)" from beg, ending with RS facing.

Fiber Therapy

UNDERSTANDING YARN BEHAVIOR

*V*ery fluffy yarns such as mohair or angora can be made to behave (before knitting or wearing) if you stick them in the Naughty Corner of your freezer for about an hour or so. This is a handy trick too if you need to frog them and they just won't rip back. If you're using a less resilient yarn such as silk or alpaca and you're working bands (around the cuffs, waist, or neck), they'll sag less if, on the wrong side, you knit through the back of all the knit stitches. You can also do this when you're picking up stitches for neckbands or armholes. Finally, cotton is going to expand, and there's nothing you can do about it, so plan ahead. *Darrow Wendoloski, Victoria, Australia*

Shape neck:

K18 (23), place these sts on holder, BO 16 (18), k to end.

P 1 row.

BO 2 sts from beg of next row, then EOR 1 (2) times—12 (17) sts.

BO rem sts.

Transfer holder sts to needle and work left shoulder as for right shoulder, reversing shaping.

FRONT

Using larger needles, with MC, CO 66 (80) sts.

Change to smaller needles and, beg with a RS row, beg working from chart; *at the same time,* work shaping as for back.

SLEEVES (MAKE 2)

Using larger needles, with MC, CO 32 (36) sts.

Change to smaller needles and, beg with a RS row, work 4 rows in St st.

Inc 1 st at each edge of next row, then every 8th row 10 times—54 (58) sts.

Work even in St st until piece measures 20" from beg, ending with RS facing.

BO 2 sts at beg of next 2 rows.

Dec 1 st at each edge of next 2 (4) rows.

Work 2 rows even in St st.

BO very loosely, using larger needles.

FINISHING

Seam shoulders.

Sew sleeve caps into armholes.

Seam sleeves and sides.

Optional: Crab st around neckline.

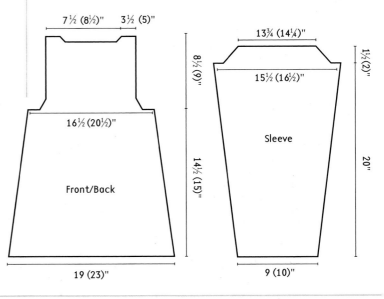

7½ (8½)"   3½ (5)"

8½ (9)"

16½ (20½)"

14½ (15)"

Front/Back

19 (23)"

13¾ (14¼)"

1½ (2)"

15½ (16½)"

20"

Sleeve

9 (10)"

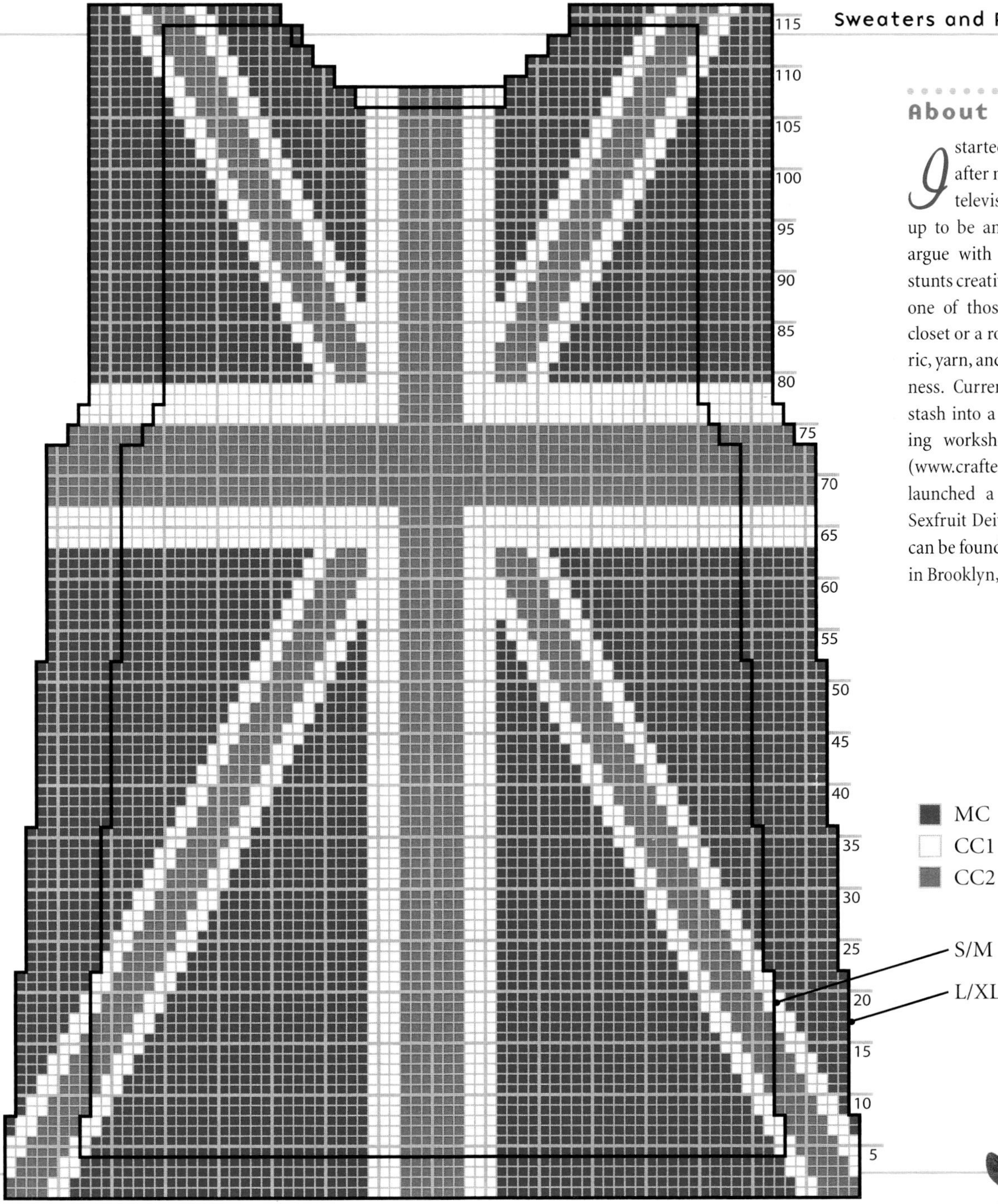

About Hannah

I started knitting as a kid after my mom got rid of the television set. Since I grew up to be an artist, I can't really argue with her theory that TV stunts creativity. I quickly became one of those people who has a closet or a room dedicated to fabric, yarn, and the pursuit of craftiness. Currently I'm turning my stash into a career: I teach crafting workshops called Crafteria (www.crafteria.net) and have launched a clothing line called Sexfruit Deity. In the meantime, I can be found learning to play bass in Brooklyn, New York.

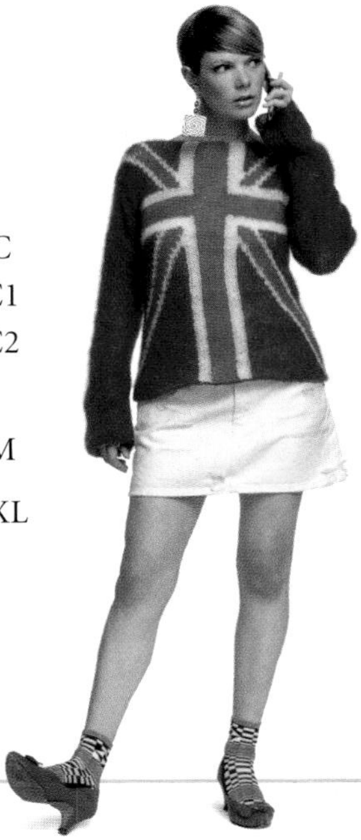

LAURA-JEAN, THE KNITTING QUEEN
Flower Power

I came up with this project after accidentally shrinking and felting a mohair sweater that made its way into the wash. I loved the texture of the fabric, so I cut it into patches for appliqués. When I was trimming the loose threads from the sewing, I realized I liked that extra bit of green mohair hanging— it actually looked like roots. Everyone who tries this loves the roots, so that's another cool part of this sweater that just happened. The shape of this sweater is a bit fitted and it has longer-than-average sleeves. It's the kind of thing you can just throw on with jeans or a skirt and go! It's comfy and cozy and fun—what more could you want in a sweater?

DIRECTIONS
BACK
With MC, CO 81 (86, 90, 95) sts. Work in St st until piece measures 2¾ (3½, 4½, 5½)" from beg, ending with RS facing.

Dec 1 st at each edge of next row, then foll 4th and 8th rows—75 (80, 84, 89) sts.

Work 1 row even.

Inc 1 st at each edge of next row, then every 10 (10, 9, 9)th row 9 times—85 (90, 94, 99) sts.

Shape armholes:

BO 3 (4, 4, 6) sts at beg of next 2 rows.

Dec 1 st from each edge of every row 3 (3, 4, 4) times, then EOR 3 (3, 4, 4) times—67 (70, 70, 71) sts.**

Size
Women's XS (S, M, L)

Finished bust: 34 (36, 38, 40)"

Finished length: 21 (22, 23, 25)"

Materials
MC: Brown Sheep Nature Spun Worsted (100% wool; 100g/245 yds), 5 (6, 7, 7) skeins #N46 Red Fox

Katia Ingenua Mohair (78% mohair, 13% nylon, 9% wool; 50g/153 yds)

CC1: 1 skein #20 Hot Pink

CC2: 1 skein #21 Light Pink

CC3: 1 skein #14 Olive Green

US 6 (4mm) straight needles, or size needed to obtain gauge

Sewing machine

Stitch-N-Tear stabilizing backing

Sewing thread complementary to CC1, CC2, and CC3

Gauge
19 sts and 26 rows = 4" in St st with MC

18 sts and 22 rows = 4" in St st with CC1

Work even in St st until piece measures 21 (22, 23, 24)" from beg.

BO.

FRONT

Work as for back to **.

Work even in St st until piece measures 19½ (20½, 21½, 22½)", ending with RS facing.

K13 (14, 14, 14), place these sts on a holder, BO 41 (42, 42, 43), k13 (14, 14, 14).

Dec 1 st from neck edge on this row, then EOR 3 (4, 4, 4) times. BO.

Transfer holder sts to needle and work as for left side, reversing shaping.

SLEEVES (MAKE 2)

CO 48 (48, 50, 52).

Working in St st, dec 1 st at each side of every 3rd row 4 times— 40 (40, 42, 44) sts.

Work even in St st until piece measures 3½" from beg, ending with RS facing.

Inc 1 st at each side of next row, then every 6 (5, 5, 6)th row 15 (19, 20, 17) times—72 (76, 82, 86) sts.

Shape cap:

Working in St st, BO 3 (4, 4, 6) sts at beg of next 2 rows.

Dec 1 st from each edge of every row 4 (4, 6, 6) times, then EOR 14 times.

BO 2 sts at beg of next 4 rows.

BO rem 22 (24, 26, 26) sts.

FELTED SWATCHES

For petals, CO 48 stitches with CC1 and work for 10".

For flower center, CO 18 stitches with CC1 and work for 4".

For leaf, CO 24 stitches with CC2 and work for 3".

To felt, toss the swatches in the washer on hot until they are approximately two thirds their original size. (Petals swatch should be approximately 7" × 6½", flower center swatch should be approximately 2½" × 2½", and leaf swatch should be approximately 3½" × 2").

Using the templates on the following page, cut out petals, flower center, and leaves from the appropriate swatches. Pin them in the correct locations to front of sweater.

Twist 3 strands of CC3 tog and pin stem in place, leaving a bit hanging off the bottom for roots. The secret to sewing all this on is to back it with Stitch-N-Tear (a tear-away stabilizer). Make sure every edge, including stem, has Stitch-N-Tear behind it.

Set stitching on your sewing machine to a midlength stitch and wide zigzag; stitch down all edges of felt appliqués. Lift presser foot often and rearrange what you're sewing so it doesn't stretch strangely.

About Laura-Jean

I spent the first seventeen years of my life in Saskatoon, Saskatchewan, where it is seriously cold most of the year and access to fashion is painfully limited. So, of course, I learned to make my own cute clothes and sweaters. I've been sewing since age twelve and knitting since I was sixteen. I got serious about fashion when I moved to Toronto and needed a career. A basic "how to use a knitting machine" course got me started, and pretty soon my company Fresh Baked Goods (and my royal title, the Knitting Queen) was born. I now sell tons of sweaters (and other clothing and accessories) in my two Toronto stores and on my Web site, www.freshbakedgoods.com. I can't believe I make a living having so much fun!

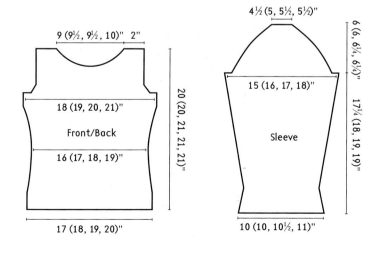

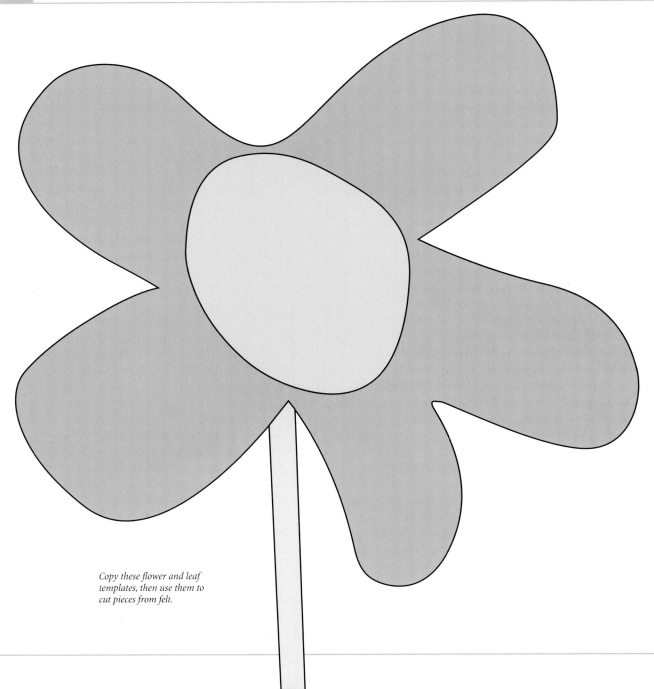

Copy these flower and leaf templates, then use them to cut pieces from felt.

You Spin Me Right Round, Baby

CHANGING A PATTERN FROM STRAIGHT KNITTING TO KNITTING IN THE ROUND

*I*f you are a circular knitting fanatic, there's nothing to stop you from knitting most of a sweater in the round even if a pattern tells you to knit it flat. You just need to make a few simple adjustments. Start with the front, casting on the total number of stitches minus 2, and place a stitch marker. Then cast on the total number of stitches for the back minus 2 stitches, place another stitch marker, and join your round. This reduction of 4 stitches—1 per side per piece—is what would have been taken up by the seams. Since you're knitting in the round, you won't need to make side seams (yay!) so you can lose those stitches.

Then just knit in the round until you get to the armhole shaping. Here you'll have to accommodate your changes in the pattern for the missing seam once again, and the number of bound-off stitches to start the armhole shaping will have to be reduced by 2 on each side. So, if the bind-off for each side is 5 stitches, meaning 10 stitches for the entire armhole (front and back combined), knit to 4 stitches before the stitch marker, remove the marker and bind off 8 stitches, then knit to 4 stitches before the next stitch marker, bind off 8 stitches again, and remove the second stitch marker.

Knit the remainder of the sweater back and forth in the usual way. Just put all the stitches for the first side on a spare circular needle or scrap yarn and work the front and the back of the sweater separately.

● There are a few important things to take into account when altering a flat-knit pattern for knitting in the round. First, your gauge for knitting in the round may be tighter than for knitting back and forth. If this is true for you, knit the back-and-forth parts on a smaller needle so that your gauge is consistent. Second, if you're working with a stitch pattern other than stockinette, you'll have to make sure that the pattern works all the way around. There is some leeway in the number of stitches you can decrease, as long as you make sure you take that into consideration when you bind off for the armholes. Finally, any shaping that is done in the body of the sweater has to be done at least a couple of stitches in from the stitch marker on either side to make the sides flow smoothly. *Marney Anderson, New York, NY*

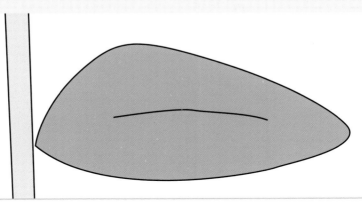

MELISSA WHERLE

Lucky

CLOVER LACE WRAP

Size

Women's XS (S, M, L, XL)

Finished bust: 32 (36, 40, 44, 48)"

Finished length: 19 (19½, 20, 20½, 22)"

Materials

Rowan 4-Ply Cotton
(100% Cotton; 50g/186 yds), 8 (8, 10, 10, 11) skeins #129 Aegean

US 2 (2.5mm) straight needles

US 3 (3mm) straight needles,
or size needed to obtain gauge

Tapestry needle

2 yds 1" ribbon in complementary color

Gauge

26 sts and 32 rows = 4" in clover lace st

Special Skill

LACE

this wrap cardigan was inspired by fashion's return to femininity. In my daily uniform of T-shirt, jeans, and Chuck Taylors, I am not much of a spokesperson for girliness, so it might seem strange that I enjoy designing and knitting lacy, femme sweaters. This is the perfect sweater to throw on over a little slip dress, or you can keep it casual with a T-shirt and jeans. It's knit out of cotton, my favorite fiber, and it is light enough for warmer spring days, which ensures a long season of wear.

STITCH PATTERN

CLOVER LACE

Rows 1 and 7: K.

Row 2 and all WS rows: P.

Row 3: K2, yo, sl1, k2tog, psso, yo, *k5, yo, sl1, k2tog, psso, yo*; rep from * to * to last 2 sts, k2.

Row 5: K3, yo, ssk, *k6, yo, ssk*; rep from * to * to last 2 sts, k2.

Row 9: K1, *k5, yo, sl1, k2tog, psso, yo*; rep from * to * to last 6 sts, k6.

Row 11: K7, *yo, ssk, k6*; rep from * to * to end.

Row 12: P

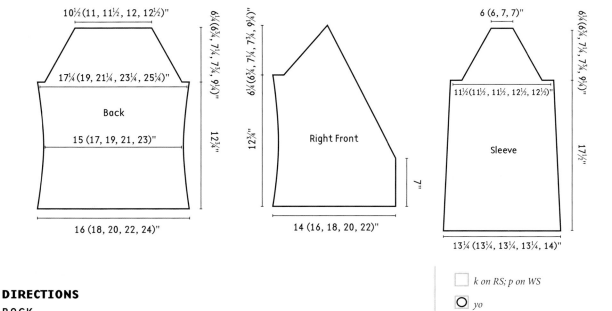

10½ (11, 11½, 12, 12½)"

6¼ (6¾, 7¼, 7¾, 9¼)"

17¼ (19, 21¼, 23¼, 25¼)"

Back

15 (17, 19, 21, 23)"

12¾"

16 (18, 20, 22, 24)"

6¼ (6¾, 7¼, 7¾, 9¼)"

12¾"

Right Front

7"

14 (16, 18, 20, 22)"

6 (6, 7, 7)"

6¼ (6¾, 7¼, 7¾, 9¼)"

11½ (11½, 11½, 12½, 12½)"

Sleeve

17½"

13¼ (13¼, 13¼, 13¼, 14)"

DIRECTIONS

BACK

With smaller needles, CO 106 (119, 132, 145, 158) sts.

Work 4 rows in 1 × 1 rib. Change to larger needles. P next row on WS. Work 2 rows in clover lace st.

Maint cont of st patt, dec 1 st at each edge of next row, then every foll 9th row 3 times more—98 (111, 124, 137, 150) sts.

Work even in st patt for 1".

Inc 1 st at each edge of next row, then every foll 7th row 6 times more—112 (125, 138, 151, 164) sts.

Work even in patt until piece measures 12¾" from beg.

Shape raglan:

BO 7 sts at beg of next 2 rows.

Dec 1 st each edge of every 2nd row 6 (14, 22, 30, 34) times, then every 4 (4, 4, 0, 4)th row 9 (6, 3, 0, 1) times—68 (71, 74, 77, 80) sts.

BO.

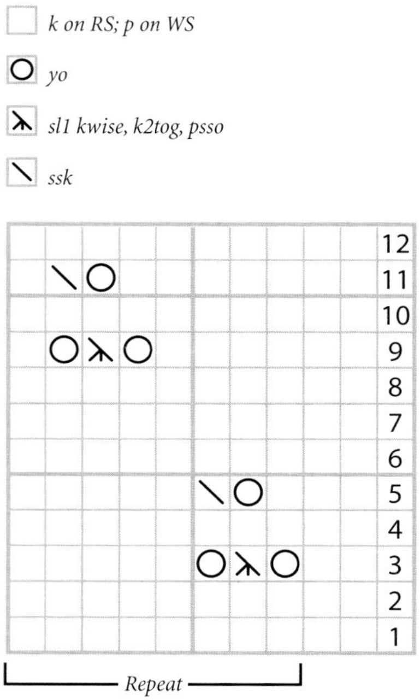

☐ k on RS; p on WS

O yo

⅄ sl1 kwise, k2tog, psso

＼ ssk

						12
＼	O					11
						10
O	⅄	O				9
						8
						7
						6
			＼	O		5
						4
			O	⅄	O	3
						2
						1

└──── *Repeat* ────┘

Clover lace

RIGHT FRONT

With smaller needles, CO 91 (104, 117, 130, 143) sts.

Work 4 rows in 1 × 1 rib. Change to larger needles. Working 4 sts in 1 × 1 rib at right edge (RS facing) of every row, p next row on WS. Work 2 rows in clover lace st. Shape waist as foll:

Dec 1 st at waist edge of next row, then every foll 9th row 3 times more—87 (100, 113, 126, 139) sts.

Work even in st patt for 1".

Inc 1 st at waist edge of next row, then every foll 7th row 6 times more—94 (107, 120, 133, 146) sts.

At the same time, when piece measures 7" from beg, shape neckline:

BO 4 sts at neck edge of next row.

Dec 1 st at neck edge every row 22 (34, 46, 58, 64) times.

Then dec 1 st at neck edge every other row 46 (42, 38, 34, 36) times.

At the same time, when piece measures 12¾" from beg, shape raglan:

BO 7 sts at beg of next row.

Dec 1 st at armhole edge every 2nd row 6 (14, 22, 30, 34) times, then every 4 (4, 4, 0, 4)th row 9 (6, 3, 0, 1) times.

LEFT FRONT

Work as for right front, reversing shaping.

SLEEVES (MAKE 2)

With smaller needles, CO 86 (86, 86, 92, 92) sts.

Work 6 rows in 1 × 1 rib.

Change to larger needles and working in clover lace patt, dec 1 st at each edge of every 21st row 3 times, then every 22nd row twice—76 (76, 76, 82, 82) sts.

Work even in patt until piece measures 17½" from beg.

Seams Sew Right

MAKING PERFECT SIDE-TO-SIDE SEAMS

My seams used to look terrible, but now they're scarily perfect, and yours can be too. When preparing to sew seams together, just run a smaller-gauge circular needle through the line of stitches you're using for each seam edge (figure 1) (this means two seam edges need two circular needles), and then sew back and forth between the two edges (figure 2). When you've finished the seam, all you have to do is pull out the two circulars, pull the sewing yarn tight, and weave in the ends. I find this makes it easier for me to pick up and sew the stitches with my yarn needle and allows me to connect them row to row more evenly. In a pinch (if you don't have two spare circulars kicking around, for instance), you can use a smooth cotton or rayon contrasting yarn instead. *David Demchuk, Toronto, Canada*

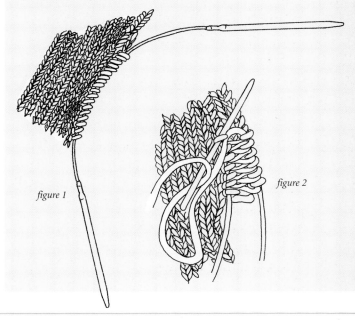

figure 1

figure 2

Shape raglan cap:

BO 7 sts at beg of next 2 rows.

Dec 1 st at each edge of every 4 (4, 4, 4, 6)th row 9 (7, 5, 3, 8) times, then every 6 (6, 6, 6, 8)th row 2 (4, 6, 8, 3) times. BO rem sts.

NECK BAND

With smaller needles, CO 13 sts.

Work in 1 × 1 rib until band measures 62½" from beg.

SIDE TIE

With smaller needles, CO 13 sts.

Work in 1 × 1 rib until tie measures 18" from beg.

FINISHING

Block all pieces.

Sew sleeves to fronts and back along raglan armhole seams.

Sew neck band to neck beg at left front edge, leaving 17" at right front edge for tie.

Sew side and underarm seams.

On left side of garment, 5½" up from hem, sew side tie into side seam.

On left front at edge on inside and on right side seam inside, sew in ribbon for tie.

Weave in ends.

About Melissa

I'm originally from southern New Jersey and moved to New York City to study at the Fashion Institute of Technology, where I majored in fashion design and specialized in knitwear. Today I am a sweater designer for a women's fashion company. My grandmother taught me how to knit when I was eight years old, but after knitting tons of Barbie tube dresses, I got a little bored. I revived my relationship with needles again during my first year of knitwear specialization in college, and the weekly meetings of my Long Island City Stitch 'n Bitch group keep me inspired and challenged. My only problem now is so many projects, so little time!

STITCH 'N BITCH ACROSS THE NATION
The South

AUSTIN, TEXAS, SNB

Before moving to Austin, I had started an L.A. chapter of SnB, where I was thrilled to have a group of intelligent, funky, fantastically crafty women working on projects and discussing everything from careers to birth control. We were gloriously open to one another's differences, so the offense some took to our group was surprising. One incident involved a gal leaving the coffee shop, refusing to share space with women who would actually be seen knitting. Another time, we were assailed by a young man who asked, "Why can't you call yourselves a more acceptable name like 'Stitch and Discourse'?"

In my new hometown, the term Stitch 'n Bitch and all it embodies are totally embraced. The Austin SnB is thriving and we've already outgrown two different venues. Onlookers often give us a thumbs-up and a smile when they see the strange mélange of coeds in cat's-eye glasses mingling with middle-aged professionals, Gen-X hipsters, and kindly grandmothers. We've become not only a knitting informational support system for each other, but also an invaluable social outlet. Stitch 'n Bitch has become an institution for those teetering on the line between social acceptance and creative anarchy.

Although the purpose may vary slightly, the result is the same: the coming together of diverse, kick-ass people to relate, shatter stereotypes, and revel in our craftiness.

Vickie Howell

CHAPEL HILL, NORTH CAROLINA, SNB

The savvy stitchers of SnB Chapel Hill came together in the summer of 2002 after founding member Gwen Schlicta read the article in *BUST* about the joys of stitching and bitching. She and four friends KIPed (knitted in public) in local coffee shops to encourage other knitters to join in. Word of mouth spread quickly, and the small Sunday afternoon knitting circle blossomed into a group with 127 members and three knitting circles a week.

In addition to the lovely moral support our group provides whenever someone has to completely frog a sweater-in-progress, SnB has become an incredible social network for its members. The women, few of whom knew each other before joining, have formed fast and lasting friendships. When we're not obsessing over the latest Rowan yarn, our conversations range from relationships to theses, pink shoes to politics. In fact, the political performance art group Keys of Resistance was formed by four Stitch 'n Bitchers after knitting chats revealed a common interest in helping people express their political views to government officials. Wearing

Austin, Texas

Chapel Hill, North Carolina

1940s secretarial dress and using antique typewriters, they set up temporary "offices" in public spaces (such as the March for Women's Lives in Washington, D.C.) and take dictation from anyone wishing to write a letter to an elected official. Another spinoff group was formed by SnBers' nonknitting male partners who frequently found themselves home alone. The guys go to their Kitsch 'n Bitch to watch terrible movies, gnaw on beef jerky, and drink orange soda.

Despite these extracurriculars, for us it always comes back to the simple joy of the click of needles, the pull of yarn through our fingers, and the company of women. The wine, cheese, coffee, happy hours, and political action groups are just the pom-pom on the hat.

Sara Daily

DALLAS, TEXAS, SnB

Stitch 'n Bitch Dallas may very well be the first knitting circle ever to count both a research scientist and a professional wrestler among its ranks, along with a few less surprising professionals: a technical writer, a restaurant owner, a teacher, a university fund-raiser, and a librarian. Our organization was formed in March 2004 with a posting on a Web site looking for kindred knitting spirits in the north Texas area, since amazingly, there was no Stitch 'n Bitch group. We figured that in a city as big as Dallas, surely there must be other knitters out there—we just needed to find them! Since then, the group has grown to more than thirty members. On average, seven to thirteen knitters show up for the twice-monthly gatherings, filling the community room at Central Market with knitting and crocheting, laughter and fun. SnB Dallas knitters range in age from twenty to fifty-something. Some have been knitting for years, while others come to learn how to start knitting and purling. When in the Dallas area, drop in and cast one on!

Chris Ingle

LEXINGTON, KENTUCKY, SnB

I wanted my granny to teach me to knit, but granny was not a knitter. So I used the money she gave me for Christmas of 2002 to buy some acrylic yarn, a pair of needles, and a hideous book titled *I Can't Believe I'm Knitting*. After a few torturous months, I more or less had the hang of knit and purl, but I wanted to learn more. Being the geek girl I am, I started posting messages on the Internet, looking for other Lexington knitters. Enter Renee Rigdon.

Dallas, Texas

Unlike me, Renee was a total craft-whore crunchy goddess who had been knitting on and off for years, along with dressmaking, bag sewing, and cloth diapering. The first SnB book had inspired her to seek out other knitters who could appreciate her wacky DIY drive. Renee and I joined forces through the Knitting Meetup Web site, and when Debbie Stoller came to town for a book signing, we showed up with fliers advertising our brand-new Stitch 'n Bitch group.

As press about the national knitting phenomenon grew, many people joined in to make the SnB Lexington group a fabulous fifty-member forum for knitters in the Bluegrass State. To counterbalance the hedonism of knitting for ourselves, we started quarterly charity projects that focus on the principle of thinking globally and acting locally.

Zabet Stewart

RALEIGH, NORTH CAROLINA, SNB

Our Stitch 'n Bitch was started following the "if you knit it, they will come" philosophy—two or three of us would sit in a popular coffee shop and KIP (knit in public), trawling for new members. Unfortunately, that didn't work, so we put fliers in the LYS and hipped the staff to our group. The store sent some very bitchin' members our way, and we moved to a more popular café with a spectacular DJ. We have now grown to more than fifty members.

We range in age from twelve to forty-nine, with about a dozen of us—professional women, grad students, feminists, and environmental activists—meeting every Wednesday night at Helios Coffee Company in downtown Raleigh. Many of us participated in a knitathon to benefit a local women's shelter, others donate knit items for fund-raisers for causes such as the NC Conservation Network and the Student Action with Farmworkers, and we hope to collaborate on much more "craftivism."

Our turn-ons include red wine, handbags, world-beat remixes, easy shawl patterns, and cute baristas. Our turn-offs include bad art shows that stay on exhibit for months on end, double-pointed needles, and mood lighting.

Raleigh, North Carolina

SnB Raleigh is proudest of member Nicole, who engineered a hands-free tea-sipping knitting helmet with her genius boyfriend, Les. Next, we plan to invent a DJ cozy to keep DJ Keith toasty warm while he spins down-tempo rhythms in synch with our knitting.

Fawn Pattison

Lexington, Kentucky

ERIN WECKERLE

Spiderweb Capelet

I design a lot of knitted items, and most of my patterns come from trial and error, with one project leading organically to the next. This capelet pattern came about when I wanted to make something that was more airy and delicate than the sweaters and ponchos I had been knitting all winter. The design is a combination of a simple scarf and a circular poncho. Simple shaping at the shoulders keeps it relaxed and drapey enough to fit anyone, but the lace stitch and the pom-pom ties make it a fancy, girly, vintage-inspired accessory. Purldrop, the name of my knitwear line, comes from practicing the "purl, drop" row for the spiderweb lace used in this capelet. After muttering that to myself over and over, it just clicked.

DIRECTIONS

CO 92 sts.

Row 1: K.

Rows 2 and 6: K2, *yo, k1; rep from * to last 2 sts, k2.

Rows 3 and 7: P3, *drop 1, p1; rep from * to last 2 sts, p2.

Row 4: K1, *sl2 pwise, k2tog, pass 2 slipped sts over, k1 without dropping st off needle, yo, p1 without dropping st off needle, yo, k1 without dropping st off needle, yo, p1 and drop st off needle; rep from * to last st, k1.

Rows 5, 9, and 19: P.

Size
Adult

Materials
Crystal Palace Merino Frappe (80% merino wool, 20% nylon; 50g/140 yds), 2 skeins #020B New Sage OR #145 Hibiscus

US 15 (10mm) straight needles

US F/5 (4mm) crochet hook

2" pom-pom maker or template

Gauge
10 st and 10 rows = 4" in St st

Special Skill
LACE

Row 8: K1, *k1 without dropping st off needle, yo, p1 without dropping st off needle, yo, k1 without dropping st off needle, yo, p1 and drop st off needle, sl2 pwise, k2tog, pass 2 slipped sts over; rep from * to last st, k1.

Rows 10–17: Rep rows 2–9.

Row 18: *K3, k2tog; rep from * to last 2 sts, k2—74 sts.

Row 20: K1, *yo, k2tog, k2tog; rep from * to last st, k1—56 sts.

Row 21: P.

BO.

FINISHING

With crochet hook, chain two 10" lengths of cord.

Attach one cord to each of the top corners.

Make two 2" pom-poms and secure one to each of the cord ends.

Weave in ends.

Show me your tips! *All Laced Up*

KEEPING TRACK OF YOUR LACE WORK

When working in a complicated lace pattern, place markers between every pattern repeat. It makes finding mistakes easier. Also, if you are having real trouble and need to unravel a lace pattern periodically, knit in a piece of nylon or mercerized cotton yarn (it is important that it be slippery) every ten rows or so. If you need to unravel, you can put your needle in along this piece of yarn before unraveling to that spot. It will keep you from dropping yarnovers. If you get past the ten rows with no problem, simply pull the guide yarn out and knit it in again on the next row.

Lucy Lee, Cambridge, MA

About Erin

I grew up in Pittsburgh, moved to Philadelphia to attend Tyler School of Art, then moved to New Haven to get my M.F.A. at Yale. While there, my best friend, who was studying photography, taught me how to knit, both as an alternative to the stress of the studio and as a complement to our art practice. I made scarves for all my friends that Christmas but it wasn't until I moved back to Philly and was working at a record store that I had time to practice my new skill. I would just listen to music and knit all day. Soon I started selling my stuff at local shops. In October 2002 my friend Rebekah Maysles and I opened a hand-made and vintage clothing shop in the back room of another store in Philly. I launched www.purldrop.com this year and we moved the shop, Sodafine, to Brooklyn, New York, in February.

In a Bind

BINDING OFF WITH A CROCHET HOOK

Here's my unconventional way of binding off. I find it easier than passing stitches over each other with two needles, and it produces a neatly finished edge. If the piece is knit with straight needles, when you come to the row to be bound off, just knit it onto a circular needle of the same size (or larger if you want to be sure to bind off loosely). Don't actually bind off the stitches. Push all the stitches to the right. Holding the knitting needle in your left hand and an appropriate-size crochet hook in your right, insert the hook into the first stitch purlwise and take the stitch off the needle. Then use the hook to pull the second stitch off the needle and through the first one (as if you are making a crochet chain). Continue with all stitches until you get to the end, then pull the yarn end through the last loop. Done! *Edina Tien, Vancouver, WA*

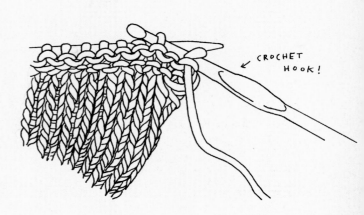

← CROCHET HOOK!

Loosen Up

HOW TO BIND OFF AND CAST ON MORE LOOSELY

As a new knitter I cast on and bind off *way* too tightly. But casting on over two needles, as is often suggested, results in stitches that are too loose for my taste. I compromise and cast on and bind off with a needle a few sizes larger than the one I knit with. Problem solved. *Crissy Hatfield, Winetka, CA*

MELANIE SCOLES
That Seventies Poncho

Size
Adult

Finished neck circumference: 27"

Finished length: 25½"

Materials
Lion Brand Cotton-Ease (50% cotton, 50% acrylic; 100g/207 yds)

A: 3 skeins #113 Cherry Red

B: 3 skeins #102 Bubblegum

C: 2 skeins #133 Orangeade

D: 1 skein #153 Licorice

E: 1 skein #100 Vanilla

US 10 (6mm) circular needle with interchangeable cords OR 1 each 16", 24", and 36", or size needed to obtain gauge

US 4 (3.25mm) double-pointed needles (set of 2)

Stitch markers

Gauge
17 sts and 19 rows = 4" in St st

A n eye-catching color combination adds interest to this otherwise simple poncho. It is worked from the neck down: The first 17 rows are worked flat to form a split neckline, then the piece is joined and worked in the round. Switch to longer needles when needed as the piece increases in diameter. For texture, random rounds are purled. New colors should be started in the front center. It's helpful to use different-colored markers to identify the front once the piece is joined. An I-cord laced through the eyelets completes the neckline.

STITCH PATTERN
COLOR SEQUENCE
8 rows A, 4 rows D, 10 rows/rnds B, 16 rnds C, 10 rnds A, 6 rnds E, 18 rnds B, 12 rnds A, 10 rnds C, 6 rnds D, 4 rnds A, 8 rnds B, 4 rnds E, 1 rnd A.

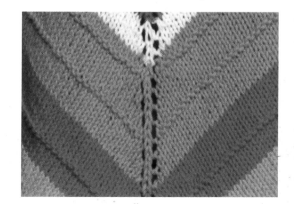

DIRECTIONS

With shortest circular needle and A, CO 115 sts. Working in color sequence, cont as follows:

Work flat in St st for 2 rows.

Row 3: K1, pm, yo, k56, yo, pm, k1, pm, yo, k56, yo, pm, k1.

Row 4: P.

Row 5: K1, sm, yo, k to next marker, yo, sm, k1, sm, yo, k to next marker, yo, sm, k1.

Rep rows 4 and 5 six times, maintaining color sequence.

Join into round, working first and last st tog.

Rnd 1: K.

Rnd 2: K1, sm, yo, k to next marker, yo, sm, k1, sm, yo, k to next marker, yo, sm.

Rep rnds 1 and 2, maintaining stripe sequence, to end of color patt—35 sts.

Optional: Randomly p a few of the k rnds to create texture.

With A, BO pwise.

About Melanie

I've been living in Seattle most of my life and have been knitting for a year and a half of it. I'd been wanting to learn since I was a teenager, but no one in my family knits. Finally, I took a beginning knitting class through my local community college, and I don't think I'll ever fail to be amazed by what can be created with just two needles and a hank of yarn. Lately I seem unable to make anything that doesn't have the color orange in it.

Extreme Measures

IMPROMPTU RULERS

*I*f you find yourself without a ruler while knitting, you can do pretty well with a standard 8½" × 11" piece of paper, index cards (3" × 5" or 4" × 6"), or a dollar bill (approximately 2" × 6"). Fold them in halves, thirds, or quarters to get smaller measurements.

Evelyn Rowe, Washington, D.C.

● When casting on the first row of a sweater or any other knit item, make sure you leave a tail of yarn long enough to cut to the length of the piece that you are knitting. For example, if the sweater is to be knit to 24", make the tail 24" long. That way, if you are out or are not near your tape measure, you have a way of measuring how much more you need to knit.

Cindy Kuo, Northbrook, IL

● Measure your hand. That's right, your hand. There may be some portions of it that can be measured in even increments of centimeters or inches. If you know what these measurements are, you can measure your knitting whenever you want, whether or not you remembered to bring a tape measure.

For instance, I know that my hand (either one—mine are both the same) is 4" from wrist to end of palm; my middle finger is 3" long; my little finger is 2" long. From my wrist to the end of the first joint of my middle finger is roughly 5", and to the end of the second joint is roughly 6". From wrist to end of middle finger is 7". With these measurements, I can do almost anything, adding them together when necessary. When instructions get very precise and it's down to half inches, of course, I do use a tape measure. *Luanne Redmond, Chicago, IL*

TIES

With dpns and A, CO 2 sts. Work in I-cord with A for 10", then in D for 1½", then in B for 2¼", then in D for 1½", and then in A for 10".

Break yarn and draw tail through sts.

FINISHING

Weave in ends on poncho and ties.

Thread ties through every other eyelet at the neck opening in the front.

SHARE ROSS

Bam 13

Shortly after I learned to knit, I made a beautiful cashmere scarf for my husband, Bam, and we both agreed it was just too "nice" for him. That's when he said the magic words. "Why don't you knit things that you'd never find in a shop? Scarves that look like rags instead of looking perfect. Sweaters that appear torn instead of flawless." I thought he'd hit on something interesting, and I set out to find the best yarn combination for this new concept. I started with a loosely knit scarf using a combination of a rag and chenille yarn, and that led to this sweater. I struggled a lot with the design and worked hard to figure out how to write the pattern, especially with such a big gauge. In fact, knitting these two yarns together is a little bit like wrestling, and it requires a good bit of manhandling to get it. Every few rows, you should give the whole piece a good tug downward to get the stitches a little more settled. But be prepared: No matter what you do, the rows *will* look uneven. That's why it's punk!

STITCHES

W&T (WRAP AND TURN)

Sl the next st pwise, bring the yarn between the needles to the front of the work, and sl the st back to the left-hand needle. Turn the work, and begin working in the opposite direction. When you get to the wrapped st on the next row, sl the needle through both the wrap and the wrapped st kwise, and k them tog.

Size

Men's S (M, L, XL)

Finished chest circumference:
36 (40, 44, 48)"

Finished length: 24 (25, 26, 27)"

Materials

A: Colinette Tagliatelli (90% merino wool, 10% nylon; 100g/175 yds), 3 skeins #141 Zebra

B: Sirdar Snowflake Chunky (100% polyester; 50g/137 yds), 3 skeins #380 Black

US 35 (20mm) 32" circular needle, or size needed to obtain gauge

Gauge

6 sts and 8 rows = 4" in garter st

Special Skill

SHORT ROW SHAPING

Pne-Knitual Agneement

AVOIDING THE CASE OF THE LOVE SWEATER

I'd heard so many horror stories about the curse of the love
sweater that I asked my fiancé to sign a pre-knitual agreement. Prior to casting on for his sweater, I had him promise to:

1. Appreciate all the work I put into the sweater by
   lavishing much praise on my knitting skills

2. *Not* pretend to like the finished product if he doesn't
   (I don't want "pity" wear)

3. Give the sweater back to me if, God forbid,
   we ever break up

I am hoping that this will take some of the pressure off of us
both, so I can happily knit away without fear that I am inadver-
tently bringing about the end of our relationship.
Chelsea Fowler-Biondolillo, Rockville, MD

DIRECTIONS

BACK

**With 1 strand of A and B held tog, CO 27 (30, 33, 36) sts.

K 1 row.

Next 2 rows: K to last 2 sts, W&T. (Tip: You may want
to tie a piece of waste yarn onto the wrapped yarn.
It's much easier to figure out which yarn is the
wrap later when you need to knit it.)

Next 2 rows: K to last 3 sts, W&T.

Next 2 rows: K to last 4 sts, W&T.

Next 2 rows: K across, working wrap sts tog
with sts as you pass them.

Work in garter st until piece measures 16 (17, 17½, 18)"
from beg.

Shape armholes:

BO 2 (2, 3, 3) sts at beg of next 2 rows.

BO 1 st at beg of next 2 rows—21 (24, 25, 28) sts.**

Work in garter st until piece measures 6 (6, 6½, 7)" from
beg of armhole shaping.

Shape shoulders:

BO 3 (3, 3, 4) sts at beg of next 2 rows.

BO 4 sts at beg of 2 next rows.

BO rem 7 (10, 11, 12) sts.

FRONT

Work as for back from ** to **.

Work in garter st until piece
measures 3 (3, 3½, 4)" from beg
of armhole shaping.

Next row: K8 (9, 9, 10), join
a second ball of yarn
(1 strand of each),
BO 5 (6, 7, 8), k
to end.

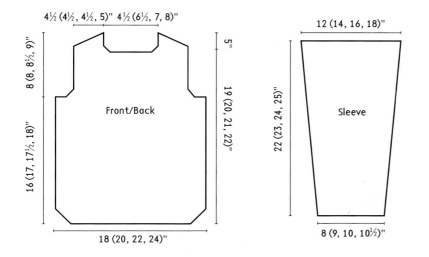

4½ (4½, 4½, 5)" 4½ (6½, 7, 8)"

8 (8, 8½, 9)"

5"

Front/Back

19 (20, 21, 22)"

16 (17, 17½, 18)"

18 (20, 22, 24)"

12 (14, 16, 18)"

Sleeve

22 (23, 24, 25)"

8 (9, 10, 10½)"

Working both sides at the same time, dec 1 st from neck edges EOR
1 (2, 2, 2) times.

BO 3 (3, 3, 4) sts at beg of next 2 rows.

BO 4 sts at beg of next 2 rows.

Mattress st shoulders of front and back tog.

SLEEVES

With 1 strand of each yarn and body laid flat with RS
facing, pu 18 (22, 24, 28) sts around armhole.

Work in garter st for 3 rows.

Dec 1 st at each edge on next row, then every foll 10th row 2 (3, 3, 4) times—
12 (14, 16, 18) sts.

Work in garter st until piece measures 22 (23, 24, 25)" from beg.

BO.

FINISHING

Mattress st sleeve and side seams.

Wet-block to measurements.

JENNA ADORNO

Ultra Femme

Size

Women's XS (S, M, L, XL)

Finished bust: 30 (33, 35½, 38½, 41)"

Finished length: 20 (21, 22, 23, 24)"

Materials

A: Rowan All Seasons Cotton
(60% cotton, 40% acrylic; 50g/98 yds),
2 (3, 3, 4, 4) skeins #202 Light Pink

B: GGH Soft Kid (70% kid mohair,
25% nylon, 5% wool; 25g/154 yds),
2 (2, 2, 3, 3) skeins #005 Light Pink

US 5 (3.75mm) double-pointed needles
(set of 5)

US 7 (4.5mm) double-pointed needles, or
size needed to obtain gauge (set of 2)

US 5 (3.75mm) 16" circular needle

US 7 (4.5mm) 16" circular needle,
or size needed to obtain gauge

2 yds 2"-wide ribbon, black

Stitch holders

Gauge

16 sts and 22 rows = 4" in St st with A
and larger needles

28 sts and 34 rows = 4" in St st with B
and smaller needles

A t 5 feet, 100 pounds, I rarely find clothes that fit. Likewise, clothes knit from patterns often drape poorly or fall off my tiny frame. So when I was shopping recently in a trendy boutique and noticed the body-skimming fuzzy sweaters, I knew my only hope of having one that fit was to design it myself. Several swatches and attempts at the perfect belt loop later, I had created my favorite sweater to date. A sweater that makes people ask "Where did you buy that?" instead of "Did you make that yourself?"

This sweater, knit totally in the round, has a simple, seamless construction that requires minimal finishing. And for petite women everywhere, I have included my original extra-small pattern, a size that (I know from experience) is rarely included in knitting books.

DIRECTIONS

With A and larger circular needle, CO 120 (132, 142, 154, 164) sts.

Pm, join, and work 2 rnds in St st.

Next rnd: *Yo, k2tog; rep from * to end.

Work 2 rnds in St st.

Next rnd: Fold hem in half at the eyelet row and *pu 1 st from the CO edge and k tog with 1 st from the needle; rep from * to end.

Next rnd: *Work 10 (11, 10, 11, 10) sts, m1; rep from * 12 (12, 14, 14, 16) times, work 0 (0, 2, 0, 4) sts—132 (144, 156, 168, 180) sts.

Work even in k2, p2 rib for 9 (9½, 10, 10½, 11)".

Swatch Watch

Show me your tips!

GETTING AN ACCURATE GAUGE FOR CIRCULAR KNITTING

Your gauge in stockinette stitch on circular needles (knit every row) can be significantly different from your gauge on straight needles (knit one row, purl one row), because many of us make our knit stitches tighter than our purl stitches. Usually, trying to figure out what your gauge is in circular knitting requires that you knit something in the round, which will need many more stitches than a flat-knit swatch and can take up considerable time. Some people say to just start knitting the first sleeve of your project and measure to see if you're getting the right gauge; if you are, at least you already have some work done on the sweater.

But if you're picking up and knitting the sleeves from the top down or knitting a tank top, you won't be able to do this. Instead, you can make what I call a "pseudocircular swatch." To do this, cast on the number of stitches you'd use for knitting a flat swatch (usually 20 or so), and then cast on several extra. (The stitches at the edges will be too sloppy to get a realistic gauge, so you want to cast on enough stitches to avoid getting anywhere near those edge stitches when you're measuring the swatch.)

Next, knit across your swatch. At the end of the row, do *not* turn your work. Instead, keep your work facing you and go back to the right edge, leaving a long strand of the yarn hanging loose across the back of your swatch. You want enough "free" working yarn across the back so that you'll be able to flatten your swatch to measure it, without having these "floats" across the back pulling or distorting the swatch. This is sort of like making I-cord, only you're not pulling the working yarn tight. Continue knitting in this manner until you have a swatch you can live with, then check your gauge, keeping well away from the edges. You've just made a stockinette swatch using only knit stitches, without having to knit it in the round!

Chris Silker, Minneapolis, MN

BELT LOOPS

Next rnd: *With larger dpns, inc1 into the next 2 sts—4 sts. With these 4 sts, work in I-cord for 11 rows. BO and break yarn, leaving a 6" tail.

Join yarn to the sts on the circular needle, work 10 sts in est patt. Rep from * to end of round—11 (12, 13, 14, 15) belt loops.

TOP OF BODY

With B and smaller circular needle *k1, inc1 in next st; rep from * to end of round, pu sts along back of each belt loop and working them in inc patt as est as you pass them—198 (216, 234, 252, 270) sts.

Work even in St st for 5 (5½, 6, 6½, 7)".

K42 (45, 49, 53, 56); place next 15 (18, 19, 20, 23) sts on holder for underarm.

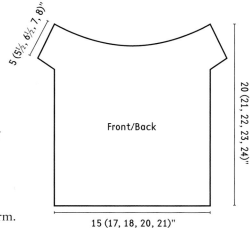

5 (5½, 6½, 7, 8)"

20 (21, 22, 23, 24)"

Front/Back

15 (17, 18, 20, 21)"

LEFT SLEEVE

With a new ball of CC and smaller dpns, CO 70 (78, 82, 89, 96) sts and divide among needles.

Join and work in St st for 1½ (2, 2½, 3, 3½)". Place first 15 (18, 19, 20, 23) sts of rnd on holder for underarm.

JOIN SLEEVE TO BODY

With smaller circular needle holding body sts, k55 (60, 63, 69, 73) sts of the sleeve from dpns. K84 (90, 98, 106, 112) body sts. Place rem 15 (18, 19, 20, 23) sts on holder for underarm.

RIGHT SLEEVE

Work as for left sleeve, place first 15 (18, 19, 20, 23) sts of rnd on holder, and join sleeve to body by knitting across sleeve sts with smaller circular needle holding body sts.

Work rem 42 (45, 49, 53, 56) body sts to complete round— 278 (300, 322, 350, 370) sts.

Work even in St st for 3½ (3½, 4, 4, 4½)".

Next rnd: *K1, k2tog; rep from * to end of rnd.

BO.

FINISHING

Stitch belt loops to body.

Graft underarms with kitchener st.

Weave in ends.

Thread ribbon through belt loops and tie. Trim ends if desired.

About Jenna

I learned to knit from my grandmother when I was eighteen, although it did not turn into an obsession until I was twenty-six, when my partner and I were trying unsuccessfully to conceive. In need of an outlet for my unquenched maternal urge, I knit baby clothes with a passion. Today my long-awaited four-year-old son and my partner are regular recipients of my knitting. With a degree in sociology and women's studies, I have a love of and interest in traditional female crafts. You can find me (and all of my knitting) online at www.thisgirlknits.com. I work in the software industry in Seattle, but dream of being paid fabulously to design knit garments full-time.

KIMBERLY FAIRCHILD

Sexie

Size

XS (S, M, L, XL)

Finished bust: 19 (23, 27, 31, 35)"
(see Note)

Finished length: 15 (16, 16½, 18½, 20)"

Materials

Berroco Glacé (100% rayon; 50g/75 yds)

MC: 5 (6, 8, 10, 11) skeins #2562
Emulsion (#2655 Cool Red)

CC: 1 skein #2422 Plum (#2012 Black)

US 7 (4.5mm) straight needles,
or size needed to obtain gauge

US 7 (4.5mm) double-pointed needles
(set of 2)

US G/6 (4mm) crochet hook

Stitch holders

Gauge

20 sts and 28 rows = 4" in St st

Note: The Berroco Glacé knits up to a very
silky, stretchy material, and the eyelets in
back also stretch out, meaning that this
halter can comfortably fit a chest that is
10" larger than the finished measurements
above.

W ho thought the inspiration for a halter top could come from a male comedian? This halter's original design was created while watching the very sexy Eddie Izzard perform his standup show "Sexie." After some experimenting and tweaking, the final product is a hot little number that can be dressed up or down, but will always inspire that sexy, sassy self-confidence that Eddie displays onstage.

This halter is a quick one-piece knit with little finishing needed. The lace is created by a simple yarn-over pattern, and the center eyelets line up in a column thanks to a clever p2tog on the wrong side. The ribbon yarn adds a nice shine. Experiment with your own color combinations to create something unique. The back tie can be tightened or loosened to give a perfect fit and an open or closed look.

DIRECTIONS

With MC, CO 90 (110, 130, 150, 170) sts.

Row 1 (RS): K2, yo, p2tog, *k2, p2; rep from * to last 4 sts, p2tog, yo, k2.

Row 2: P2, *k2, p2; rep from * to end.

Row 3: K1, *yo, k2tog; rep from * 6 (6, 6, 9, 9) times; k30 (40, 50, 54, 64), yo, k30 (40, 50, 54, 64), **ssk, yo; rep from ** 6 (6, 6, 9, 9) times, k1.

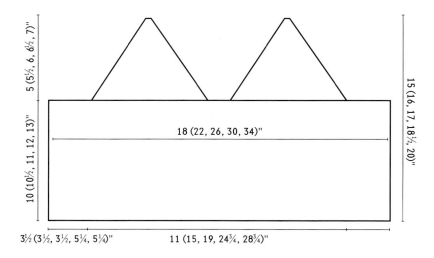

5 (5½, 6, 6½, 7)"

10 (10½, 11, 12, 13)"

18 (22, 26, 30, 34)"

15 (16, 17, 18½, 20)"

3½ (3½, 3½, 5¼, 5¼)"   11 (15, 19, 24¾, 28¾)"

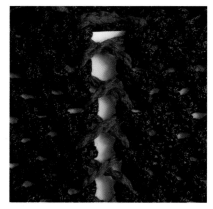

Lace up the back as tightly or as loosely as you want.

Rows 4 and 8: P44 (54, 64, 74, 84), p2tog, p to end.

Rows 5 and 9: K.

Row 6: P.

Row 7: K2, *yo, k2tog; rep from * 6 (6, 6, 9, 9) times; k29 (39, 49, 53, 63), yo, k29 (39, 49, 53, 63), **ssk, yo; rep from ** to last 2 sts, k2.

Row 10: P.

Rep rows 3–10 until work measures 10 (10½, 11, 12, 13)" from beg (measured over St st center panel) and end with a row 6 or 10.

Next row: K2, yo, p2tog, *k2, p2; rep from * 2 (2, 2, 3, 3) times; k29 (39, 49, 55, 65), yo, k29 (39, 49, 55, 65), **p2, k2; rep from ** 2 (2, 2, 3, 3) times, p2tog, yo, k2.

Next row: *P2, k2; rep from * 3 (3, 3, 4, 4) times; k1, p27 (37, 47, 53, 63), p2tog, p27 (37, 47, 53, 63), k1, **k2, p2; rep from ** to end.

Next row: BO 17 (17, 17, 23, 23) sts in 1 × 1 rib, k27 (37, 47, 53, 63), BO 2, k27 (37, 47, 53, 63), p1, work in 1 × 1 rib to end.

Next row: BO 17 (17, 17, 23, 23) sts in 1 × 1 rib, p27 (37, 47, 53, 63), join new yarn to left side and p27 (37, 47, 53, 63).

Next row (RS, working both sides at the same time): K1, k2tog, k to last 3 sts, ssk, k1.

Next row: P.

Rep last 2 rows until 5 (5, 7, 9, 11) sts rem.

Next row: K1 (1, 2, 3, 4), k2tog, k2 (2, 3, 4, 5).

Next row: P.

Next row: K1 (1, 1, 2, 3), k2tog, k1 (1, 2, 3, 4).

Next row: P.

Place rem sts on holders.

FINISHING

With CC, RS facing, and beg to the right of the live stitches of the right side, SC around neck from the right side to the live sts of the left side. *Make 1 extra sc loop and transfer this and the live sts to a dpn.

Next row: K1, k2tog 1 (1, 2, 2, 3) times, k1 (1, 1, 2, 2).

Work in I-cord on rem sts until cord is long enough to comfortably tie around your neck (approx. 10").*

With RS live sts, rep from * to *.

With CC, crochet a chain 60" long.

Lace the tie up the back, starting with rib hole at bottom and lacing into each side hole from the k2 yo rows (skip the k1 yo rows).

Weave in ends.

About Kimberly

To reduce my boredom in graduate school, I got my grandmom to teach me to knit. Since then, I've created sweaters, scarves, and bags and developed a strong addiction to yarn, needles, and knitting magazines and books. When I'm not satisfying my knitting jones, I'm taking classes and conducting research on my way to a Ph.D. in social psychology from Rutgers University. I've been lucky enough to teach my own classes, my favorite of which is the psychology of women. Next semester I'll even be teaching a knitting class! Now if only I could find a way to do the psychology of knitting. . . . You can keep up with my knitting adventures at www.eden.rutgers.edu/~kfairchi/knitting.html.

Don't Get Your Knitters in a Twist

WORDS TO KNIT BY

There are no mistakes, only unique variations in the design.

Design something. Even if it's just a coaster.

Patterns are guidelines, not absolute rules.

Knit at lunchtime; it'll calm you for the afternoon. *Ali Hawke, St. Louis, MO*

● If you can't decide whether an error in your knitting needs to be frogged or can be ignored, just remember what we say in my knitting group: "If you couldn't spot it from a prancing pony, it isn't that big a deal." It is unclear, however, if you are viewing the object from the prancing pony or if you are watching it go by on said prancing pony. *Lucy Lee, Cambridge, MA*

● My tip, as a beginner, is to have a glass of wine to sip on while you knit. Your stitches might not be perfect but you'll be feeling relaxed, and, hey, isn't relaxation one of the major benefits of knitting? *Andrea Nold, St. Louis, MO*

STITCH 'N BITCH ACROSS THE NATION
The Southwest

Boulder, Colorado

BOULDER, COLORADO, SnB

Set in the shadow of the breathtaking flagstone peaks of the Flatirons, the Boulder Stitch 'n Bitch group mirrors its eclectic, laid-back town. After moving here, I knit my first hat on Thanksgiving Day of 2002. A year later, I started a Stitch 'n Bitch group with a handful of knitters, and within six months we had grown to nearly fifty. We meet three times a month at a trendy teahouse or an Irish pub, which kind of sums up our group—

we're a tea and Guinness crowd. Among our members are teachers, college students, obsessive knitters, free-form ("What's a gauge, anyway?") knitters, pattern knitters, sparkly-yarn knitters, and knitters who can't believe there will ever be a day when they can knit without looking. We make even our lone crocheter feel at home. Tara Jon Manning, who authored *Men in Knits*, is an inspiring member of our group. Many of us have completed projects from her book, and we enjoy having her

around to hit up for tips and suggestions. We urge all visiting knitters to join in the stitching and bitching when they're in town.

Brenda Payne

DENVER, COLORADO, SnB

Our group is relatively new, having started in March 2004, but Denver Stitch 'n Bitch has more than fifty members, with a core group of six and some out-of-state knitters who just want to connect with a sisterhood. When we started the group we didn't know what we were getting into, who would be interested, or how much fun it would be. We tend to draw comments wherever we go. Our favorite reaction was from a woman

Denver, Colorado

who frantically knocked on the window
of the coffee shop to get our attention and ran inside to tell us how cool
she thought the meeting was.

We've gone on field trips to visit
local yarn stores, and we get regular
updates on one member's ex-husband.
We call him "H," and because of his ever-
present personality, we've thought of
changing the group name to Stitch 'n H.
Another bonding activity is hating on our
LYS yarn Nazi.

We've been amazed by the immediate
bond we've formed with one another,
how big needles can be, our members'
willingness to explore and share secrets,
why felted bags shrink one way and not
the other, and how many male knitters
there are. Our favorite meeting place is
Lisa Marie's Coffee and Tea House, but for
summer gatherings, we are looking for
a great margarita-with-a-patio spot.

Amber Bell

PHOENIX, ARIZONA, SNB

I got the urge to knit when my mother-
in-law, who hails from Northern
Ireland, knit a roll-neck sweater for my
daughter. About that time, I moved to
Portland, Oregon, for six months, took
classes at Northwest Wools, and fell in
love with knitting. I was sad to have to
leave such a knitter-friendly city, and I
was concerned that in the Arizona climate
there would be little interest in knitting.

Phoenix, Arizona

I needn't have worried—Phoenix Stitchin'
and Bitchin's first meeting, at the end of
2003, drew about thirty very enthusiastic
knitters and crocheters, and we now have
a growing e-mail list of more than one
hundred. Our members span an incredible
range of ages from eighteen-year-old
newbies to experienced grandmas. We
have a loose requirement that members
knit one item a year for charity. The first
beneficiary was Banner Desert Hospital
in Mesa. We knit lap robes, blankets, hats,
and booties for preemie babies and cancer
patients, then collected the items in early
December and delivered them for
Christmas.

Kim Dallas

SALT LAKE CITY, UTAH, SNB

Salt Lake City is such a conservative
place that just meeting in a coffee
shop can peg you as some sort of revolutionary. But that's cool with SLC SnB. Our
nearly forty members are outspoken,

witty, blatant, daring, kind, and supportive. Our ages span thirty-plus years, and
we are married, single, straight, bi, young,
young at heart, mothers, grandmothers,
teachers, midwives, stand-up comedians,
Web-site developers, librarians, feminists,
thinkers, as well as knitters.

Some of us travel more than forty
miles for the Tuesday knit nights—it's that
much fun! Sometimes I don't get much
knitting of my own done because I'm too
busy admiring someone else's project,
teaching a newbie the basics, or knitting
a few rows for another knitter, but I
always enjoy the experience. We all do.
The warmth, the sharing, the openness,
the raucous laughter . . . It's all there
and it's all good. We're having a ball.

Laurie Oberg Hadden

Salt Lake City, Utah

JENNA ADORNO

Mud Flap Girl Tank Top

Remember when Thelma and Louise first tackled the mud flap girl in that great chick flick? When they lured an offensive truck driver with a girl-clad truck off the road, women everywhere cheered. But in the end our unfortunate heroines died. On *Sex in the City,* liberated Samantha sported a mud flap girl necklace. She went on to stay happily single, remaining carefree and proudly alive. Now, *that's* worth commemorating on a mud flap.

This tank was designed for all the strong, sassy, female-positive women everywhere. What's better than a sexy girl sporting a sexy girl image and taking it as her own?

DIRECTIONS
BACK
With MC, CO 80 (90, 100, 110, 120) sts.

Next row (RS): P 1 row.

Beg with a p row, work in St st until piece measures 2" from beg, ending with RS facing.

Next (dec) row: K1, k2tog, k to last 3 sts, ssk, k1.

Working in St st, rep dec row every foll 4th row to 64 (74, 84, 94, 104) sts.

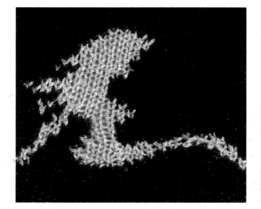

Size
Women's XS (S, M, L, XL)

Finished bust: 32 (36, 40, 44, 48)"

Finished length: 20 (20, 21, 21, 22½)"

Materials
MC: Brown Sheep Cotton Fleece (80% cotton, 20% wool; 100g/215 yds), 3 (4, 4, 5, 5) skeins #CW005 Cavern

CC: Berroco Metallic FX (85% rayon, 15% metallic; 25g/85 yds), 1 skein #1002 Silver

US 6 (4mm) straight needles, or size needed to obtain gauge

US G/6 (4mm) crochet hook

Stitch holders

Tapestry needle

Gauge
20 sts and 28 rows = 4" in St st using MC

Special Skill
INTARSIA

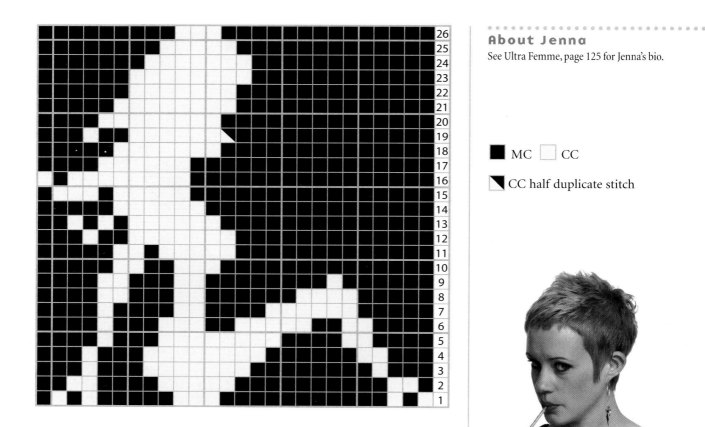

About Jenna
See Ultra Femme, page 125 for Jenna's bio.

■ MC □ CC

◣ CC half duplicate stitch

Work even in St st until piece measures 7" from beg, ending with RS facing.**

Next (inc) row: K1, m1, k to last 2 sts, m1, k1.

Working in St st, rep inc row every foll 4th row to 80 (90, 100, 110, 120) sts.

Work even in St st until piece measures 12½" from beg.

Shape armholes:

BO 4 (4, 5, 6, 6) sts at beg of next 2 (4, 4, 2, 4) rows, 3 (3, 3, 5, 5) sts at beg of next 2 (2, 4, 2, 4) rows, 2 (2, 0, 4, 0) sts at beg of next 4 (2, 0, 4, 0) rows. Dec 1 st at each edge of EOR to 44 (48, 50, 52, 54) sts.

Shape neck:

K16 (18, 19, 19, 20), place these sts on a holder, BO 12 (12, 12, 14, 14), k to end.

Next row: P to end.

Next row: BO3, k to end.

Next row: P to end.

Next row: BO2, k to end.

Next row: P to end.

Dec 1 st from neck edge every row 3 (5, 5, 5, 5) times—8 (8, 9, 9, 10) sts.

Work even in St st until piece measures 7½ (7½, 8, 8, 8½)" from beg of armhole shaping.

Place sts on st holder.

Transfer left strap sts to needles and work as for right strap, reversing shaping.

FRONT

Work as for back to **.

Next (inc) row: K1, m1, k to last 2 sts, m1, k1.

Working in St st, rep inc row every foll 4th row to 80 (90, 100, 110, 120) sts; *at the same time,* when piece has been increased to 76 (86, 96, 106, 116) sts, beg working from chart as foll with RS facing.

Next row: K25 (30, 35, 40, 45), work 26 chart sts, k25 (30, 35, 40, 45).

Cont as est for back, working from chart while shaping.

FINISHING

Join front and back straps with kitchener st.

Sew side seams.

Crab st around armholes and neckline.

Add single half duplicate stitch for nose.

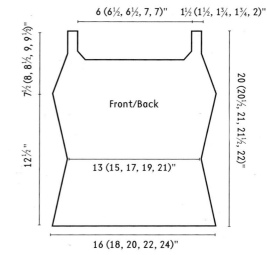

6 (6½, 6½, 7, 7)"   1½ (1½, 1¾, 1¾, 2)"

7½ (8, 8½, 9, 9½)"

20 (20½, 21, 21½, 22)"

Front/Back

12½"

13 (15, 17, 19, 21)"

16 (18, 20, 22, 24)"

Slip Up

MAKING A NICER DECREASE

The next time a pattern calls for an ssk decrease (slip as to knit, slip as to knit, then knit both together), try making a spk instead: Slip as to knit, slip as to purl, then knit both together. It seems to make a smoother-lying decrease. *Margene Merrill Smith, Salt Lake City, UT*

JOAN MCGOWAN-MICHAEL

Quick and Dirty
2-NEEDLE FISHNET STOCKINGS

Size
One size

Materials
Cascade Fixation (98.3% cotton, 1.7% elastic; 50g/100 yds relaxed, 186 yds stretched), 2 balls #6185 Hot Pink OR #8990 Black

US 6 (4mm) straight needles, or size needed to obtain gauge

US 8 (5mm) straight needles

Tapestry needle

Stitch markers

Elastic thread (optional)

Gauge
20 sts and 32 rows = 4" in St st on smaller needles.

ven the knitter who is double-pointed-needle- or lace-impaired can bang out these sexy, seamed, lacy stockings in a weekend. They're worked from the toe up, so simply stop knitting and add some ribbing when they're the length you want. Then, to keep these thigh-highs from falling down, wear them with garters (sexy!).

When asked if this stitch had a name, I had to think for a moment, and realized that this was a pattern that I'd used to make windowpane vests for my Barbie doll in the late '60s. Since I don't recall seeing it in any stitch dictionaries, it may very well be the product of a seven-year-old mind. In any event, when stretched over a shapely leg it becomes an attractive openwork stocking pattern.

STITCH PATTERN
WINDOWPANE STITCH
*K1, return same st to left-hand needle, k same st again, return same st to left-hand needle, k same st again for total k3 times each st; rep from * across row.

DIRECTIONS
TOE
With smaller needles, CO 12 sts.

P 1 row.

Next row: K3, pm, k6, pm, k3.

Work in St st, increasing 1 st before first and after second marker on every RS row 4 times—20 sts.

P 1 row.

Work in windowpane st until piece measures 4" from beg, ending with RS facing.

Next 2 RS rows: K1, m1, work in windowpane st to last st, m1, k1—24 sts.

Work 1 row even in windowpane st.

Dec 1 st at each edge on next, then EOR 3 times—16 sts.

Work in windowpane st for 5", ending with RS facing.

Change to larger needles.

Next (inc) row: K1, m1, work in windowpane st to last st, m1, k1—18 sts.

Work in windowpane st for 3", ending with RS facing.

Rep inc row next, then every 4th row 2 times—24 sts.

Work in windowpane st until piece measures 27" from beg (or to desired length), ending with RS facing.

Next row: K, picking up 1 st between each st—47 sts.

Change to smaller needles.

Work in 2 × 2 rib for 1½".

BO in rib patt.

FINISHING

Fold stocking so that seam is centered in back; seam across toe. Loosely seam back leg.

Lightly press with cool iron.

Optional: Sew elastic thread invisibly through WS of ribbing.

About Joan

I like to knit and I like to make clothes. Thankfully, I can do both from my recliner. For the past twenty years, I've been designing clothing professionally, including a lengthy stint at Frederick's of Hollywood. My company, White Lies Designs, specializes in romantic (and provocative!) knitting patterns for a wide range of sizes. I've had designs and articles published in *Vogue Knitting, Interweave Knits, Knitters, Cast On,* and other knitting publications, and keep a Web site at www.whitelies designs.com.

Block Out with Your Sock Out

HOW TO MAKE A SOCK BLOCKER
FROM A WIRE HANGER

*S*tart with your average triangle-shape wire hanger. Imagine that the hook is point A, the left-hand corner is B, and right-hand corner is C. Place your index finger halfway between B and C and pull away from A, creating a diamond shape. Now push B in toward C, so that the point is concave instead of convex, and voilà—you have a sock shape. These hangers are great when you don't have the space for all those wool socks you've knit to lie flat to dry; just hang them up on a shower rod or anywhere else that's easy. *Amanda White Berka, Fort Collins, CO*

Show Me Your tips!

A

B

C

PUSH!

B

A

C

:PULL
& down

ZOE SARGENT

Itsy-Bitsy Teeny-Weeny Purple Polka-Dot Tankini

L ast winter I made the bikini from the first *Stitch 'n Bitch* book and added my own polka-dot pattern. I liked it a lot, but wanted something a little different, and even more dots. Several revisions and a billion polka dots later, this tankini was born. The top can work with shorts or a skirt off the beach, too.

The yarn I used has a bit of elastic for a nice snug fit. I modeled the bottoms on my favorite, best-fitting underwear. They have a good amount of coverage but won't make you look like you're wearing granny panties. It's perfect for sunbathing and frolicking on the beach. Have fun, and don't forget your sunscreen!

DIRECTIONS

TOP FRONT

With MC, CO 90 (98, 106) sts.

Rows 1–3: Work in 1 × 1 rib.

Row 4: P.

Rows 5–17: Work from chart for 12 rows, working first and last st of every row in MC.

Next (dec) row: K2, k2tog, k to last 4 sts, ssk, k2.

Rep dec row every 10th row twice more—84 (92, 100) sts.

Work even in St st until piece measures 6 (6½, 7)" from beg, ending with RS facing.

Size

Women's S (M, L)

Finished bust: 28 (31, 33)"

Finished hip: 28½ (30, 32½)"

To fit bust: 34 (36, 38)"

To fit hips: 36 (38, 40)"

Materials

Cascade Fixation (98.3% cotton, 1.7% elastic; 50g/186 yds)

MC: 4 (5, 6) skeins #2406 Light Purple

CC: 1 skein #6388 Dark Purple

US 3 (3.25mm) straight needles, or size needed to obtain gauge

Stitch holder

2 yards ¼" elastic

Sewing needle and thread

Gauge

24 sts and 40 rows = 4" in St st

Special Skill

FAIR ISLE

Next (inc) row: K2, inc1, K to last 3 sts, inc1, k2.

Rep inc row every 9th row twice more—90 (98, 106) sts.

Work from chart 2 for 5 rows, working first and last st of every row in MC.**

Knitting the first and last sts of every row, shape left side of halter as follows, while maintaining the integrity of the chart:

Next row (RS facing): K45 (49, 53), place rem sts on holder.

Next row: K3, p2tog tbl, p to last 3 sts, k3.

Setup row: K4 (6, 8), work from chart, k3 (5, 7).

Cont to work garter edges in MC and center sts from chart as est, shape left side of halter:

Rows 1, 3, 15, 17, 19, 29, 31, 37, and 39: P.

Rows 2, 14, 16, 18, 20, and 22: K to last 5 sts, ssk, k3.

Rows 4, 6, 8, 10, 12, 24, 26, and 34: K.

Rows 5, 7, 9, 11, 13, and 21: K3, p2tog tbl, p to last 3 sts, k3.

Rows 23, 25, 27, 33, and 35: K3, p2tog tbl, p to last 5 sts, p2tog, k3.

Rows 28, 30, 32, 36, 38, and 40: K3, k2tog, k to last 5 sts, ssk, k3.

Row 41: K3, p2tog tbl, p to last 5 sts, p2tog, k3.

Medium and large only:

Next row: K3, k2tog, k to last 5 sts, ssk, k3. Next row: K3, p2tog tbl, p to last 5 sts, p2tog, k3.

Large only:

Rep last 2 rows once.

All sizes:

Next row: K2, k2tog, ssk, k2—6 sts.

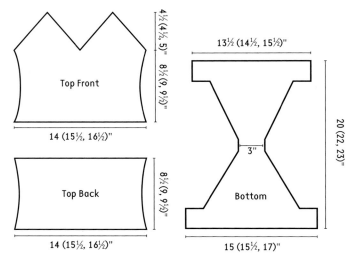

Strap:

Work in garter st on rem 6 sts for 16" or to a length that will tie comfortably around the neck. BO.

Right side of halter:

Work as for left side, reversing shaping and chart.

TOP BACK

Work as for front to **.

Work in 1 × 1 rib for 3 rows.

BO.

BIKINI BOTTOM

With MC, CO 82 (88, 94) sts.

Rows 1–3: Work in 1 × 1 rib.

Row 4: P.

Rows 5–17: Work from chart for 12 rows.

Work in St st for 2 (2½, 3)", ending with RS facing.

Next row: K52 (55, 59) beg with a k st, work in 1 × 1 rib to end.

Next row: Work in 1 × 1 rib for 30 (33, 35) sts, k22 (22, 24), rib to end.

Rep last row once.

Next row: BO 27 (30, 32), rib 2 sts, k24 (24, 26), rib to end.

Next row: BO 27 (30, 32), rib 2 sts, p to end.

P the first and last st of every row, cont as follows:

Next (dec) row: P3, k2tog, k to last 5 sts, ssk, p3. Rep dec row every 6th row 4 (4, 5) times more.

Work even in St st for 2 (2, 3)".

P 1 row.

Inc 1 st on each edge, 3 sts in from edge of next row, then EOR 25 (27, 29) times more, then EOR 10 (10, 12) times more—90 (94, 102) sts.

Next row: K1, p1, k to last 2 sts, p1, k1.

Next row: P1, k1, p to last 2 sts, k1, p1.

Next row: K1, p1, k to last 2 sts, p1, k1.

Work even in St st for 2 (2½, 3)".

Work from chart 1 for 12 rows.

Work in 1 × 1 rib for 3 rows.

BO.

FINISHING

Seam top sides.

Seam bottom sides.

Weave in ends.

Attach elastic:

Turn the bottom inside out. On the inside top edge along the ribbing, attach one end of the elastic to a side seam with a safety pin. Thread tapestry needle with several feet of doubled MC and secure end underneath elastic. Work in herringbone st over elastic around entire waistband.

Try the bottom on and adjust elastic to fit. Sew elastic ends tog with thread.

MC

CC

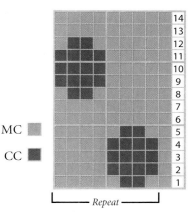

— Repeat —

About Zoe

I started knitting at age seven at a Waldorf School, and all the scarves, socks, and swimsuits I've knitted since then could probably reach around the globe—or at least around the block a couple of times (but it's a large block). The tankini is my ultimate creation so far. Tentative future plans include knitting sweaters for my pet chickens to protect them from the frigid Boston winters. I'm a recent graduate of the Sudbury Valley School and hope to pursue a career that involves my passion for all things crafty and to continue my other interests—gardening, yoga, and belly dancing.

JAMIE CHUPICK

Accidentally on Purpose
DROP STITCH VEST

Size
Women's S (M, L)

Finished bust: 30 (39, 48)"

Finished length: 23 (24, 25)"

Materials
Patons Grace
(100% mercerized cotton; 50g/136 yds), 5 (7, 9) skeins #438 Fuchsia

US 5 (3.5mm) straight needles, or size needed to obtain gauge

Stitch holder

Tapestry needle

Gauge
24 sts and 26 rows = 4" in St st

16 sts and 26 rows = 4" in drop st patt

Abbreviations
DBO2: Drop next st, lift up resulting ladder, k into front of ladder, k into back of ladder, BO first st, BO next st.

On WS, work as for RS but p into front and then back of ladder.

t his vest was originally designed to be machine knit with much finer yarn. But it's so versatile that any weight of yarn may be used, and it can be worn in various ways. It's casual and funky worn with a long- or short-sleeved T-shirt underneath, and totally sexy with just a camisole. The smooth and silky cotton yarn makes a sleek, stretchy fabric, and it's fun to knit, too. The stitch pattern only happens as you are binding off stitches at the very end. It's a lot like turning a hole in your stocking into a "ladder," except the stitches will "run" down from the neck instead of upward.

There's no shaping needed for the armholes or the back (even at the neck). So, even though the directions look complicated, it's a breeze. You get to drop stitches all the way down to the bottom—on purpose!

DIRECTIONS
FRONT
CO 60 (78, 96) sts.

Work even in St st until piece measures 21 (22, 23)" from beg, ending with RS facing.

Little Miss Marker

IDEAS FOR IMPROVISED STITCH MARKERS

I have a large collection of unused earrings. Some I grew out of, others were fashion no-nos, and some became single after their buddy was lost. I've been able to give those abandoned and orphaned earrings new life. You see, like Wonder Woman, they have a secret identity—they're not just earrings, they're stitch markers! Those with a hook or post can be used as row markers by simply slipping them gently through stitches in your work, while hoops or those with kidney-style findings can be used to mark stitches on your needles.
Marie Irshad, Cardiff, Wales

● Plastic-coated paper clips (not to be confused with all-plastic paper clips) make dandy markers and can be purchased in large quantities at any office supply store.
Evelyn Rowe

● You can always use one of your old rings that doesn't fit anymore as a stitch marker. It's a great way to see it every day and get some joy out of it—rather than keeping it tucked away in a drawer. *Catherine Clift, Melbourne, Australia*

● I use the very small "ouchless" hair elastics—those elasticky circles, about ¾" across, and sold in a bag of a hundred—as stitch markers. They come in many colors, which makes it easy to keep track of which part you're marking.
Anne Leonard

Shape neck, right side:

Small:
Next row: K26 and place these sts on a holder, DBO2, BO6, DBO2, k26.

Next and all WS rows: P.

Next row: BO1, DBO2, BO1, k to end.

Next RS row: BO4, k to end.

Next RS row: BO1, DBO2, BO1, k to end.

Next RS row: DBO2, BO2, k to end.

Next RS row: BO4, k to end.

Next RS row: DBO2, BO1, DBO2, BO6.

Medium:
Next row: K33 and place these sts on a holder, DBO2, BO1, DBO2, BO6, DBO2, BO1, DBO2, k33.

Next and all WS rows: P.

Next RS row: BO4, k to end. Next RS row: BO2, DBO2, BO1, k to end.

Next RS row: DBO2, BO3, k to end. Next RS row: BO3, DBO2, k to end.

Next RS row: BO1, DBO2, BO1, k to end.

Next RS row: BO3, k to end.

Next RS row: BO2, DBO2, BO1, DBO2, BO6.

Large:
Next row: K41 and place these sts on a holder, BO1, DBO2, BO1, DBO2, BO6, DBO2, BO1, DBO2, BO1, k41.

Next and all WS rows: P.

Next RS row: BO3, k to end.

Next RS row: BO2, DBO2, k to end.

Next RS row: BO1, DBO2, BO1, k to end.

Next RS row: BO3, k to end.

Next RS row: BO2, DBO2, k to end.

Next RS row: BO1, DBO2, BO1, k to end.

Next RS row: BO3, k to end.

Next RS row: BO2, DBO2, BO1, k to end.

Next RS row: DBO2, BO3, k to end.

Next RS row: BO3, DBO2, BO1, DBO2, BO6.

Shape neck, left side:

Transfer holder sts to needle and work as for right side, connecting yarn at neck edge and beg with a WS (p) row, reversing shaping.

BACK
CO 60 (78, 96) sts.

Work even in St st until piece measures 23 (24, 25)" from beg, ending with RS facing.

Next row: *BO 6, DBO2, BO1, DBO2; rep from * 5 (7, 9) times, BO 6.

FINISHING
Seam shoulders.

Seam sides from CO edge to 7 (8, 8½)" below beg of shoulder BO.

10 (13, 16)"   2½ (3¼, 4)"

Front/Back

23 (24, 25)"

15½ (19½, 24)"

About Jamie

My grandmother taught me how to knit and crochet when I was seven, but I never imagined I would be pursuing it as a career. In fact, it wasn't until I was eighteen and moved from Dallas to Los Angeles to study textile design that I discovered my passion for knitting. I am currently developing Little Ditties, a line of sweaters, ponchos, wristbands, legwarmers, and other accessories. They are available at chocosho.com, a forum where designers and artists sell their creations. When I'm not busy knitting, I work as a designer of quilting fabrics.

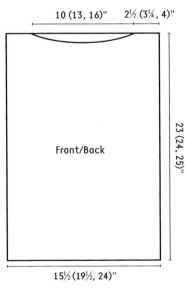

STEFANIE JAPEL

Totally Tubular

MINISKIRT/BOOB TUBE

t he idea for this pattern came to me while packing for a trip last spring. I travel a lot and was thinking that if one piece of clothing could have multiple uses, it would cut down on the number of things I'd have to take in my suitcase. Then I remembered the "modular clothing" of the mid-'80s: simple tubes, rectangles, and squares and combined in an infinite number of ways. A shirt could be a skirt or be scrunched up into a belt. Here's my take on that concept—a multifunctional piece of clothing that can go from boob tube to miniskirt. On a cool evening, it can be a shoulder warmer. On a hot day, you can wear it as a skirt.

STITCH PATTERNS

LACE PATTERN (TUBE 1 ONLY)

Rnd 1: *K2tog, yo; rep from * 9 times.

Rnds 2 and 4: K.

Rnd 3: *Yo, k2tog; rep from * 9 times.

BOBBLE STITCH (TUBE 1 ONLY)

K3 into next stitch, turn, p3, turn, k3, turn, sl1, k2tog, psso.

LACE PATTERN (TUBE 2 ONLY)

Rnds 1, 3, 5, and 7: Yo, k2tog, yo.

Rnds 2, 4, 6, and 8: K.

Rnd 9: yo, k2tog.

Size

Finished waist or shoulder: 27 (31, 35, 39)"

Finished length: 18 (18, 19, 19)"

Materials

Berroco Cotton Twist (70% mercerized cotton, 30% rayon; 50g/85 yds)

Tube 1

7 (7, 8, 9) skeins #8311 True Red

Tube 2

7 (7, 8, 9) skeins #8387 Soul

US 5 (3.5mm) 24" circular needle

US 8 (5mm) 24" circular needle, or size needed to obtain gauge

Gauge

20 sts and 24 rows = 4" in St st with larger needle

24 sts and 36 rows = 4" in St st with smaller needle

Special Skill

LACE

DIRECTIONS, TUBE 1

With smaller needle, CO 160 (180, 200, 220) sts.

Join and pm to mark beg of rnds, work 5 rnds in garter st.

Work in St st until piece measures $4\frac{1}{2}$ ($4\frac{1}{2}$, $5\frac{1}{2}$, $5\frac{1}{2}$)" from beg.

Change to larger needle and K 1 rnd.

Next rnd: Work in lace patt for 20 sts, pm, k40 (50, 60, 70), pm, work in lace patt for Tube 1 for 20 sts, pm, k80 (90, 100, 110).

Circular Logic

TIPS FOR WORKING WITH CIRCULAR NEEDLES

*T*o alleviate the "crazed serpentine" nature of circular needles, dip the plastic cords that connect the needle points into boiling water for just a second to release them and soften them up. I pull them straight while they cool, and it seems to make them less twisty and much easier to work with. *Katy Burns, Chicago, IL*

● With circular needles, the place where the plastic cable joins the needle is often smoother on one side than it is on the other. Reserve the smoother join for the needle you are knitting *from*, since this is the end where you'll be pushing stitches from the cable onto the needle, and any imperfections in the join will snag your stitches. The end you are knitting *to* has stitches just worked sliding from the needle to the (smaller) cable, so it usually doesn't matter much if this join isn't as nice. *Joan Dyer, New York, NY*

● When starting a piece of circular knitting, cast on one more stitch than is required for the pattern. When getting ready to join (on the first row of knitting), slip the extra stitch from the right needle to the left, then knit these first two stitches together (the first cast-on and the last cast-on "extra stitch"). This will leave the correct number of stitches on your needles and will give a great, almost invisible join at the beginning of the work. *Catherine Clift, Melbourne, Australia*

Cont as est, working lace patt at sides and St st between, until piece measures 16 (16, 17, 17)" from beg.

TRIM

Work 5 rnds in garter st.

Work 2 rnds in St st.

Next rnd: *K4, make bobble; rep from * to end of round.

Work 2 rnds in St st.

Work 5 rnds in garter st.

BO.

DIRECTIONS, TUBE 2

With smaller needle, CO 160 (180, 200, 220) sts.

Join and work 5 rnds in garter st.

Work in St st until piece measures 3 (4, 4, 4½)" from beg.

Change to larger needle and work 5 rnds in St st.

Next 9 rnds: K10, work lace patt for Tube 2, k to end.

Work 5 rnds in St st.

Next 9 rnds: K15, work lace patt, k to end.

Work 5 rnds in St st.

Cont as est, working 5 more sts before lace patt with every rep until 30 sts have been worked before lace patt.

Work 5 rnds in St st.

Work 5 rnds in garter st.

BO.

About Stefanie

I was born in Wichita, Kansas, and lived in eight different towns before my parents settled in Pleasant Hill, Iowa, when I was in third grade. I've got two postgraduate degrees in geology and currently live in Mainz, Germany, where I'm a research scientist in high-pressure mineral physics. I was first taught to knit when I was eight by my grandmother but I didn't become completely obsessed until I was twenty and playing drums in an all-girl punk band (called Period). I had to have cool stuff to wear at our performances so people would see me way back there behind three hot guitar players! Even though I'm older now (thirty-three), I still knit with that punk aesthetic in mind. Individuality is the key to happiness. I have a knitting weblog at www.glampyre.com.

HEATHER DIXON

Candy Stripers

MESSENGER AND LAPTOP BAGS

L ike a lot of women I know, I carry a ton of completely necessary stuff around with me every day, so last year, when my favorite multicolored leather patchwork shoulder bag bit the dust, I decided to try my hand at designing a felted knit replacement. I had seen patterns for felted bags around, but I needed something a little more substantial that I could throw over my shoulder to leave both hands free. Now this stripy orange and pink messenger bag, my new favorite, goes everywhere I go. The laptop version is made in the same way, just altering the measurements, and it looks so pretty in springtime colors!

Proportions are based on my leather shoulder bag. Directions for messenger bag are followed by directions for laptop bag in parentheses; italic type indicates directions for messenger bag only. Where there is only one direction, it applies to both.

STITCH PATTERN

HORIZONTAL HERRINGBONE STITCH

Row 1: K1, *s1, k1, raise sl st with left-hand needle but do not drop it, k into back of raised st, drop from needle; rep from * to last st, k1.

Row 2: *P2tog, then purl first st again, slipping both sts off needle tog; rep from * to end.

Size

Finished measurements:

Messenger bag: 10" × 6½" × 4½"

Laptop bag: 16" × 10½" × 2¼"

Materials

Brown Sheep Lamb's Pride Bulky (85% wool, 15% mohair; 113g/125 yds)

MESSENGER BAG

MC: 2 skeins M22 Autumn Harvest

CC1: 1 skein M38 Lotus Pink

CC2: 1 skein M105 RPM Pink

CC3: 1 skein M155 Lemon Drop

LAPTOP BAG

MC: 2 skeins M120 Limeade

CC1: 2 skeins M52 Spruce

CC2: 1 skein M155 Lemon Drop

CC3: 1 skein M10 Crème

US 15 (10mm) straight needles, or size needed to obtain gauge

10 (16)" zipper to match CC1

One 2" metal ring

Stitch markers

Tapestry needle

Gauge

10 sts and 15 rows = 4" in St st

STRIPE SEQUENCES

Front panel:

8 rows MC, 6 rows CC1, 2 rows CC2, 2 rows CC3, 2 rows CC2, 4 rows CC1, 8 rows MC (8 rows MC, 4 rows CC1, 2 rows CC2, 2 rows CC3, 2 rows MC, 2 rows CC2, 2 rows CC3, 4 rows CC1, 2 rows CC2, 6 rows MC, 4 rows CC1, 2 rows CC2, 2 rows CC3, 2 rows MC, 2 rows CC2, 2 rows CC3, 4 rows CC1, 2 rows CC2, 4 rows MC).

Back panel:

6 rows MC, 4 rows CC1, 2 rows CC2, 2 rows CC3, 2 rows MC, 2 rows CC2, 2 rows CC3, 4 rows CC1, 2 rows CC2, 6 rows MC (10 rows MC, 6 rows CC1, 2 rows CC2, 2 rows CC3, 2 rows CC2, 4 rows CC1, 8 rows MC, 6 rows CC1, 2 rows CC2, 2 rows CC3, 2 rows CC2, 4 rows CC1, 8 rows MC).

To adjust the pattern to fit your laptop, just add or subtract CO stitches from the front and back panels.

DIRECTIONS

BASE

With MC, CO 20 (12)sts. Work in horizontal herringbone st, alternating 2 rows MC and 2 rows CC1 for 30 (50) rows.

BO.

FRONT PANEL

With RS of base facing and MC, pick up 30 (50) sts from one long base edge. Beg with a RS row, work in St st foll stripe sequence for front panel.

Change to CC1 and BO.

BACK PANEL

Work as for front panel, foll stripe sequence for back panel.

FIRST SIDE PANEL

Messenger bag only:

Stripe sequence: 4 rows MC, 4 rows CC1, 2 rows CC2, 2 rows CC3, 2 rows CC2, 2 rows CC1, 6 rows MC.

With RS of base facing and MC, pick up 20 (10) sts from base CO edge.

Working in horizontal herringbone st, foll stripe sequence above (***alternate 2 rows of MC and 2 rows of CC1 for 158 rows, pm at each edge of row 36; BO).

Messenger bag only:

Next row: With CC1, k2tog, then work horizontal herringbone st to last 3 sts, k1, k2tog.

Next row: P1, then work horizontal herringbone st to last st, p1.

Rep these 2 rows, alternating 2 rows of MC with

*2 rows of CC1 until 8 sts rem, and pm at each edge of second row of MC stripe in dec patt.***

Cont in stripe sequence as est, working even in horizontal herringbone st for 20 more rows.

BO.

SECOND SIDE PANEL

Messenger bag only:

Stripe sequence: 2 rows MC, 2 rows CC1, 2 rows CC2, 2 rows CC3, 2 rows CC2, 6 rows CC1, 6 rows MC.

Work as for first side panel to **, foll stripe sequence above. Cont in stripe sequence as est, work even in horizontal herringbone st for 80 more rows (work as for first side panel to ***, alternating 2 rows of MC and 2 rows of CC1 for 58 rows). BO.

With WS tog (so that the seams are on the outside), pin front and back to side panels so that top of front and back line up with the markers on side panels.

Back st these 4 seams.

TOP

Wind off about a small apple-sized ball of MC (piece requires working 2 sections at the same time).

With MC, pu 8 (10) sts from wrong side of shorter side panel at top of dec shaping (6 rows up from markers).

Work 2 (4) rows even in St st.

Messenger bag only:

Cont in St st, inc 1 st at each edge of next row, then EOR to 14 sts, ending with RS facing.

Divide for bag opening:

K7 (5), join new ball of MC and use to k7 (5).

Next row: With new ball of MC, p7 (5); with first ball of MC, p7 (5).

A Very Kinky Girl

WHEN TO SHOWER WITH YOUR YARN

*I*f you've unraveled yarn from a project and would like to reuse it, here's one way to remove the kinks. Wrap the yarn loosely around a wide piece of cardboard, then take this giant loop off the cardboard and hang it over a plastic coat hanger. Hang the yarn in the bathroom the next time you take a shower. The bathroom will fill up with steam, and by the time you finish your shower, all the kinks in the yarn will have loosened up and it will be nice and workable again. *Amy Singleton, Galveston, TX*

Rep these 2 rows 18 (39) times.

Join bag opening:

With first ball of MC, k all 14 (10) sts. Break 2nd ball of yarn.

Work 1 (3) rows even in St st.

BO.

Messenger bag only:

Dec 1 st at each edge of next row, then EOR to 8 sts, ending with RS facing.

Work 2 rows even in St st.

BO.

FINISHING

WS tog, pin top section to top of bag so that BO edge matches CO edge at opposite side panel and top edges of front and back are neatly in place. Backstitch tog.

Weave in ends.

To felt, place bag in a zippered pillow case and run through a hot wash cycle. Wash until desired felting has occurred (this may take 2 to 3 washes). Optional: Add a few pairs of jeans to the cycle to help with agitation.

Once your bag is the size you like, pull corners and squeeze seams to form a boxy bag shape and leave in warm and airy place to dry fully.

Pin one side of zipper into opening so that only the teeth will show from the outside.

Sew zipper in place close to edge of bag opening and again at outer edge of zipper tape.

Repeat on other side of bag opening, being careful not to stretch edges.

Thread metal ring over shorter strap, fold strap to inside, and firmly sew down BO edge to start of top section.

Take longer strap and thread it through metal ring. Fold end of strap to length required and sew firmly, close to ring and at BO edge.

About Heather

See Valentine's Hat and Mittens pattern, page 54, for Heather's bio.

That Felt Great

A FEW GOOD FELTING IDEAS

A member of Chicago Stitch 'n Bitch once told me that using Dawn dish detergent for felting works best. When I tried it on a felted purse, it worked like a charm. *Jen Mindel, Chicago, IL*

● I have a washing machine in my rented Brooklyn apartment, but I'm wary of clogging the pipes with all the little bits of fuzz that come off when you felt. I've found that placing the article in an old pillow case and then folding over and pinning the edge closed with safety pins keeps the little fuzzies inside. Tossed in the washer with a couple pairs of old jeans, it still provides enough agitation for felting. *Jen Greely, Jersey City, NJ*

● All the felting instructions I've come across are for home, top-loader machines, where they tell you to check on the progress every ten minutes. But there's no reason why we laundromat-dependent people can't felt too. Just stick your finished product into the machine (in a pillow case or some such), along with something to create friction (jeans), put your quarters in, and relax. It'll take a couple of runs. Keep washing until you're happy with the result. *Valentina, Nakic, NY*

● Long, skinny items felt more evenly if you put them in a small-ish bag, a bit smaller than a pillowcase. That way they won't get wrapped around the agitator or pulled out of whack from the water they're holding, and end up longer than before felting. *Kate Pickering Antonova, New York, NY*

● When choosing yarn for a felted project, beware of using very light colors, especially white. White and very pale yarns have often been bleached, which damages the fibers too much for them to felt well. *KPA*

● Felting by hand can get pretty boring and definitely splashy. I prefer to combine it with another favorite evening activity—a soak in the tub. I take in with me a short tub on a tray (for small items), or a big bucket (for larger projects). Make sure it's a clean bucket, obviously, and put in your soap, vinegar, and any other tools you might need (such as a wooden spoon for agitating). Hot and cold water are as convenient as can be, and I use a nice-smelling, gentle soap for both the tub and the felting bucket, so I don't mind all the splashing around. *KPA*

● In my experience, it doesn't make anything felt faster or better to use painfully hot water, or to agitate so vigorously that it either tires your hands or—if you're rubbing against something, like a cookie rack—unnecessarily rips the wool. Simply kneading the wool like bread dough, in comfortably hot water with plenty of soap, works just as fast and never does any damage. *KPA*

● Felted slippers can be slippery to walk in. An alternative to buying expensive slipper bottoms is to paint a pattern on the bottom of the slippers with puffy fabric paint (found in any crafts store for about 99¢ per bottle). Try painting concentric circles or flowers on the heels and toes. For my grandpa, who lives in the Alzheimer's ward of a nursing home, I painted his name and washing instructions on the bottom of each slipper. *KPA*

● If you accidentally felt too much, it's remarkably easy to stretch the item back to where you want it as long as it's still warm and wet. If you've already let it dry, try dipping it back in warm, slightly soapy water until it's soaked (but don't agitate). Then stretch it, fix it onto some object, and let it dry. *KPA*

158

Size

Finished height: 6 (8)" + handles

Finished width: 10 (14)"

Finished depth: 3½ (5)"

Materials

SMALL BAG

Cascade 220 (100% wool; 100g/220 yds)

MC: 2 skeins #7919 Turquoise

CC: 1 skein #8505 White

US 8 (5mm) straight needles,
or size needed to obtain gauge

US 8 (5mm) double-pointed needles
(set of 2)

7" white zipper

LARGE BAG

Brown Sheep Lamb's Pride Worsted
(85% wool, 15% mohair; 113g/190 yds)

MC: 2 skeins #M-38 Lotus Pink

CC: 1 skein #M-05 Onyx

US 11 (8mm) straight needles,
or size needed to obtain gauge

US 11 (8mm) double-pointed needles
(set of 2)

12" black zipper

BOTH BAGS

2 stitch holders

Sewing needle

Thread to match MC

Gauge

Small bag: 17 sts and 22 rows = 4" in St st

Large bag: 12 sts and 16 rows = 4" in St st

GEORGIA A. COLEMAN

Letter Have It

I'm crazy about the new initial craze! I want one of everything with a big ole G right smack in the middle. Only, I've encountered a little problem: Nobody sells anything with a G on it. I've found plenty of Ks and a ton of Js. But c'mon, we aren't all Kimberly or Jessica! This bag is my tribute to all the unpopular initials out there, and its shape is inspired by my love of 1950s bowling bags. Best of all, by simply changing the needle size, you can make the bag big or little. The bigger bag is perfect for toting around knitting projects, and the little one is just the right size for your wallet and keys. It makes a perfect personalized gift.

DIRECTIONS

FRONT

With MC and straight needles, CO 48 sts.

Beg with a RS row, work in St st for 10 rows.

Row 11: K14, work row 1 of chart, k14.

Row 12: P14, work row 2 of chart, p14.

Cont as est until row 12 of chart has been completed.

Next row: K2, k2tog, k10, work row 13 of chart, k10, k2tog, k2.

Next row: P13, work row 14 of chart, p13.

Cont as est, working decs on RS rows, until all rows of chart have been completed.

Next row: K2, k2tog, k to last 4 sts, k2tog, k2.

Next row: P.

Rep last 2 rows once—30 sts.

BO loosely.

BACK

With MC and straight needles, CO 48 sts.

Beg with a RS row, work in St st for 22 rows.

Next row: K2, k2tog, k to last 4 sts, k2tog, k2.

Next row: P.

Rep last 2 rows 8 times more—30 sts.

BO loosely.

CENTER PANEL

With MC and straight needles, CO 16 sts.

Work in garter st for $38\frac{1}{2}$ (42)".

Next row: K8, place rem sts on holder.

Work in garter st on these 8 sts for 9 ($10\frac{1}{2}$)". Place sts on 2nd holder. Break yarn, leaving a 6" tail.

Join yarn to sts on 1st holder. Work in garter st on these 8 sts for 9 ($10\frac{1}{2}$)".

Next row: K8 from left-hand needle, then k8 from holder. Work in garter st on all 16 sts for $1\frac{1}{2}$".

BO loosely.

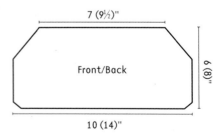

7 ($9\frac{1}{2}$)"

Front/Back

9 (8)"

10 (14)"

Smaller needles make a smaller bag; larger needles make a bigger one!

About Georgia

I can't remember a time when I didn't want to knit. The only problem was that I didn't know how. Around three years ago I finally got the chance to learn—a woman I was working with showed me how to cast on and how to make the knit stitch. After about a hundred garter stitch items I decided it was time to learn the rest, and I have been knitting everything from lace to Fair Isle ever since. About a year ago I started a blog, www.onmymind.blogdrive.com, to chronicle my knitting journeys. In my real life I am a full-blooded Chicagoan and a third-year college student. Although crazy school schedules often keep me from attending the Chicago Stitch 'n Bitch, I have unofficial knitting get-togethers all the time.

HANDLES (MAKE 2)

With MC and straight needles, CO on 7 sts.

Work in garter st until piece measures 8 (9½)" from beg.

BO loosely.

PIPING (MAKE 2)

With CC1 and dpns, CO on 3 sts.

Work in I-cord for 41 (54)".

Place sts on a holder. Break yarn, leaving a 9" tail.

FINISHING

With MC, sew the CO and BO edges of the center panel tog.

Sew the front and back to the center panel, ensuring that the zipper opening is centered along the top.

With CC1, sew I-cord along the outer edges of the front and back.

If necessary, adjust length of piping by taking sts off holder and working in I-cord or ripping back to appropriate length. Draw tail through sts and secure ends of piping tog.

Sew handles right next to piping on the center panel, placed at the beginning and end of the BO edge.

Weave in ends.

FELTING

Place the bag in a zippered pillow or laundry bag, then in the washer on the hot cycle with a tablespoon of dish soap or laundry detergent. Stop occasionally to check the bag. If it is not completely dense after one cycle, run it through again until it is.

When felted, remove excess water by letting the bag go through the spin cycle.

Remove the bag from the washer, shape, and stuff with plastic bags. Set the bag on a towel and allow it to dry completely.

Pin the zipper in place and sew it in by hand.

We All Cord for I-cord *show me your tips!*

MAKING I-CORD ON CIRCULAR NEEDLES

*F*or my current project, I desperately needed to make an I-cord. After getting directions from a friend, I set out to look for double-pointed needles. Despite the number of craft stores in Austin, I was unable to find the right size. That's when I realized that if the right circular needle is used, you can create I-cord with only one needle. Simply move the I-cord from one side of the needle to the other as you knit. I call it "I-cord for the desperate."

Jennifer Mailloux, Austin, TX

Initial charts continued on next page ⟶

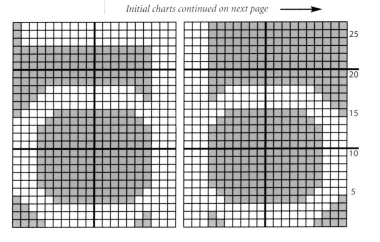

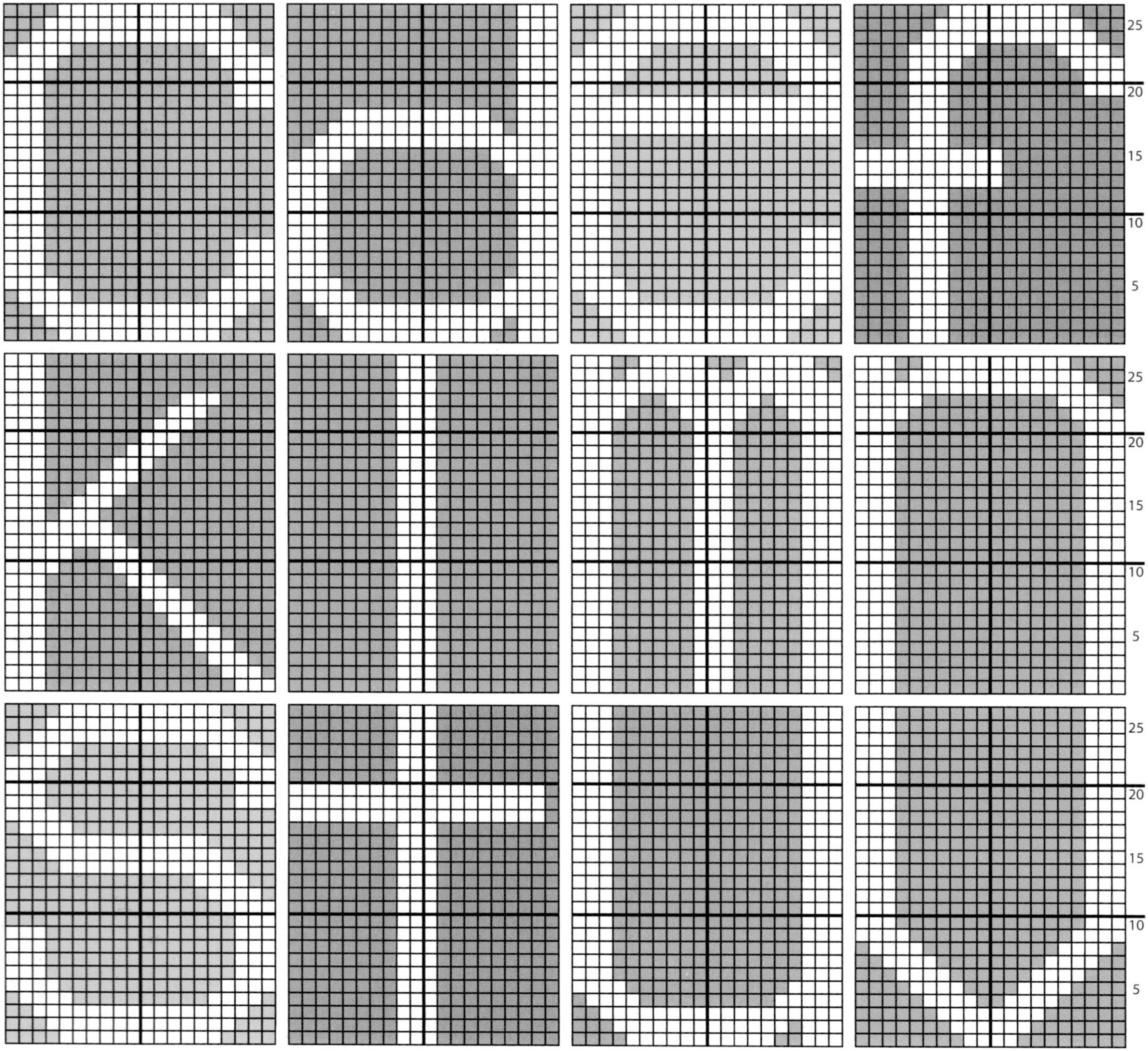
25
20
15
10
5

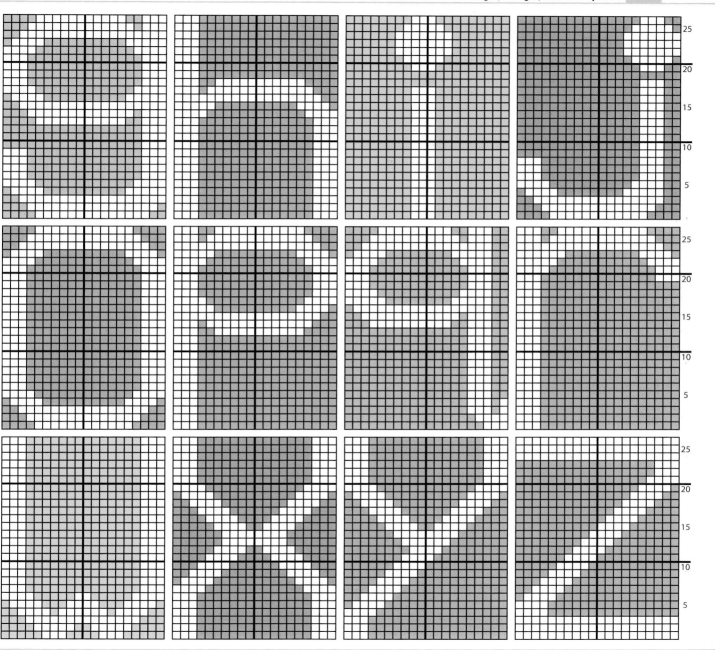

DEBBIE STOLLER

Poster Boy

these days, everyone's carrying interesting little tote bags with images screenprinted onto them. Poster boy came about when I was trying to figure out if there was a way to make a similar image in knitting. I wanted to make a two-color image that was not as regular as the kind usually done in Fair Isle patterns, yet not as simple as those often made using the intarsia method.

Poster Boy is knit using the Fair Isle method, where the color not in use is carried along behind the working color, but is twisted with the other yarn about every five stitches so as to avoid long strands hanging at the back of your work. Just about any black-and-white image that isn't too complicated can be knit this way. Start by taking an image into Photoshop and making it 11" wide, with a resolution of only 6 pixels per inch. Play around with the brightness and contrast so that the image is reduced to black and white but is still recognizable. Print out the image, get yourself some knitter's graph paper, and lay the pixelated image underneath it on a lightbox. Color in your chart with a pencil. Then grab your needles and make that poster boy come to life!

DIRECTIONS
BAG
With CC and circular needle, CO 112 sts.

Join and work in the round as follows:

Row 1: P1, pm, k55, p1, pm, k55.

Work 3 more rows in St st, with 1 p st before markers as est.

Size
Finished width: 11"

Finished length: 12"

Materials
Brown Sheep Lamb's Pride Worsted (85% wool, 15% mohair; 113g/125 yds)

MC: 1 skein M81 Red Baron

CC: 1 skein M105 Black

US 8 (5mm) 16" circular needle, or size needed to obtain gauge

US 7 (4.5mm) straight needles

1 yd lining fabric

Sewing thread to match lining

Gauge
18 sts and 26 rows = 4"

Special Skill
FAIR ISLE

Row 5: Beg working from chart, 1 rep on each side of the markers. Carry color not in use loosely behind work, catching it in place with working yarn every 5 sts. Vary the placement of yarn twists on each rnd.

Working from chart, cont in St st, maintaining p sts as est, until all chart rows have been worked.

Break CC and cont in MC, working 3 rnds in St st.

P 1 rnd.

K 3 more rounds in St st.

BO loosely.

STRAPS (MAKE 2)

With MC and straight needles, CO 13 sts.

Work in St st until piece measures 27" from beg.

BO.

FINISHING

Fold straps in half, WS tog, and mattress st tog along lengthwise edge.

Seam bottom of bag closed.

Fold top of bag toward WS at purl row; stitch down hem.

Fold straps so that the seams are centered on the back side of straps. Attach one strap to the front of the bag and the other strap to the back of the bag, with the ends of the straps 1½" in the outer edge of the bag.

Cut the lining fabric into two 12" × 13" pieces. With RS tog, sew seam across bottom and sides, ½" from edge.

Press top ½" of lining to outside (WS).

Place lining bag inside knit bag and, with sewing thread, sew the top of the lining to the hem of the knit bag.

About Debbie

My mother taught me to knit when I was six. When I was twenty, I was retaught by my grandmother—a woman who knit for ninety of her 103 years. But I didn't enjoy the process and quickly gave up the hobby. Then, about fifteen years later—in 1999—I picked up an unfinished sweater and worked on it during a three-day, cross-country train trip, and finally it all clicked. Suddenly I was hooked, and couldn't get enough of the craft, reading about it, studying it, and, of course, practicing it. I also quickly became aware of knitting's relatively low regard in our culture and went on a mission to "Take Back the Knit"—writing about knitting in my magazine, *BUST*, and starting a Stitch 'n Bitch group in NYC to teach as many people as I could the myriad joys of knitting. When I'm not knitting, working on my magazine, or writing knitting books—I'm sleeping!

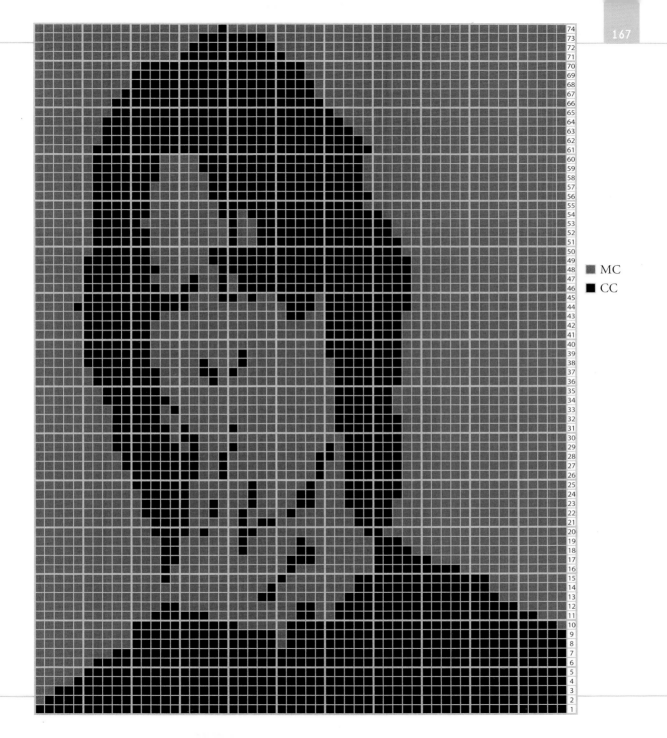

MC

CC

STEPHANIE MRSE

Om Yoga Mat Bag

I came up with the idea for this bag while looking at patterns for knit mesh shopping bags. At the same time, I was getting back into yoga and noticing that you can buy yoga mat bags online for outrageous amounts of money!

This lace pattern looks impressive, but it is easy to memorize and knit. The sturdy cotton yarn can be purchased inexpensively at almost any craft store.

Size
22" long × 11" in diameter

Materials
Lion Brand Lion Cotton
(100% cotton; 142g/236 yds),
2 skeins #148 Turquoise

US 9 (5.5mm) straight needles

US 8 (5mm) straight needles,
or size needed to obtain gauge

1 yd white drawstring cord

Gauge
16 sts and 22 rows = 4" in diagonal
lace st, slightly stretched, on smaller
needles

Special Skill
LACE

STITCH PATTERN
DIAGONAL LACE STITCH
Rows 1, 3, 5, and 7: P.

Row 2: K2, *yo, sl1, k2tog, psso, yo, k1; rep from * to last 2 sts, k2.

Row 4: K2, *k1, yo, sl1, k2tog, psso, yo; rep from * to last 2 sts, k2.

Row 6: K1, k2tog, *yo, k1, yo, sl1, k2tog, psso; rep from * to last 5 sts, yo, k1, yo, ssk, k2.

Row 8: K2, k2tog, *yo, k1, yo, sl1, k2tog, psso; rep from * to last 4 sts, yo, k1, yo, ssk, k1.

DIRECTIONS
STRAP
With larger needles and 2 strands of yarn held tog, CO 6 sts.

Work in 1 × 1 rib, slipping the 1st st of every row kwise, until piece measures 29" from beg.

BO.

BAG

With smaller needles, CO 80 sts.

Work in diagonal lace st until piece measures 13½" from beg.

BO kwise.

FINISHING

Mattress st CO edge to BO edge.

Thread yarn in and out through the bottom, pull tails tight to the inside, and secure.

Sew CO edge of strap to the top end of the bag, along the seam line. Sew BO edge of strap 3 inches from the bottom of the bag, along the seam line.

Weave in all ends.

Thread drawstring in and out through the lace patt along the top edge of the bag. Tie overhand knots at each end of the drawstring.

About Stephanie

My grandmother taught me to knit when I was a child. I loved spending the night at her house because she always had something crafty to keep me occupied. I started knitting seriously again when I was in graduate school and decided I wanted to learn to knit socks. In real life I am a chemist and live in San Diego with my wonderful husband and cute dog. When I'm not knitting, I'm usually sewing, cross-stitching, or watching sports.

Show me your tips! *Knowing Right from Wrong*

HOW TO REMEMBER WHICH SIDE OF YOUR WORK IS WHICH

Having different-colored same-size needles—say, a pair of blue and a pair of red US 9s—makes working with every-other-row-type patterns easier. Using one red and one blue needle, I just keep in mind which one works the second row of a pattern, and then when that needle is in my right hand, I know to work the second row. Or I remember that red equals the right side, blue equals the back. This has helped me loads when I pick up my knitting in the middle of a row and am not sure which row of my pattern to start working again. *Tricia Mitchell, Johnston, PA*

STITCH 'N BITCH ACROSS THE NATION
The Midwest

Akron, Ohio

Cedar Rapids, Iowa

AKRON, OHIO, SNB

We like to say "If you can do it sitting in a chair, bring it and come hang out." Launched in January 2004, the Akron Stitch 'n Bitch grew quickly, due largely to a newspaper article that was written by one of our knitters. We meet weekly at Square Records to share knitting projects and skills, as well as donated homemade treats and coffee. Although shoppers sometimes give us surprised looks, Square Records is a great environment for our meetings, with exhibits of local artists' work and great music

playing. Being surrounded by so many art forms encourages our creativity. A lot of nights we go home having made progress on our projects—and with a few new records, too!

Our knitters are mostly in their twenties and thirties, but Akron SnB has drawn all ages and skill levels, as well as crocheters, spinners, cross-stitchers, and sewers. We've taught a few dozen people to knit (including at least five guys), and even if we don't see these new knitters every week, we know that they carry their knitting skills with them.

Moving beyond Wednesday-night meetings, we took a summertime trip to shear alpacas and spin the donated fleece, which we used to knit clothing for local shelters for the upcoming winter. We've also spawned two other Stitch 'n Bitch groups in nearby Canton and Barberton.

Megan Marucco, Rae Nester, and
Juniper Sage

CEDAR RAPIDS, IOWA, SNB

The Cedar Rapids Stitch 'n Bitch may be one of the smallest groups around—there are only three of us—but we're probably one of the most loyal. We first met around fall of 2003 at Coffeesmiths, a place where we can spread out on comfy chairs in front of a burning log fire. Although we're stymied by the lack of local yarn shops here in the heartland,

Chicago, Illinois

the Cedar Rapids SnB trio keeps up on the latest yarn and pattern trends through visits to the excellent yarn shops within a few hours' drive and by checking out Internet sites and knitting blogs.

The biggest challenge for us is just making the time for knitting. We've found our gatherings a haven, a wonderful time to deepen friendships while sharing our precious projects. We're planning knitting weekends away from our kids and husbands, and knit-along ventures as well.

Ann Rushton

CHICAGO SNB

The Chicago Stitch 'n Bitch wasn't the first SnB chapter, but if you look at mailing list numbers, we're definitely the largest, with more than one thousand subscribers. Luckily, we draw only about fifteen or twenty people a week, and it's not always the same twenty people, which keeps things fresh. My guess is that many of the list members don't even live in Chicago, but in cities without SnBs, so they sign up for the feeling of being a part of a like-minded group, a community that shares their love of the craft. I felt that way myself until I ventured out of my comfort zone (I'm more of a wallflower than a social diva) and organized my own group, which turned out surprisingly well.

I'm constantly amazed at the life force of the Chicago group and at the quality, generosity, and passion of the people it has attracted. I want to encourage the non-Chicagoans lurking on the list (you know who you are) to take the next step and start a group of your own. Don't be daunted by it, don't overthink it, don't be afraid to be a leader; just pick a place to meet and tell a few friends who will tell a few other friends. You'll be amazed at how many people there are just like you, waiting for a group to join, and who will jump at the chance to hang with you. Once the group starts meeting regularly, you'll see that it will take on a personality and direction all its own—and that's when the real fun begins.

In our first four years, Chicago members taught beginners at Ladyfest Midwest, knitted afghans for fire stations, were featured on a local TV show and in various publications, and even produced a one-hour cable access show of our own. But the coolest thing we've done is pass on our love and knowledge of the craft to others: curious nonknitters who walked by our meeting one week and joined the group the next; beginners who are now teaching their own classes; people who read about our group and bought a book to teach themselves. That's the power of groups like ours, and like the one you're going to start in your own town. Once you get the ball rolling and watch the group take on a life of its own, I'm sure you'll discover—as I have in the years I've been part of this phenomenal group of Chicago people—that there's nothing knitters can't do.

Brenda Janish

CLEVELAND, OHIO, SNB

With the help of *Stitch 'n Bitch: The Knitter's Handbook*, I taught my friend how to knit (and she taught me how to crochet). Then, with our newfound skills and needles in hand, we began enlisting others in our crafting crusade. We meet at Capsule, an Internet "cybar" that provides the architecture and atmosphere of a 1970s sci-fi TV series: orange circular couches, cosmic backdrops, blue drinks, and moody lighting. (No rocking chairs, please!) Metal, punk, and indie-rock DJs provide the necessary rhythm for knitting the night away.

Our group was soon joined by crocheters who were already making loads of products for local craft shows. There's a rumor out there about an age-old grudge between knitters and crocheters, but it's not so with the Cleveland SnB, who strive for a mutually respectful atmosphere. We knitters have learned to appreciate the speed of crocheting and the look of different projects. (In the wild, crotcheters and knitters are natural enemies, but if you raise 'em together as pups . . .)

We've also attracted nonknitting writers and artists, who have been put to use making center-pulled balls of yarn. We've taught several beginners some basics and were surprised by how few people knew how to tie square knots.

Teachers, small-business owners, Ph.D. candidates, financial advisers, graphic designers, and advertising reps all unite for the love of yarn and yarns, and we encourage quiet people to get loud by frequently interrupting meetings with the chant "Less stitching, more bitching."

In addition to a group Web site and a Yahoo group, our members sell their handiwork on our merchandise site, www.there-she-goes.com. We offer quality handmade bags and accessories. Schemes in the works include visits to the Akron and Chicago SnBs and attracting a cross-dressing cross-stitcher to the group.

Susan Ensor

Cleveland, Ohio

LESLIE BARBAZETTE

Saucy Tote

Size

Finished height: 9" (+ straps)

Finished width: 12"

Materials

Caron Craft & Rug 3 Ply
(100% polyester; 39.7g/60 yds)

MC: 3 skeins #105 Medium Pink

CC: 1 skein #658 Christmas Green

US 11 (8mm) 24" circular needle,
or size needed to obtain gauge

Clear plastic canvas: two 9" × 11½"
pieces, two 4¼" × 9" pieces, one
4¼" × 11½" piece

Cotton fabric: one 35" × 12" piece,
one 6" × 14" piece

2 yds string or embroidery floss

Tapestry needle

Pointed large-eyed needle

12 large paper clips

One 2" button

Gauge

12 sts and 16 rows = 4" in St st

originally made this bag for my friend Melissa's twenty-seventh birthday. Mel's mom calls her saucy, hence the name. I wanted a knit bag that had a clean and defined shape (no sagging allowed). After trying to shape it with cardboard and foam from craft stores, I finally figured out that by using plastic canvas I could keep the shape of the bag and have it still be washable. Kits for making this bag are available at my Web site, www.citizenbags.com.

DIRECTIONS

BODY

With MC, CO 100 sts.

Pm and join, work in St st until piece measures 8½" from beg.

BO and break yarn, leaving a 36" tail.

STRAP (MAKE 2)

With MC, CO 8 sts, leaving a 12" tail.

Work in St st until piece measures 15" from beg.

BO and break yarn, leaving a 12" tail.

BUTTON FLAP

With MC, CO 11 sts, leaving a 20" tail.

Work in St st until piece measures 4" from beg, ending with RS facing.

Next row: K4, BO 3, k4.

Next row: P4, CO 3, p4.

Work in St st until piece measures 5½" from beg.

BO.

BOTTOM

With CC, CO 34 sts.

Work in St st until piece measures 4½" from beg.

BO and break yarn, leaving a 36" tail.

FINISHING

Body assembly:

With 24" lengths of white string and leaving at least a 6" tail, whipstitch the 9" sides of the plastic canvas tog. Tie the top and bottom of the strings tog to secure (**figure 1**).

Place the large piece of fabric WS up under the canvas and lay the plastic canvas flat on top of it. Fold the ends of the fabric over the canvas and use paperclips to hold everything tog.

Fold this in half with RS facing. With the sharp needle and 1 yd of MC, whipstitch the 2 ends of the bag tog through both the layers of fabric and plastic canvas (**figure 2**).

Slip the knitted body of the bag over the interior, with the BO being the top of the bag. Rearrange the paper clips to hold the knit piece to the interior. Beg with the top, using the BO tail, whipstitch the top edge of the bag through both the knit piece and the plastic canvas. Rep on the bottom edge.

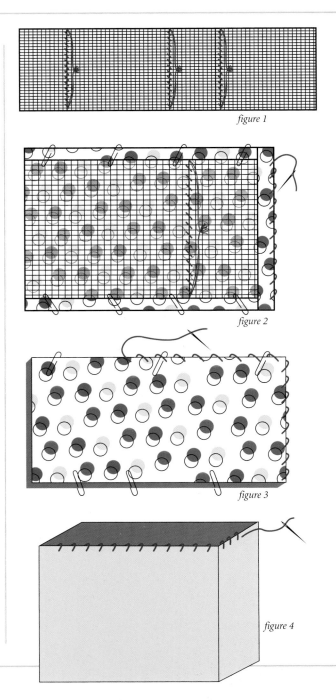

figure 1

figure 2

figure 3

figure 4

Bottom assembly:

Place the 6" × 14" fabric WS up and lay the 4¼" × 11½" plastic canvas on top of it, then fold the ends of the fabric over the plastic canvas, using paper clips to hold the pieces tog. Then lie the knit bottom WS up, place the fabric-covered mesh bottom on top of it with the fabric facing up, and adjust the paper clips to hold all 3 layers tog. Using the long tail and the sharp needle, whipstitch along the edges (**figure 3**).

With MC, whipstitch the knit bottom of the bag to the knit body of the bag (**figure 4**).

Mattress st the strap to the top of the bag 1" from each end. Rep on other side.

Mattress st the flap to the top center of the back.

Sew button to correspond with buttonhole on flap, sewing through the plastic canvas but not the fabric interior.

Weave in ends.

About Leslie

I taught myself how to knit in the back of my parents' olive-green Volkswagen bus during a road trip to Truckee, California, when I was eight. I've had some really clever moments since then, like when I believed one ball of yarn would make me a whole sweater. The sadness that ensued when I ran out of yarn and couldn't find more of the same color made me stop knitting for a few years. I caught the knitting bug again upon returning to the Bay Area after living in London for five years. This bug grew into a small handbag company called Citizen Bags. I live in Oakland, California, with my husband, who feeds every cat in the neighborhood. My first book, *Viva Poncho,* which includes poncho and capelet patterns, comes out in spring 2005.

Have Yarn, Will Travel

MAKING A STASH SAMPLE CARD

I made a card that has a strand of yarn from each of my "on hand" skeins that I keep tucked away in my purse (you never know when you'll be able to pop into the yarn shop). Take a 3" × 5" piece of white, sturdy cardboard, and make notches every ½" on the 5" edge. Then wind about 12" of each yarn around it by color, leaving some open spaces. Now you have the ability to pick up additional yarns to add into projects for pizzazz or to find that complementary yarn you need without having to carry your entire supply along. *Lili Brandt, San José, CA*

TRINITY MULLER

Going Out with a Bag

Swinging insouciantly from the wrist, this bag is the perfect size to hold your essentials when you're out for a night on the town or tearing it up on the dance floor. The pattern I give here can be varied endlessly. You can change the size or shape, use the leftover yarn in your stash, pick funky colored zippers, string buttons on it instead of beads, use ribbon for the wrist strap, add a fabric lining, or any other variation you can think of. Really, make this project yours! It knits up quickly and makes a great gift. And you never have to worry about the fit.

Instructions for the pink colorway are followed by instructions for the black colorway in parentheses. Where there is only one number, it applies to both bags.

Sparkly crystal beads and soft, fuzzy yarn make this bag glamour-rific!

SPECIAL INSTRUCTIONS

To string beads with a helper thread: Thread the needle with thread as normal, then thread the needle from the opposite direction to create a loop of thread. Thread B yarn through the thread loop and string the beads using the needle and thread to get the beads on the B yarn. Once the beads are on the B yarn, separate the yarn from the thread.

Size
Finished width: 5"

Finished length: 4"

Materials
A: Katia Danubio
(76% wool, 24% nylon; 50g/100 yds),
1 skein #10 Light Pink (#2 Black)

B: Jaeger Siena (100% mercerized cotton; 50g/153 yds), 1 skein #403 Marshmallow (#418 Black)

US 6 (4mm) straight needles, or size needed to obtain gauge

37 8mm Swarovski crystal beads, Clear (Amethyst), from Bead Diner, www.beaddiner.com

4" (10 cm) zipper, Pink (Black)

Sewing thread to match B

Sewing needle

Tapestry needle

Gauge
20 sts and 28 rows = 4" in St st

Abbreviation
Pb: Place bead. Slide 1 bead up B and place tightly next to last k st.

DIRECTIONS

BAG

String 31 beads onto B using a helper thread.

Slide beads down and CO 24 sts with 1 strand of A and B held tog, leaving a 12" tail.

Beg with a RS row, work in St st for 6 rows.

Row 7: K6, pb, sl next st pwise, *k5, pb, sl1 st pwise; rep from * once, k5.

Row 8: P.

Row 9: K3, pb, sl1 pwise, *k5, pb, sl1 pwise; rep from * twice, k2.

Row 10: P.

Rep rows 7 to 10 until all beads have been worked, ending with row 8.

Work in St st until piece measures 8" from beg, ending with RS facing.

BO, leaving a 12" tail.

WRIST STRAP

Cut three 30" strands of B. Beg 6" from ends, braid strands tog until braid measures 14" from beg.

FINISHING

Fold the piece in half lengthwise with WS tog. With CO and BO tails, mattress st sides tog. Weave in ends.

Sew zipper into bag using back st.

Attach strap to bag by threading one end of the braid through zipper pull hole. Knot the loose strands from either side of the braid tog. With a helper thread, thread one bead onto each loose strand. Tie the yarn off below the beads, varying the lengths of the yarn that the beads hang from. Cut off any extra yarn.

About Trinity

My knitting addiction began in Minneapolis and moved with me to Boston. I'm a self-taught knitter who thought she'd never grow tired of small projects. Though I recently completed my first poncho and have moved on to designing a queen-size knitted blanket, I still love the satisfaction of a quickly knit-up project like this one. I also make beaded jewelry, thanks to my friend Jamie, who got me hooked on beads in return for my teaching her to knit. Using both crafts doubles the pleasure and the design possibilities.

The Mile-High (Knitting) Club

TIPS FOR FREQUENT FLIERS

In the wake of September 11, 2001, the question of whether one can bring one's knitting needles aboard an airplane has become the most frequently asked question on knitting e-mail lists and bulletin boards. The answer is that today you should have no problem knitting your way past airport security check-points, but not all your knitting supplies may pass muster. According to the Transportation Security Administration (TSA), as of June 23, 2004, knitting needles and crochet hooks are allowed on planes in carry-on luggage as well as checked lug-gage. It recommends that needles in carry-on be less than 31 inches in total length and that they be made of bamboo or plastic (take metal needles in your checked luggage). Just in case the screener still won't let your needles through, the TSA suggests that you take along a self-addressed stamped enve-lope so you can have them mail your supplies to you, and that you carry a crochet hook so you can quickly bind off the project if your needles are confiscated. Finally, metal scissors with pointed tips—most embroidery scissors would fall into this cate-gory—are not allowed in hand luggage, but you can take them in your checked luggage. Even those cute little circular yarn cut-ters with a blade inside are a no-no in your carry-on bag.

For the latest info, check the TSA's Web site at www.tsa.gov and be sure to look at the "Special Considerations" page, where the topic of knitting supplies is specifically addressed, or call them at 866-289-9673. *DS*

● Even though my size 15 Brittany wooden needles made it past security on my last flight, I received evil looks from other pas-sengers and a flight attendant accused me of being Buffy the Vampire Slayer. When I travel next, I'm going to take only small projects (on small needles) to avoid attention. Knitting keeps me sane on long flights! *Amy Secrest, Chandler, AZ*

● When flying, I always carry a pack of dental floss with my knit-ting. You can cut even thick wooly yarn under the floss cutter, and it's 100% airline friendly! *AS*

● I travel a lot and usually need a scissors in the middle of a flight. So I always take along my nail clippers, which are allowed on planes. If I need to break my yarn, I just clip it! I haven't met a yarn it hasn't worked on. *Jamie Kennealy, Austin, TX*

Show Me Your Tips!!

RENEE LADD

The Bead Goes On
BEADED WRIST CUFFS

love knitting with beads and am always looking for new ways to combine beads and yarn. I took a class at Arnhild Hillesland's knitting studio in 2001 and learned about traditional Norwegian pulse warmers (more commonly known as wrist warmers). I made a pair to warm my hands in my very cold office (they really do work!), then decided my sixteen-year-old niece would love a pair. After seeing the Skully sweater in *Stitch 'n Bitch,* I knew the combination of girly pearls and edgy skulls would be perfect for her. I've also included an alternative broken heart design for the sixteen-year-old in all of us.

STITCH PATTERN
KNITTING WITH BEADS
Sl a bead before each st marked in black on the chart by pushing a bead as close to the right needle as possible. K the next st as normal, securing the bead between two k sts. The bead will be on the RS of the work as you are working the WS. The following row (the RS row) will be knit without beads.

DIRECTIONS
With beading needle, thread 172 beads for the skull (283 for the heart) onto your yarn. Push the beads down on the yarn and CO 25 sts.

Work in garter st, without beads, until piece measures 1½" from beg. Work in garter st, k with beads, foll chart, until all chart rows have been completed.

Size
Adult

Finished circumference: 6½"

Finished width: 3"

Materials
Sandnes Lanett
(100% merino wool; 50gr/213 yds),
1 skein #1099 Black

3 US 0 (2mm) straight needles,
or size needed to obtain gauge

172 silver (283 red) size 8 seed beads

Twisted wire collapsible-eye beading needle

Gauge
24 sts and 66 rows = 4" in beaded garter st

Work in garter st until piece measures 6½" from beg.

Break yarn, leaving an 18" tail, and keep sts on needle.

FINISHING
Pu all 25 sts from CO edge with a third needle. With RS together, join the picked-up sts to the final row using a 3-needle BO.

Weave in ends and turn RS out.

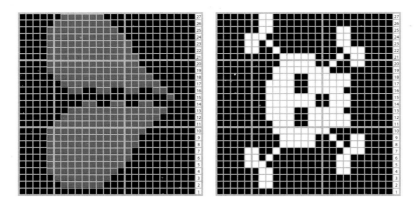

Note: *The chart shows only the RS (beaded) rows.*

About Renee
I am a thirty-five-year-old attorney living in St. Paul, Minnesota. When I was in college, I lived across the street from a yarn store and was drawn to the beautiful yarns and creativity of knitting, but it all seemed too expensive for my student budget. After jealously watching a fellow student knit during our law school classes, I finally took a community ed class. A great and unending love was born. I've dabbled in quilting, scrapbooking, beading, needlework, and other crafts, but I always return to the magic of two sticks and a string. When I'm not working or knitting, I am cheering on the Minnesota sports teams or indulging my love of good food, great conversation, books, and movies.

Show me your tips! **Point Taken**

HOW TO MAKE YARN INTO A BEADING NEEDLE
When knitting with beads it can be really hard to find a needle that is both small enough to go through the bead and has an eye large enough to thread the yarn through. Try putting clear nail polish on the end of the yarn where you'll be threading the beads and, as it dries, shape it into a point. It can take a few applications to get it stiff enough, but it's much easier than trying to find a needle that fits the bill. *Vanessa Hays, Durham, NC*

Good Wool Hunting

RECYCLING YARN FROM THRIFT-STORE SWEATERS

Good-quality yarns, especially those that contain luxury fibers such as mohair, cashmere, or silk, can cost you an arm and a leg. But there are bargains to be had at your local thrift store if you're willing to recycle old yarn from a second-hand sweater instead of buying brand-new yarn. Begin by visiting your favorite thrift store and looking through the sweater rack for something made in a yarn you like. I find that mohair, wool, and various novelty yarns (fuzzy, sparkly, what have you) are pretty easy to come by; I've also found nice cotton yarns and interesting ribbon yarns. Before you lay down your $3 for the sweater, check the seams! Some cheap sweaters are made by cutting pieces out of machine-knit cloth; these pieces are then serged together with what looks like a zigzag stitch. If you took apart a sweater like that, you'd just have lots of little lengths of yarn. So make sure that the inside seams of the sweater look like knit edges, sewn together. This means that each piece of the sweater was individually knit (by hand or machine) and should come apart into one or two lengths of yarn.

To take the sweater apart:

Most sweaters come apart into four pieces: front, back, and two sleeves. Some have a collar or other elements. You're going to reduce the sweater to these component parts by undoing all the seams. Turn the sweater inside out and start with a side seam because it's the easiest. Find the thread that's holding the seam together. It will be a different type of thread from the yarn (a bit like embroidery floss, but thinner) and will show up *on one side of the seam* as a row of little Vs. Follow the *tops* of those Vs to one end of the seam. Then use small, pointed scissors to cut through one side of one of the Vs, as close to the end of the seam as you can. Then, with the scissors' point or a knitting needle, pull up on the same side of the next V down; that should pull up the end of the thread you just cut. Grab that loose end with your fingers and pull. It should undo all of the Vs (which turn out to be little loops) down the entire seam. If it catches and stops, just pull the two sides of the seam apart with a sharp but gentle tug, and things should loosen up. If you get really stuck, you can always pick another V and start again with a new loose end. Repeat this process with all the seams until you have four (or more) flat pieces of knit fabric. (*Note:* Sometimes a shoulder or neck-edge seam will be bound with some kind of stitching or is especially difficult to undo. You can, in a pinch, cut along the top of a knit piece and take that seam off; you'll only lose a few yards of the yarn that way. But *never, ever cut along a side seam!*)

Pick one piece and start unraveling:

If you can, find the loose end at one top corner of the piece and undo it; otherwise you can just cut into the top row somewhere and start pulling it apart. If the yarn catches a bit at the end of a row, a gentle tug should loosen it. As you unravel, wind the yarn into a ball. The yarn will be kinky, but this won't affect the ease of knitting with it or the way it looks once it's reknit. And you've got yourself three or four or five balls of some really cool yarn for the price of one skein of cheap acrylic! *Miranda Hassett, Carrboro, NC*

TRACI TRUESDALE

Roller Girl Legwarmers

ten years ago, when I was in college, I worked at a coffee shop connected to *the* music venue in town. I frequently wore my roller skates to work, hoping my moves would encourage better tips. Wanting to celebrate my former love for everything rollerskates and the resurgence of '80s fashion, I made myself a pair of these legwarmers. I even brought out the old skates for a test drive. This pattern is perfect for beginners who are yearning to flex their creative muscles on a project that is a little more challenging than a basic scarf. So knit up these legwarmers, find an old pair of skates, and shake your groove thang.

STITCH PATTERN
STRIPE SEQUENCE
7 rows MC, 4 rows CC, 4 rows MC, 4 rows CC, 7 rows MC.

Size
Women's S (M, L)

Finished circumference (upper calf): 12 (14½, 17½)"

Finished length: 16 (17, 18)"

Materials
Cascade 220 (100% wool; 100g/220 yds)

MC: 2 (2, 3) skeins #2410 Purple

CC: 1 skein #7814 Chartreuse

US 8 (5mm) double-pointed needles (set of 5) or US 8 (5mm) 16" circular needle, or size needed to obtain gauge

Gauge
20 sts and 28 rows = 4" in St st

DIRECTIONS (MAKE 2)

With MC, CO 60 (72, 88) sts. If using dpns, divide sts among 4 dpns, 15 (18, 22) sts on each.

Join and, foll stripe sequence, work 26 rnds in 2 × 2 rib.

With MC, work in St st until piece measures 16 (17, 18)" from beg.

BO.

FINISHING
Weave in ends.

Get a Hold of Yourself
SHOW ME YOUR TIPS!

USING DPNS AND CIRCULARS TO HOLD LIVE STITCHES

Use circular and double-pointed needles instead of stitch holders. Since they operate from both ends, these needles eliminate the tedious slipping back and forth of stitches from traditional stitch holders. This is particularly useful when you intend to use the three-needle bind-off at the shoulders and when you are picking up stitches around the neck. I use short-row shaping for the shoulders if it's needed, instead of binding off to shape them, and put them on double-pointed needles when they're done so I can use the three-needle bind-off to connect them. The same works for the neck edge: Put the stitches for the front of the neck on double-pointed needles rather than binding them off and picking them up again later. Wrap a rubber band around each end of the double-pointed needles to keep the stitches from falling off. *Lindsay Woodel, Providence, RI*

About Traci

I live in Chicago with my husband and daughter. I started knitting several years ago when a coworker's mother dropped by the office while our boss was out of town. Knowing that she had an eager pupil, she brought me my first pair of bamboo needles and some delicious fluffy green yarn. I caught on pretty quickly and was immediately impressed with how easily my scarf grew. After I knit diligently all afternoon under the close supervision of my teacher, I then forgot all that I had just learned while trying to knit on the train ride home. An emergency trip to the knitting section at the library put me back on course. Today, with my habit fully in control of my life, I fantasize about knitting professionally someday and continue to try out my designs on unsuspecting friends and family.

STITCH 'N BITCH ACROSS THE NATION
California

Berkeley, California

BERKELEY, CALIFORNIA, SNB

On a Friday night in January of 2004, five friends and I gathered in my living room to remember or learn how to knit. We were armed with a copy of *Stitch 'n Bitch,* several skeins of yarn, and some old needles—the only situation in which it's okay to share them. Little did we know that in less than six weeks we'd outgrow the living room with more than one hundred members in our SnB group.

Most of our group's early members were seminary students and staff from the Pacific School of Religion and the Graduate Theological Union, both in Berkeley, who were drawn to the craft for its meditative nature. Then UC Berkeley students showed up and brought friends,

and it became an eclectic group of stitchers from all over the East Bay.

We've knit for charities such as Afghans for Afghans (crafting to assist the people of Afghanistan), the Knitter Critters Knitathon (making blankets for shelter animals), and a prayer shawl ministry (creating special shawls that the knitter infuses with prayers). Right now, we're planning a stitcher's retreat to explore knitting and other handwork as spiritual practice. For us, knitting is stress release and community-building. It develops patience, awareness, and much more.

Miss JoJo St. Purl

LOS ANGELES, CALIFORNIA, SNB

When *Stitch 'n Bitch* was published last year, the *LA Times* covered the LA SnB, and our membership soared. What started with seven girls knitting at a coffeehouse in Santa Monica in 2002 has since grown to four hundred girls and boys throughout the greater Los Angeles region. Six other branches of SnB L.A. have cropped up in the far-flung corners of the city, and our calendar now shows events just about daily.

If you're a member of a Stitch 'n Bitch in Los Angeles, you basically have to agree

to pretend there is winter. We send wooly scarves and sweaters to friends in Vermont and Seattle, and make ourselves felted slippers and afghans for the few really cool nights a year here. We use summer cottons and light acrylics all year long. Our natives have thin blood and wear knitted hats in 68-degree weather. And most of our SnB crew is so hard core, we continue knitting and crocheting through the 110-degree days of mid-September.

Because so many group members are designers, our talk often revolves around the licensing, copyrighting, and pricing of our products, as well as where to get labels and dress forms. Also, L.A. has more than

Los Angeles, California

thirty LYSs, so a lot of our bitching tends to be about the best and worst yarn stores around. Mostly, we are a bunch of like-minded girls and boys making new friends and getting caffeinated. Many of us don't have other friends who do what we do. But we're Stitch 'n Bitch—and we recruit.

Faith Landsman

San Francisco, California

SAN FRANCISCO, CALIFORNIA, CHICKS WITH STICKS

San Francisco Chicks with Sticks was born in the fall of 2002 when roommates Gabrielle Pope and Kathy Barobs invited a few women over to their apartment for a night of knitting. After they spent more time watching *The Bachelorette* and drinking wine than knitting, they decided to look for a place without a TV. They chose Bliss Bar, in Noe Valley. Happily, the owner offered them the use of the back room, on one condition: They had to share the room on the last Monday of every month with a group called Munch,

which meant that the SnB chicks found themselves knitting once a month surrounded by a group of S&M enthusiasts. Surprisingly enough, it was the knitters who got the oddest looks!

Typically, twenty to thirty members show up for a good three hours of knitting and chatting, and, if they're lucky, Cabaret Chocolates contributes gourmet goodies for knitting energy. Though some members have been knitting for years, quite a few show up with no experience at all. Now people who have learned how to cast on at SFCWS are teaching the next set of knitters. The members inspire one another to try harder projects—and not to fear their favorite cheer: "Rip it out! Rip it out!" As one member put it, "I used to hate Mondays, and now they're my favorite night of the week!"

Kathy Barobs

SAN FRANCISCO PENINSULA, CALIFORNIA, SnB

If you're having trouble recruiting knitters to your SnB group, follow our example: Schedule meetings in the lounge of a local restaurant or bar, don't require an RSVP, and they will come. We have more than fifty members and two weekly meetings of newcomers and lifelong knitters alike. We have fun trying to recruit the curious men who ask what we're doing; no luck yet, but we'll keep trying.

San Francisco Peninsula, California

We relish seeing the completed projects of our fellow knitters, since being involved from the beginning makes us feel as if we gave birth to ten projects instead of just one. And projects tend to catch on like wildfire: First it was felted bags, then scribble scarves, then "poncho-palooza." Who knows what next season will bring?

Knitting with the group has given each of our members the confidence to do more than she'd do on her own. Together we've learned:

1. There is always someone out there with a larger stash than yours.
2. If you know how to knit a scarf, you are absolutely ready for a sweater.
3. Knitting without a pattern isn't as scary as you think (some people prefer it).
4. Weaving in your ends is overrated—if you're the only one who sees them, let 'em hang!

Leslie Harrison

SAN JOSÉ, CALIFORNIA, SNB

If you've read anything about Silicon Valley, then you must know that life has been a roller coaster for us. Watching as friends and family lose their jobs, businesses, and sometimes their homes is devastating. But it seems that the more we are challenged, the more we strive to achieve, and many of us find ourselves doing things we never thought possible. Take me, for instance. I wanted to start a knitting group in September 2003, and even in the midst of schoolwork, charity knitting, and selling my line of knitting handbags to yarn stores, I did it.

Not much happens on a Sunday afternoon in the valley, but if you take a closer look, you'll see a cluster of tables, bobbing heads, and clicking needles—it's the Stitch 'n Bitch, that odd mix of ladies talking nonstop and knitting. The ones discovering talent that some of them never knew they had. The ones giving advice to those who ask for it (move over, Dr. Laura), swapping tried-and-true patterns and making up new ones, planning group projects, and giggling. The members of our little group are as varied as the stitches on your granny's afghan, but they do have a common thread—the art of knitting. We ooh and aah over every newly completed scarf, sweater, blanket, felted purse and hat, and even fish for compliments the way a mother does over photos of her new baby.

Jordana Paige

SANTA CRUZ, CALIFORNIA, SNB

The Santa Cruz Stitch 'n Bitch was born in September 2003, when best friends Gunilla and Babs pored over their regular knitting schedules and couldn't come up with a single day that week on which they could get together and have coffee and knit. "We should set a specific time and just do it—have a Stitch 'n Bitch like every Saturday afternoon," said Gunilla. "That's a damn good idea!" said Babs. Today they hold regular knitting sessions with about ten regulars every Saturday afternoon at their usual hangout, the 120 Union coffee shop. They all cheer one another on, no matter how crazy the project. Help is always readily available, and they welcome visitors and beginners into the flock. The first hit's always free. (No—wait! That didn't sound right. . . .)

One newcomer, a young, male UCSC student, showed up wanting to knit a hat with a ball of brown sheep wool worsted and size 10 circulars at the ready. Gunilla showed him how to cast on and how to knit Continental style (she's from Sweden, after all). He quickly got the hang of it, and under Gunilla's direction, he finished the hat the next day. He hasn't returned to SnB, but he was spotted at a yarn shop where he was getting materials for his next project, a felted hat. Future plans for Santa Cruz SnB include a Purl 'n Hurl—knitting's response to the pub crawl.

Gunilla Leavitt

Santa Cruz, Califonia

San José, California

Finished size

Women's M

Materials

MONSTER

A: Brown Sheep Lamb's Pride Bulky (85% wool, 15% mohair; 113g/125 yds), 3 skeins #M110 Orange You Glad

B: Lion Brand Fun Fur (100% polyester; 50g/60 yds), 2 skeins #195 Hot Pink

US 13 (9mm) 24" circular needle

1 sheet red craft felt

1 sheet white craft foam

Four 1½" (40mm) wiggle eyes

Glue

PLAIN

A: Brown Sheep Lamb's Pride Bulky (85% wool, 15% mohair; 113g/125 yds), 3 skeins #M38 Lotus Pink

B: Lion Brand Fun Fur (100% polyester; 50g/60 yds), 2 skeins #191 Violet

US 13 (9mm) 24" circular needle

US 13 (9mm) double-pointed needle (1 needle)

Gauge

12 sts and 16 rows = 4" with A, but exact gauge is unimportant for this project

Special Skill

SHORT-ROW SHAPING

AMY SWENSON

Felted Furry Foot Warmers

t hese fun slippers are great for keeping your toes toasty while appealing to your inner child. Knit a pair of happy monsters with gaping mouths, pointy felt teeth, and giant googly eyes. Or knit a pair that's plain (but far from boring). Knit with bulky wool and fun fur and then felted, the slippers are thick and fluffy and perfect for shuffling around in on a lazy weekend morning. They're also a great quick-to-knit gift.

STITCH

W&T (WRAP AND TURN)

Sl the next st pwise, bring the yarn between the needles to the front of the work, and sl the st back to the left-hand needle. Turn the work, and begin working in the opposite direction. When you get to the wrapped st on the next row, sl the needle through both the wrap and the wrapped st kwise, and k them tog.

Violet variation

⚞ *The Long and Winding Yarn*

KEEPING YOUR YARN STILL WHILE YOU WIND IT UP

*I*f you buy a skein of yarn that is center-pulled, but no matter how much you search you can't find the inside end, you may want to rewind it. To work quickly without the yarn flying all over the place while you're winding, just put the yarn into a wide and deep plastic hamper. Or try an empty CD holder: Packs of blank CDs come stacked in a plastic container, with a bar sticking up in the center. Simply place your yarn on the bar as if it were a spool and wind away. *Diana Camden, Costa Mesa, CA*

DIRECTIONS

SOLE

With A, CO 9 sts.

Working in St st, shape sole:

Row 1: K.

Rows 2–3: Inc 1 st at each edge.

Row 4: P.

Row 5: Inc 1 st at each edge.

Rows 6–8: Work even in St st.

Row 9: Inc 1 st at each edge.

Work even in St st until piece measures 14" from beg, ending with RS facing.

Dec 1 st from each edge of next row, then EOR once.

Next (turning) row (WS): K.

Inc 1 st from each edge of next row, then EOR once.

Work in St st until piece measures 13½" from turning row, ending with RS facing.

Next row: Ssk, k to last 2 sts, k2tog.

Work 3 rows even.

Dec 1 st from each edge of next row, then EOR once—9 sts.

BO; do not break yarn.

Fold sole with WS tog (the turning row becomes the heel edge). Beg at toe end, pu sts through each half of the sole as foll:

Pu 53 sts along left edge of sole, 13 sts along heel edge, 53 sts along right edge, and 9 sts along toe edge—128 sts.

Join B, and with 1 strand of each yarn held tog, k 1 rnd even.

Next rnd and cont with both yarns tog: K30, BO 59, working 2 sts tog 5 times evenly across BO, k39—69 sts.

MONSTER ONLY

K 1 row, turn.

Shape as follows:

K34, w&t, sl1, k34. Turn work.

K28, w&t, sl1, k40, turn.

K34, w&t, sl1, k34, turn.

K28, w&t, sl1, k40, w&t.

Next row: Sl1, k11, k2tog, w&t.

Rep last row 9 times more—59 sts.

Next row: Sl1 st, k4, k2tog, k5, k2tog, w&t.

Next row: Sl1, k10, k2tog, w&t.

Rep last row 4 times more—52 sts.

Next row: Sl1, k4, k2tog, k4, k2tog, w&t.

Next row: Sl1, k9, k2tog, w&t.

Rep last row 4 times more—45 sts.

Next row: Sl1, k3, k2tog, k4, k2tog, w&t.

Next row: Sl1, k8, k2tog, w&t.

Rep last row 3 times more—39 sts.

Next row: Sl1, k3, k2tog, k3, k2tog, w&t.

Next row: Sl1, k7, k2tog, w&t.

Rep last row 5 times more—31 sts.

Next row: Sl1, k2, k2tog, k3, k2tog, w&t.

Next row: Sl1, k6, k2tog, w&t.

Rep last row 4 times more—24 sts.

Next row: Sl1, k2, k2tog, k2, k2tog, w&t.

Next row: Sl1, k5, k2tog, w&t.

Rep last row 13 times more—8 sts.

Next row: Sl1, k5, k2tog, pu 5 sts along side of top and 1 st on sole edge. Turn work.

Next row: Sl1, k10, k2tog, pu 5 sts along side and 1 st on sole edge. Turn work.

BO.

PLAIN ONLY

K 2 rows even.

Next row: K30, place rem sts on spare needle.

Work in garter st on first 30 sts until slipper top is 6" from sole edge.

Use 3-needle BO to attach 30 live sts to 30 sts on spare needle.

Graft the 9 rem live sts to toe edge of slipper top.

FINISHING

Loosely tack any yarn ends to prevent unraveling, then felt slippers to desired size.

Monster only:

The still wet felted slipper will have an extra bulge of fabric at the top of the toe. Push this in to form a mouth and let dry. Cut out tongue and teeth as desired from felt and craft foam, and glue in place. Glue on eyes where desired.

About Amy

Although I grew up in Chicago, I now live in Calgary, Alberta, where warm slippers are useful practically year-round. I finance my overwhelming addiction to yarn through my work as a business requirements analyst for a leading interactive services agency. More information about my line of original knitting patterns can be found at www.indiknits.com.

RENEE RIGDON

Hurry Up Spring Armwarmers

S now on the ground; ice on my sidewalk—I'd had enough of winter and it was only January. In need of a pick-me-up, I headed off to my friendly LYS for my favorite drug, Noro Kureyon. While I fondled its woolly goodness, I tried to envision vines and leaves sprouting, banishing the snow for another year. These armwarmers are as close as I could get to changing the seasons with a wave of my hand. They are a little bit earth goddess and a whole lot of sass on a brisk day, with just enough coverage to keep your hands toasty, but still leave you use of your fingers.

Because everything but the thumb gusset and the section that's knit from the chart is ribbed, shaping is unnecessary and these armwarmers fit just about anyone. They kept me warm while I dreamed of spring and will do the same for you.

DIRECTIONS

RIGHT ARMWARMER

CO 32 sts.

Divide sts among 3 dpns with 11 sts on 1st needle, 10 sts on 2nd, and 11 sts on 3rd.

Join and, beg and ending with k1, work in 2 × 2 rib until piece measures 1½" from beg.

Cont rib on 1st and 3rd needles, work from chart on 2nd needle until 30 chart rows have been worked.

Size

Women's M

Finished circumference: 6½"

To fit: Up to 10½" circumference

Materials

Noro Kureyon (100% wool; 50g/110 yds), 2 skeins #88 (green/brown/orange/yellow) OR #130 (pink/purple/yellow/red)

US 7 (4.5mm) double-pointed needles, or size needed to obtain gauge (set of 4)

Cable needle

Stitch markers

Stitch holder

Gauge

16 sts and 24 rows = 4" in St st

Maintaining rib and chart patt as est, beg thumb gusset on 3rd needle:

Rnd 1, needle 3: P2, k1, pm, m1, pm, cont in patt as est.

Rnd 2, needle 3: Sm, m1, k1, m1, sm, cont in patt as est.

Cont to work gusset by k into the back and front of the first and last sts between the markers on each rnd to 13 sts between markers.

Place gusset sts on holder.

Cont in the round, work in patt until all chart rows have been completed.

Work in 2 × 2 rib for 1".

BO.

Use color #130 to make these sunset-colored warmers.

−	= p
□	= k
I	= ktbl
M	= m1
	= sl1 st to cn, hold in front, p1, k1 from cn
	= sl1 st to cn, hold to back, k1, p1 from cn
	= sl1 st to cn, hold to front, k1, k1 from cn
	= sl1 st to cn, hold to back, k1, k1 from cn
	= sl right needle through next 3 sts as if to k, k through the front, back, and front of all 3 sts
	= sl right needle through next 2 sts as if to k through the back, k through the back and front of both sts
	= p2tog

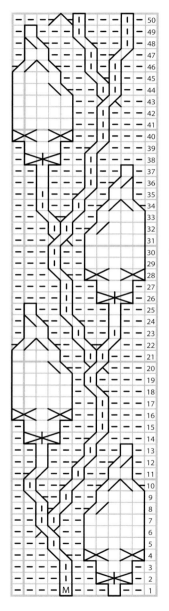

Thumb:

Divide holder sts between 3 dpns.

Join new yarn and k first and last gusset sts tog.

Work in St st for 2 rnds, then in 2 × 2 rib for 2 rnds.

BO.

LEFT ARMWARMER

Work as for right armwarmer, reversing chart.

Reverse placement of thumb gusset as follows:

Rnd 30, needle 1: K1, p2, k2, p2, k1, pm, m1, pm, k1, p2, work to row 30 of chart. Cont left armwarmer as for right armwarmer.

FINISHING

Weave in ends, using tail from thumb BO to seam the hole between the thumb gusset and the palm.

About Renee

When I was five years old, my nana taught me how to crochet. I'm sure that my snakelike chains, some extending the length of my yard, were a portent of the fiber addiction that would take hold when I taught myself to knit thirteen years later. Now I balance knitting time with caring for my seventeen-month-old, "Monkey Boy" Cayden, and his sidekick, Dog Wonder, and thwarting my husband's evil plans. I helped start the Lexington, Kentucky, Stitch 'n Bitch and intend to own a kickass yarn shop within ten years.

Wet It and Forget It

JOINING YARN WITH THE SPIT-SPLICE METHOD

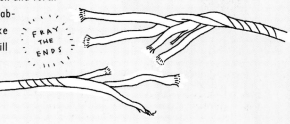

When you need to start a new ball of wool, rather than tying the old and new ends together, you can attach them to each other almost invisibly by using your own God-given saliva. This method works only with 100% wool yarns. First, fray the two ends of the yarn to be joined, then use a pair of scissors or your hands to remove a little bit of yarn from each end. Suck on the ends (this is the "spit" part). Lay the ends across each other so that they overlap slightly. Then rub them rapidly back and forth with the palm of your hand against a fabric that has a little texture to it, like your jeans. The friction and heat will make the fibers stick together (it can take a couple of minutes). Then just go right on knitting!

Meg Poehler, Portland, OR

CARRIE COLLINS
Belt de Jour

during a monthlong job hiatus last winter, I did nothing but knit for three weeks straight. I had acquired a hefty stash of yarn and had to come up with dozens of ways to use it. It wasn't hard, until I came across a beautiful sweater pattern with a cable pattern running down the front. I didn't have enough yarn for the sweater and had already spent my entire yarn budget for the year. But as I started knitting the cable pattern, just to try it out, I discovered that it was the perfect width for a belt. It's a great cheap project and an easy introduction to cables.

Size

Length: To fit

Width: 1¾"

Materials

Lamb's Pride Worsted (85% wool, 15% mohair; 113g/190 yds), 1 skein M78 Aztec Turquoise OR M120 Limeade

US 7 (4.5mm) straight needles, or size needed to obtain gauge

Cable needle

Belt buckle: One ¾" rhinestone buckle #19830 for Aztec Turquoise belt; one ¾" metal buckle #31091 for Limeade belt, both from M & J Trimming, www.mjtrim.com

Gauge

18 stitches and 22 rows = 4" in St st

STITCH PATTERN
CABLE PATTERN

Row 1: K8.

Row 2: P8.

Row 3: C4b, c4f

Row 4: P8.

Row 5: K8.

Row 6: P8.

DIRECTIONS

BELT

CO 12 sts.

Row 1: Sl1 pwise, p1, cable patt row 1, p2.

Row 2: Sl1 kwise, k1, cable patt row 2, k2.

Row 3: Sl1 pwise, p1, cable patt row 3, p2.

Row 4: Sl1 kwise, k1, cable patt row 4, k2.

Row 5: Sl1 pwise, p1, cable patt row 5, p2.

Row 6: Sl1 kwise, k1, cable patt row 6, k2.

Rep rows 1 to 6 until belt is 1" longer than desired length.

BO.

BELT LOOP (OPTIONAL)

CO 4 sts.

Work in garter st for 1½" from beg.

BO.

FINISHING

Block pieces.

Sew belt loop onto belt 5" from CO edge.

Attach belt buckle to CO end of belt.

Fold corners of BO end into a triangle and sew tog.

About Carrie

I recently moved to Chicago from San Francisco, where I teach knitting and piano. I started knitting when I was eleven or twelve years old, but then started focusing on music in my "spare" time. After my last recital, I wanted to do something completely different from playing the piano, so I picked up knitting again. My boyfriend gladly accepted my first "punk rock" scarf—aptly named for the many accidental holes and wavy sides. I've been a compulsive knitter ever since.

Ancient Chinese Secret

MAKING KNITTING NEEDLES FROM CHOPSTICKS

I came up with the idea of making chopstick knitting needles after many late nights at the China Buffet. It is a great way to save money and fill in your needle collection. To make them, you'll need:

- A pair of chopsticks (of course)
- A pencil sharpener
- Medium- and fine-grain sandpaper
- Old rag or fabric scrap
- Small amount of polymer clay
- Craft glue
- Clear polyurethane (optional)

(1) Sharpen the "food" tip of each chopstick with a pencil sharpener.

(2) Sand down the entire needle (with the grain) using the medium-grain sandpaper and then the fine-grain sandpaper. Be sure to make the tip rounded, not pointed—we don't want any knitting-related injuries, do we?

(3) When both needles have been fully sanded, rub them with your cloth until they are silky smooth.

(4) To make the ends of the needles, take a small amount of polymer clay and wrap it around each end in any fashion your heart desires. Bake the needles and clay according to the instructions on the package. Polymer clay shrinks when it cooks, so the ends should be stuck to the needles after baking. If an end falls off, simply glue it back in place with craft glue.

(5) You have a few options when it comes to finishing the needles. By far the most durable method is to coat the needles with a layer of clear polyurethane. Another way is to alternate rubbing the needle with waxed paper (until hot) and then a fabric scrap. This will make the wood satiny, and it will help fill in any spaces left by sanding. *Cassie Christenson, Oshkosh and Dodgeville, WI*

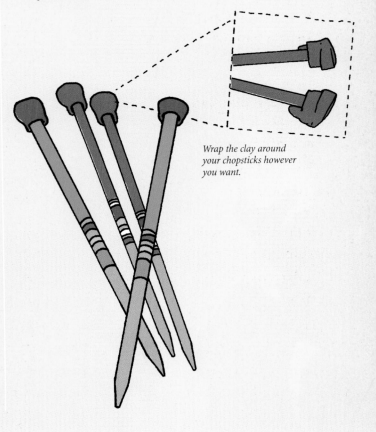

Wrap the clay around your chopsticks however you want.

MARCY NETH

Li'l Devil Pants

these pants are based on a pair of knitted baby pants my husband and I borrowed from friends for our first son. We used to call them his Mussolini pants because they looked like a pair of ski pants Mussolini had worn and made the baby resemble a tiny fascist dictator. When our second son was born I wanted similar pants, and came up with these. They are soft and easy to put on. The devil tail is in keeping with the dictator theme. (Life with my sons is not easy.) The little garter stitch devil point at the end of the tail can be reversed to be a heart shape for good, sweet babies, if any such babies exist.

DIRECTIONS

PANTS

Waist hem:

With straight needles, CO 70 (74, 78) sts.

Work in St st until piece measures 1" from beg, ending with WS facing.

Turning ridge (WS): K.

Work next 3 rows in St st, beg with a K row.

Drawstring hole:

Next row: *K8, turn.

Next row: P8, turn.

Rep from * 1 time.

Size

6 (12, 18) months

Finished waist: 17 (18, 19)"

Finished length: 15 (16½, 18)"

Materials

Sandnes Lanett Superwash (100% merino wool; 50g/213 yds), 3 (4, 4) skeins #4128 Cherry Red

US 3 (3.25mm) straight needles, or size needed to obtain gauge

US 3 (3.25mm) double-pointed needles (set of 2)

One ¾" button

Gauge

32 sts and 42 rows = 4" in St st

Next row: K8 and place these sts on a holder. Break yarn, leaving a 4" tail.

Join yarn to sts on left-hand needle and k 62 (66, 70) sts.

Work in St st on these 62 (66, 70) sts for 4 more rows.

Next row: P 70 (74, 78) sts, including sts from holder.

Top:

Work in St st until piece measures 6 (6½, 7)" from beg, ending with RS facing.

Inc 1 st at each edge of next row, then EOR 3 times, then ER 8 times—94 (98, 102) sts.

Work in St st until piece measures 7½ (8, 8½)" from beg, ending with RS facing.

Leg:

Dec 1 st at each edge of next row, then every foll 12 (14, 14)th row 6 times—80 (84, 88) sts.

Work in St st until piece measures 16 (17½, 19)" from beg, ending with WS facing.

Turning ridge (WS): K.

Work next 3 rows in St st, beg with a K row.

BO.

Make a second piece as for the first, reversing drawstring hole shaping as follows:

Next row: *K62 (66, 70), turn.

Next row: P62 (66, 70), turn.

Rep from * 1 time.

Next row: K62 (66, 70) and place these sts on a holder. Break yarn, leaving a 4" tail.

Join yarn to sts on left-hand needle and k8.

Work in St st on these 8 sts for 4 more rows.

Next row: P70 (74, 78) sts, inc 1 st from holder.

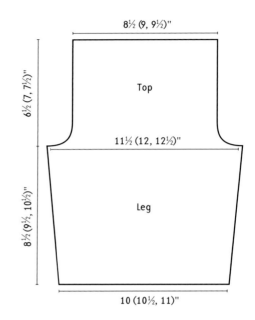

8½ (9, 9½)"

6½ (7, 7½)"

Top

11½ (12, 12½)"

8½ (9½, 10½)"

Leg

10 (10½, 11)"

TAIL

With straight needles, CO 3 sts.

P 1 row.

Inc 1 st at each edge of next row, then EOR 2 times more—9 sts.

Work in St st until piece measures 10" from beg, ending with RS facing.

Dec 1 st at each edge of next row, then EOR 2 times more—3 sts.

BO.

DEVIL POINT (MAKE 2)

With straight needles, CO 1 st.

K 1 row.

Next row: Inc1—2 sts.

K 1 row.

Next row: Inc1 twice—4 sts.

K 2 rows.

Next row: *Inc1, k to last st, inc1.
K 1 row.* Rep from * to * once more.

Next row: *Inc1, k to last st, inc1.
K 2 rows.* Rep from * to * three times more—16 sts.

Next row: K6, k2tog, turn, placing rem sts on holder.

**K 1 row.

Next row: K2tog, k3, k2tog, turn.

K 1 row.

Next row: K2tog, k1, k2tog, turn.

BO.**

Transfer holder sts to needle. Join yarn and k2tog, k6.

Rep from ** to **.

DRAWSTRING

With dpns, CO 3 sts.

Work in I-cord for 25 (27, 29)".

Break yarn, leaving a 4" tail. Draw tail through sts and secure.

FINISHING

Mattress st body and inseam of pants, leaving a ½" space open 2" down from the garter ridge at the top of the back.

Reinforce drawstring holes and back tail hole with blanket st.

Fold body hem to the inside at the turning ridge and whipstitch in place, leaving drawstring holes open.

Thread drawstring through holes.

Fold leg hems to the inside at the turning ridge and whipstitch in place.

Sew button to the tail at CO end.

Tack devil points onto either side of the rem end of the tail and sew tog.

Weave in all ends.

About Marcy

I am a lapsed librarian who is currently a stay-at-home mom. A friend taught me to knit in the 1980s when I wanted a plain black sweater and could not find one anywhere. (One day I will make that black sweater.) A long stint at the Art Institute of Chicago taught me that almost anything can be knit out of any material. As much as I love wool, I know that strings and sticks can be combined in limitless ways.

DELIA LAM

Baby's First Tattoo

Lately there has been a spate of new babies among my friends, and that means a never-ending need for baby gifts. This little sweater was developed in response to looking for something classic but contemporary and still a bit saucy to fit modern mommy tastes. It's a twist on a simple piece that offers an opportunity for a fine gauge and intarsia in a smaller project.

Classic tattoos and vintage textiles inspired the swallows, but if you omit these motifs and knit in a solid color, the cardi is still absolutely elegant due to its fine gauge. Add the motifs and the contrasting trim and the variations are endless for customizing. The directions are written for mirrored motifs on the chest, but this cardi really invites experimentation and is a great baby shower standard.

DIRECTIONS

BACK

With CC, CO 70 (76, 84, 90) sts. Work in seed st for 6 rows. Change to MC and work in St st until piece measures 4½ (5, 5½, 6)" from beg, ending with a WS row.

Size

3 (6, 12, 18) months

Finished chest: 20 (22, 24, 26)"

Finished length: 8¾ (9¾, 10¾, 11¾)"

Materials

Rowan 4-Ply Soft
(100% merino wool; 50g/162 yds)

MC: 2 (3, 3, 4, 4) skeins #377 Wink

CC: 1 skein #389 Expresso

US 3 (3mm) straight needles,
or size needed to obtain gauge

4 small snaps

Tapestry needle

Stitch holders

Gauge

28 sts and 36 rows = 4" in St st

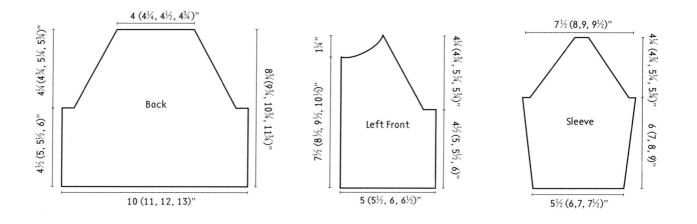

Shape raglan:

BO 3 sts at beg of next 2 rows.

Next row (RS): Sl1 kwise, k1, ssk, k to last 4 sts, k2tog, k2.

Next row: Sl1 kwise, p to end.

Rep last 2 rows until 28 (30, 32, 34) sts rem.

Place rem sts on holder.

LEFT FRONT

With CC, CO 35 (38, 42, 45) sts. Work in seed st for 6 rows.

Change to MC and work in St st last 4 sts.

With CC, work in seed st for front band to end.

Keeping in patt as established, work until piece measures 4½ (5, 5½, 6)" from beg, end with a WS row.

Work raglan shaping at side edge as for back, *at the same time,* when piece measures 7½ (8½, 9½, 10½)" from beg, end with a RS row and shape neck as foll:

BO 4 (5, 6, 7) sts and cont to dec 1 st at neck edge every row 10 times more.

RIGHT FRONT

Work as for left front, reversing all shaping.

SLEEVE (MAKE 2)

With CC, CO 38 (42, 48, 52) sts. Work in seed st for 6 rows.

Change to MC and work in St st, inc 1 st each side every 4th row 8 times—54 (58, 64, 68) sts.

Work until piece measures 6 (7, 8, 9)" from beg.

Shape raglan cap:

BO 3 sts at beg of next 2 rows.

Next row (RS): Sl1 kwise, k1, ssk, k to last 4 sts, k2tog, k2.

Next row: Sl1 kwise, p to end.

Rep last 2 rows until 12 sts rem.

Place rem sts on holder.

FINISHING

Sew raglan sleeves to back and fronts. Sew side and sleeve seams.

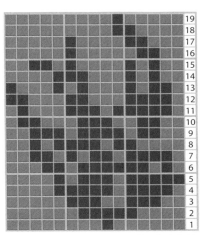

swallow for left side

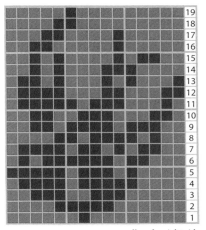

swallow for right side

About Delia

I've been knitting since I was five, thanks to my grandmother. I shared a room with her when I was little and every night I fell asleep to the sound of her needles clacking away, soothing and lulling me with their rhythm. These days, I love how many people knit—the bouncer at the bar, the hipster at the show, the student at the library, the friend, the neighbor, the boss. As a lifelong yarn junkie as well as crafting fiend, I haunt yarn shops, buy and stash more than I can sensibly knit, dream of patterns, and think of my grandmother. When not knitting, I can be found getting a late start learning how to drive a stick shift on the streets of Minneapolis and St. Paul.

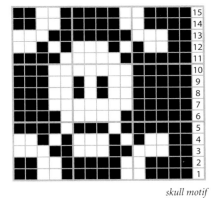

skull motif

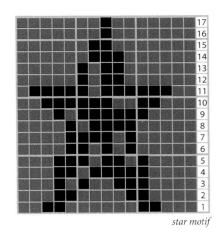

star motif

Neck band:

With CC and RS facing, pu and k15 sts up right front neck, transfer sts from holders to needle, pu and k15 sts down left front neck—82 (84, 86, 88) sts. Work in seed st for 6 rows.

BO.

St chosen motif onto left and right fronts of cardigan, beg lower right hand corner of chosen chart so that chart is centered on front and bottom edge of motif is in line with beg of raglan shaping.

JENNIFER SMALL
Bunny Hat

originally started making baby hats as gifts because they were a great return on my investment—they don't take long, and you can add lots of cute details for maximum oohs and aahs when you give them at a baby shower. I made this hat for my friend Eric's new baby girl. He is a very hip Gen-X guy, and I wanted to make something embarrassingly cute to welcome him into fatherhood. The wool in this wool- and cotton-blend yarn makes it stretchy and easy to work with, and the cotton makes it soft and light for comfort. I use short-row shaping for the ear flaps so they're extra stretchy. The hat is designed in pink with white inner ears for a girl, but you could make it in light blue or even in tan with pink inner ears for a Peter Rabbit vibe.

STITCH

W&T (WRAP AND TURN)

Sl the next st pwise, bring the yarn between the needles to the front of the work, and sl the st back to the left-hand needle. Turn the work, and begin working in the opposite direction. When you get to the wrapped st on the next row, sl the needle through both the wrap and the wrapped st kwise, and k them tog.

DIRECTIONS

HAT

With MC and dpn or circular needles, cast on 44 (56) sts.

Size
3–12 (18–36) months

Finished circumference: 14 (16)"

Materials
Rowan Wool Cotton (50% merino wool, 50% cotton; 50g/123 yds)

MC: 2 balls #951 Tender

CC1: 1 ball #900 Antique

CC2: 1 ball #908 Inky

US 5 (3.5mm) 16" circular needle, or size needed to obtain gauge

US 5 (3.5mm) double-pointed needles (set of 5)

Stitch marker

Tapestry needle

Gauge
22 sts and 32 rows = 4" in St st

Special Skill
SHORT-ROW SHAPING

Ear flaps:

Working back and forth, work 9 rows in garter st.

**Next row: K21 (27), w&t.

Next row: K.

Rep these 2 rows, working 1 less st before each wrap, until 8 live sts rem.

Turn and work to end.

Next row: K all sts, picking up wraps and working them tog with sts as you work across.**

Rep from ** to ** for second ear flap.

Body of hat:

Next row (back of hat): K19 (27), *m1, k1; rep from * 6 (2) times, k19 (27).

Without turning, pm (first marker) and CO 30 sts (front of hat)—80 (88) sts.

Pm (second marker and beg of rnd) and join, being careful not to twist sts.

Next rnd: P5, k40, p5, sl marker, p to end of rnd.

Work 6 rnds more as established, working 1 less p st every other row before first marker and after 2nd marker.

Remove first marker and work in St st until piece measures 3½ (4)" from CO edge.

Next rnd: *K6, k2tog; rep from * to end. K 1 rnd.

Rep these 2 rnds, working 1 less st bet decs until 20 (22) sts rem.

Next rnd: K2tog around—10 (11) sts.

Next rnd: K0 (1), k2tog around—5 (6) sts.

Break yarn, draw tail through rem sts and secure.

Embroidery chart

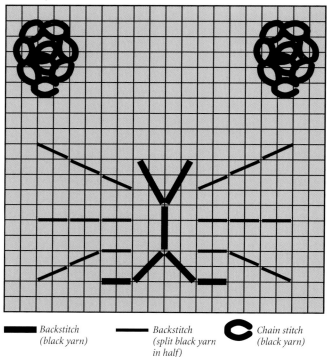

| Backstitch (black yarn) | Backstitch (split black yarn in half) | Chain stitch (black yarn) |

TIES

With dpn, pu 3 sts from bottom corner of ear flap. Work in I-cord for 10".

Repeat on second ear flap.

OUTER EAR (MAKE 2)

With MC, CO 13 sts.

Work in St st for 20 rows.

Next row: Ssk, k9, k2tog.

**Work in St st for 5 rows.

Next row: Ssk, k7, k2tog.

Work in St st for 3 rows.

Next row: Ssk, k5, k2tog.**

Rep from ** to **, working 2 less sts bet decs, until 5 sts rem.

Work in St st for 3 rows.

BO.

INNER EAR (MAKE 2)
With CC1, CO 9 sts.

Work in St st for 20 rows.

Next row: Ssk, k5, k2tog.

Work in St st for 5 rows.

Rep these 6 rows, working 2 less sts bet decs, until 3 sts rem.

Work in St st for 3 rows.

BO.

FINISHING
Steam-block earpieces.

With MC, blanket st inner ear to outer ear: Beg at the bottom of one edge, sew up to the top. At the top, there will be a few more rows of the outer ear. Seam the two tips together. Sew down the inner ear to the other outer ear edge.

Steam-block the ears flat and sew them to hat to correspond with picture.

With CC2 and tapestry needle, embroider face on front of hat to correspond with diagram.

About Jennifer

Chicago's my town, where I work as a software designer. Knitting is a great way for me to be creative with my hands and not just my brain. I've always loved fiber arts, and even have an art degree in it. I only began knitting about three years ago, and I'm delighted with its potential. I especially love shaping with knitting; it's magical that a 3-D shape can appear from my needles. I've been knitting for all of my friends' babies for the last few years, and now am eagerly expecting a baby of my own to adorn with all sorts of silly and cute items!

Presto Chango

MAKING NICER COLOR CHANGES IN RIBBING

When changing colors in a rib, knit the entire first row (even the purl stitches) of the new color. Knit the next row with the same color in the normal way for ribbing: Knit the knits and purl the purls. You will avoid that funny jog you get on the purl stitches and make a smooth color transition, and that knit row will essentially disappear. Magic!

Lucy Lee, Cambridge, MA

HEIDI NEURAUTER

One-Hour Baby Booties

before my daughter was born, I spent much of my then underappreciated free time knitting her a bunch of teensy socks and booties. The footwear in question was knit on size 0 needles using very soft, very expensive, very dry-clean-only cashmere. They were delicate, and looked so sweet stacked neatly in her dresser drawer. Of course, I birthed a guileless free spirit who couldn't be bothered with socks. Or booties. Or cashmere. Did I mention the socks were bland and slippery? How could I blame my discerning baby for rejecting them? I can only blame myself. Who in her right mind would knit something with a 2- or 3-month shelf life using size 0 needles?

Today, as a mom, I am a lot more practical, and into saving precious time and energy whenever possible. I designed these booties, which can be knit in one hour or less, to appeal to both the knitter and the infant geniuses who will wear them with pride and adulation.

Size
Newborn (3–6 months)

Materials
Lamb's Pride Bulky
(85% wool, 15% mohair; 113g/125 yds),
1 skein M115 Oatmeal

For newborn: US 8 (5mm) straight
needles

For 3–6 months: US 9 (5.5mm) straight
needles

US I/9 (5.5mm) crochet hook

Two ½" buttons

1 packet blue Kool-Aid w/ a pinch of
cherry (to mute the blue)

Gauge
13 sts and 22 rows = 4" garter st
on size 8 needles

12 sts and 20 rows = 4" on size
9 needles

Abbreviation
Inc1: K and p into the same st.

DIRECTIONS
BOOTY (MAKE 2)
CO 9 sts.

Row 1: K1, inc1, k1, inc1, inc1, inc1, k1, inc1, k1—14 sts.

Rows 2, 4, 6, 8, and 9: K.

Row 3: K2, inc1, k2, inc1, k1, m1, k1, inc1, k2, inc1, k2—19 sts.

Row 5: K3, inc1, k2, inc1, k2, inc1, k2, inc1, k2, inc1, k3—24 sts.

Row 7: K8, inc1, k3, m1, k3, inc1, k8—27 sts.

Row 10: K15, skp, turn.

Row 11: K4, k2tog, turn.

Rows 12 and 14: Sl1 pwise, p3, skp, turn.

Rows 13 and 15: Sl1 kwise, k3, k2tog, turn.

Row 16: Sl1 pwise, p4, k8.

Row 17: K.

BO.

FINISHING

Mattress st sole and heel.

STRAP

Use Kool-Aid to dye 1 oz of main yarn as directed on opposite page.

With crochet hook and dyed yarn, insert into inside instep of bootie and chain 20.

Join last 6 sts tog into a loop.

Sew button to other side of bootie to correspond with strap loop.

Rep for second bootie.

Block by wetting thoroughly with warm water and squaring the toes by inserting tissue into the front.

About Heidi

I was raised by a mother who knit, and I believe I "osmosed" the process from her. I don't remember learning how to knit or purl, but I do remember, vividly, using hideous acrylic yarn to knit various long strips that could fit the general description of a "scarf."

In 1993 I moved to New York City and discovered, among other things, a local yarn store that seduced me with its warm, fuzzy, and (most important) nonsynthetic embrace. I began knitting again as a way to minimize my erupting yarn stash. In 2002 I started a small business selling baby-related hand knits and odds and ends (www.amobaby.com). When I'm not expending all of my energy learning the ways of the world from my toddler, I sometimes act, I sometimes write, and I almost always knit.

DIY Dye

HOW TO DYE YARN WITH KOOL-AID

Kool-Aid will work only with animal fibers, so wool, mohair, angora, and silk work well, but cotton, linen, and rayon won't hold the color.

The suggested starting point for mixing the colors is 1 packet unsweetened Kool-Aid mixed with 1 cup (8 oz) of lukewarm water. (You'll probably end up using about 3 packets of each color.)

You can add 1 oz. white vinegar to help with colorfastness, although some people feel this isn't necessary, as the Kool-Aid contains citric acid. I suggest using clear measuring cups, so you'll be able to see the color clearly.

You can mix different Kool-Aid colors like watercolors; add more water to make lighter colors, or more Kool-Aid for more saturated colors. The grape color is very intense and acts like a black. When you add a very diluted solution of grape to a primary red, you'll get a raspberry color. Play around with the colors; perhaps even knit a swatch to see how the dyed yarn looks knit. If you are going to use more than 1 skein for a project, take notes about your color mixtures and dilutions so you can duplicate them.

1. Wind your yarn into hanks if it doesn't already come that way. Don't try to dye a ball of yarn, because the middle won't get the color. Try to make the hanks consistent if you are dyeing multiple skeins for a project.

2. Loosely tie the hanks in at least 4 places so they don't unwind and get tangled.

3. Soak the hanks in room-temperature water for at least 20 minutes. Don't stir your yarn or make temperature changes, as this can result in felted fibers, which you won't be able to use.

4. When you are ready to dye your yarn, carefully lift one hank at a time out of the water. Let as much water drain as possible. You can gently squeeze the bottom of the hank to get excess water out.

If you are dyeing your yarn more than one color:

1. Lay your hank(s) out on a plastic-covered surface, because Kool-Aid dyes more than just yarn.

2. Pour the Kool-Aid liquid onto your hank a little at a time. You can leave space between the colors, or let them bleed into each other.

3. Place the hank in a medium-size microwaveable casserole dish. Cover with plastic wrap that has a few holes punched in it.

4. Microwave on high for 2–4 minutes, or until the water in the dish is clear.

5. Put the yarn in your sink or bathtub and let cool. Fill the basin with lukewarm water to rinse the yarn, but don't let the force of the water hit the yarn directly.

6. Hang the yarn in the shower to dry overnight.

If you are dyeing your yarn one solid color:

1. Place the hank of yarn in a medium-size microwaveable casserole dish. Pour in the Kool-Aid, making sure to coat the yarn evenly. You can use your gloved hands to gently push the yarn down into the liquid to make sure it is evenly dyed.

2. Follow steps 4–6 above.

Martha Lazar, Brooklyn, NY

STITCH 'N BITCH ACROSS THE NATION
The Northwest

OCEAN SHORES, WASHINGTON, SIT 'N KNIT

A Group for Kids

For my thirteenth birthday, I asked my parents for a knitting lesson. I had just gotten a new dog and wanted to make him a sweater. Then in February 2004 I moved to Ocean Shores, Washington. Inspired by *Stitch 'n Bitch,* I contacted Debbie Stoller to ask if I could join the Seattle Stitch 'n Bitch. Debbie explained that the group consisted of adults who met at night in bars and that perhaps I should start a group for kids my age.

On my first day at my new school, I sat down at a table in the lunchroom and took out my knitting. Some people said, "That's for grandmas," but I told them, "I knit and I'm not a grandma." Other kids were definitely interested, and many already knew how to crochet. Our group, Sit 'n Knit, is very small, with about four members ranging in age from ten to thirteen, plus my cousin, who goes to a different school. The meetings are not always on the same day, but wherever we go, there's lots of knitting to be found. We meet at lunchtime in the library, in art class, or in people's homes. We talk about yarns, what's going on in the school, and politics. Now we're starting to recognize how things are put together. We stare at other people's sweaters and say, "I could make that."

My advice to kids who want to start a knitting group is "Just do it." I started teaching my friends to knit so they wouldn't be bored when I talked obsessively about it, and the guys are more excited than the girls. When kids get frustrated, I tell them something I read in

Portland, Oregon

Maggie Righetti's knitting book: "It's not a mistake if you know how you made it."

Joceyln Caven

PORTLAND, OREGON, SnB

You could call me the "queen bee" of the PDX Stitch 'n Bitch group (I founded it), but in reality I'm not the most knowledgeable member. In fact, I started the group for the purely selfish goal of getting master knitters into my network to teach me the knitty gritty. For some crazy reason, people liked the idea enough to join!

SnB Portland is an outlet for knitters and crocheters to meet up, vent, teach,

Ocean Shores, Washington

learn, make new friends, and best of all, create and be creative. Crocheters play well in the group too. There's always the ongoing debate between crocheters ("One stick is better than two!") and knitters ("Knitting is a science built on the foundations of counting, and crocheting is for lazy people"), but both share the addiction to yarn, so what's all the fuss is about? Plus, there are the memorable teaching lessons where you hear stuff like, "Take the hook and poke it in the part that looks like a butt!" or "Wrap the string this way, then stab it here!" In the end, we're all having fun, and in the process, we're doing a little good for the community by donating blankets and our other handmade crafts to neighbors in need.

Malia Smith

SEATTLE, WASHINGTON, PURLYGIRLS

Seattle PurlyGirls was started in January 2004 by PurlyGirl extraordinaire Nichole, whose infectious enthusiasm brought membership to 130 knitters in three months. About thirty PurlyGirls show up weekly in a private room at a swanky Seattle club, where the owners know their names and favorite drinks.

The group holds regular special events, including knitting slumber parties and tea parties, bringing in massage therapists to soothe sore knitting hands, and organizing field trips to wool festivals and yarn sales. With members from the local yarn shops, they have the inside scoop on upcoming sales and events, as well as the lowdown on the newest yarns to hit the market. Although there's a "no kids allowed" rule for the regular weekly meet-ups, the PurlyGirls have an additional Saturday group at a local playground where the kids run freely and the moms knit in peace.

One of the PurlyGirls' favorite yarn stores, Churchmouse Yarns and Teas, is a short ferry ride across Puget Sound. PGirls often gather to make the day trip together, and the store owners reserve a table in the shop and hang out the welcome sign (literally) for their arrival. The girls are always open to impromptu gatherings: small groups at coffee shops, or knitting picnics in the park on the rare sunny Seattle day.

The PurlyGirls vary in age, culture, and skill level, but no problem—from perfecting the kitchener stitch to Fair Isle to socks on circular needles—is too hard for someone in the group to solve.

Jenna Adorno

Seattle, Washington

PEGGY DEPUE

Casey's Coat

Size

S (M, L)

Finished length: 12 (16, 21)"

Finished circumference: 15 (18, 22)"

Materials

Brown Sheep Lamb's Pride Worsted
(85% wool, 15% mohair; 113g/190 yds)

MC: 1 (2, 2) skeins #M38 Lotus Pink
(#M78 Aztec Turquoise)

CC: 1 (1, 2) skeins #M110 Orange You
Glad (#M120 Limeade)

US 7 (4.5mm) straight needles

US 8 (5mm) straight needles,
or size needed to obtain gauge

US 7 (4.5mm) double-pointed needles
(set of 4)

Tapestry needle

Gauge

4.5 sts and 6 rows = 4" in St st with
larger needles

ast winter my grandmother was in the hospital on and off over several weeks. When I went to Ohio to visit her, I offered to take her little white terrier, Casey, home to New Jersey with me until Grandmother was in better health. Casey came to me wearing an orange acrylic sweater (it helped my grandmother, whose eyesight is poor, see her against her pale carpet). After a romp in the snow, Casey's sweater was soaked and I decided to make her a new-and-improved one out of wool.

This sweater was meant for a small dog, but I've resized it to fit medium-size and larger breeds as well. Measure your dog before you start to make sure the sweater will fit when it's finished. Even better, knit the sweater on circular needles and try it on the dog from time to time, adding more or fewer rows of stockinette stitch to ensure a proper fit.

At its core, this is a simple stockinette stitch dog sweater. You can make the stripe sequence as complicated or as easy as you like. Switching colors on RS rows and carrying CC behind the RS reduces the number of yarn ends to weave in.

Left Hanging

HOW TO KEEP YOUR KNITTING ON THE NEEDLES

To keep your work from falling off the needles when you are taking a break or storing your knitting, use an empty film canister. With pointy scissors, poke a small hole in the bottom of the canister. Insert the needle holding your knitting into the hole (it should fit tightly). This will keep the stitches from falling off the needle. *Wendy Robinette, Burlingame, CA*

STITCH PATTERNS

STRIPE SEQUENCE (SMALL)

4 rows MC, 4 rows CC, 18 rows MC, 2 rows CC, 4 rows MC, 2 rows CC, 2 rows MC, 6 rows CC, 4 rows MC, 2 rows CC, 6 rows MC, 2 rows CC, 2 rows MC, 2 rows CC, 2 rows MC, 2 rows CC, 2 rows MC.

STRIPE SEQUENCE (MEDIUM)

4 rows MC, 4 rows CC, 2 rows MC, 2 rows CC, 18 rows MC, 4 rows CC, 4 rows MC, 2 rows CC, 2 rows MC, 2 rows CC, 10 rows MC, 2 rows CC, 4 rows MC, 2 rows CC, 4 rows MC, 4 rows CC, 2 rows MC, 2 rows CC, 10 rows MC.

STRIPE SEQUENCE (LARGE)

4 rows MC, 4 rows CC, 2 rows MC, 2 rows CC, 28 rows MC, 2 rows CC, 2 rows MC, 6 rows CC, 2 rows MC, 6 rows CC, 6 rows MC, 2 rows CC, 2 rows MC, 2 rows CC, 24 rows MC, 2 rows CC, 4 rows MC, 2 rows CC, 4 rows MC, 4 rows CC, 2 rows MC, 2 rows CC, 11 rows MC.

DIRECTIONS

With smaller needles and CC, CO 44 (70, 80) sts.

Work in 1 × 1 rib for 2 rows.

Change to MC and work in 1 × 1 rib until collar measures 3 (3, 4)" from beg, ending with RS facing.

Beg stripe sequence and shape sweater as follows:

Next row: Inc 16 (18, 20) sts evenly across row.

Change to larger needles and work in St st until piece measures 4 (5, 7)" from beg, ending with RS facing.

Next row: K9 (12, 15), join new yarn, BO 6 (8, 10), k to last 15 (20, 25) sts, join new yarn, BO 6 (8, 10), k9 (12, 15).

Work even in St st, working the 3 pieces with separate yarn, until piece measures 2½ (3, 4)" from new yarn join, ending with RS facing.

Next row: With first ball of yarn, k9 (12, 15), CO 6 (8, 10), k to last 15 (20, 25) sts, CO 6 (8, 10), 9 (12, 15).

Break 2nd and 3rd ball of yarn.

Work even in St st until piece measures 9 (12, 15½)" from beg, ending with RS facing.

BO 6 (9, 13) sts at beg of next 2 rows.

BO 4 (3, 3) sts at beg of next 2 (4, 4) rows—40 (58, 62) sts.

Dec 1 st from each edge of next row then EOR 9 (13, 14) times—20 (30, 32) sts.

BO 4 (3, 2) sts at beg of next 2 (4, 5) rows.

BO rem sts and weave in yarn ends.

SLEEVES

With dpns and MC, pu 22 (28, 36) sts around leg opening. Work in 1 × 1 rib for 2 (3, 3)". Change to CC and work 1 row in rib.

BO.

Work second sleeve as for first, reversing colors.

FINISHING

With smaller needles and CC, pu 144 (192, 242) sts around bottom edge. Work in 1 × 1 rib for 1". BO.

Sew center seam.

Weave in ends.

About Peggy

A couple of years ago I was reading *Martha Stewart Living* and came across an article about knitting that had step-by-step instructions. I hadn't touched knitting needles since I was a five-year-old sitting on the porch with Hazel, the little old lady next door, but the steps felt familiar and I caught on again quickly. I've been addicted to knitting and buying (way too much) yarn ever since. I'm an art student living with my husband, three-year-old daughter, and eleven-month-old chocolate Lab, Lily, in a condo nestled in the mountains of northern New Jersey. I spend most of my time (what I don't spend chasing my daughter around, that is) being arty: drawing, painting, making soap, and of course, knitting and designing my own patterns. I also have a Web site, www.my-daydream.com, where I chronicle my adventures in knitting, motherhood, soapmaking, and life.

Ball of Confusion

HOW TO KEEP YOUR YARN UNDER CONTROL

Clean out your cottage cheese containers and insert a grommet in the lid to make a tidy hole for yarn to travel through. Put the ball inside, thread the yarn through the hole, and close the lid. *Amanda White Berka, Fort Collins, CO*

● Try toting cone yarns in a shoe box. Select a sturdy shoe box that is deep enough for the cone to be laid on its side. Cut a hole in each of the shorter sides of the box to accommodate a dowel. Thread the dowel through one hole, then through the cone and the opposite hole in the shoebox. The cone will be suspended and spin easily as you knit. If you don't have a dowel, use a long metal knitting needle. *AWB*

● To keep your yarn from rolling away, try using one of those 32- or 44-ounce hard plastic soda cups with a straw hole in the lid. Put the yarn inside, feed the end through the hole, and screw on the top. It works great for large skeins of yarn that unwind from the center. *Diana Camden, Huntington Beach, CA*

● When working on projects involving multiple colors of yarn, take a sandwich-size zippered plastic bag, snip off a small corner, and place each ball in its own bag. Thread the yarn end through the hole in the corner and seal the top. This can also help you keep your sanity when working with strandy and hairy novelty yarns that love to tangle upon themselves or each other. *Christina Berdoulay, San Mateo, CA*

MICHELLE AMERON

Catwarming Set

After seeing my cat promptly and viciously destroy the store-bought mouse toys that she loves so, I wondered if a more durable one might be made. I also wanted to design a gift set to welcome new baby kitties to their home—a "catwarming" set. The swishy string can be swung about or draped over a doorknob or claw-safe furniture for lots of super-fun kitty times, and the three blind mice . . . well, the possibilities are endless! While my cat doesn't really "get" catnip, I know many cats do, so instructions for adding it as part of the stuffing are included.

DIRECTIONS

MOUSE (MAKE 3, ALTERNATING WHICH COLORS ARE MC AND CC AS SHOWN)

With MC and straight needles, CO 3 sts.

Row 1: Inc1 into each st.

Row 2 and all even rows: P.

Row 3: (K1, inc1) twice, k2 (inc1, k1) twice.

Row 5: K2 (m1, k2) 4 times.

Row 7: (K3, m1) twice, k2, (m1, k3) twice.

Row 9: (K4, m1) twice, k2 (m1, k4) twice.

Rows 10–16: Work even.

Change to CC and work 2 rows.

Change to MC and work 5 rows.

Next row: (K3, k2tog) twice, k2 (k2tog, k3) twice.

Sizes

MOUSE

Finished length: 3" + tail

Finished circumference: 3¾"

STRING TOY

Finished length: 44"

Materials

Red Heart Sport
(100% acrylic; 70g/250 yds)

A: 1 skein #414 Charcoal

B: 1 skein #755 Pale Rose

C: 1 skein #918 Vermillion

US 4 (3.5mm) straight needles,
or size needed to obtain gauge

US 4 (3.5mm) double-pointed needles
(set of 2)

Tapestry needle

Polyester stuffing

Catnip (optional)

¼ yd muslin (optional)

Gauge

24 sts and 32 rows = 4" in St st

P 1 row.

Next row: *K1, k2tog; rep from * to end.

P 1 row.

Next row: K2tog; rep to end.

Break yarn, leaving a 12" tail. Draw tail through rem sts, pull tightly to the inside, and secure.

Ears (Make 6, two in each body color):

With MC and straight needles, CO 6 sts.

Work 2 rows in St st.

Next row: K2tog; rep to end.

Break yarn, leaving a 6" tail. Draw tail through rem sts and secure.

Tails (Make 3, one in each body color):

With MC and dpns, CO 2 sts. Work in I-cord until 3½" from beg.

Break yarn, leaving a 6" tail. Draw tail through rem sts and secure.

FINISHING

Using tail of body yarn, mattress st body, leaving 1" open at end.

Stuff body with polyester filling, adding optional packet of catnip (see below) and taking care not to add too much filling, just enough to retain desired shape.

Mattress st opening closed.

Optional:

Cut two 5" × 5" squares of muslin diagonally in half. Fold 3 pieces in half, with shorter ends meeting, and seam along each short end, forming a cone. Fill with catnip. Fold sides of open end in toward middle and sew shut. Machine sewing is recommended to keep the catnip secure. Trim excess fabric. Add to mouse when stuffing, with pointed end toward the nose, and mattress st seam.

Sew ears to top of mouse heads about halfway between the nose and the contrast stripe with RS of ears facing forward. Pull the string that was threaded through the last 3 sts of ears to make them curve slightly to the front.

Attach tail, using yarn tail to secure.

Stitch eyes and nose in contrasting color.

Weave in ends.

STRING TOY

(When alternating colors, carry yarn up to next stripe rather than breaking yarn after each color change.)

Ball (Make 2):

With A and straight needles, CO 9 sts.

Alternating 2 rows A, 2 rows B, 2 rows C, shape ball as follows:

Row 1 and every odd row: P.

Row 2: *K1, m1; rep from * to end.

Row 4: *K2, m1; rep from * to end.

Row 6: K3, m1, (k5, m1) 4 times, k4.

Work 9 rows even in St st, cont to alt colors as est.

Row 16: K2, *k2tog, k4; rep from * to end.

Row 18: *K1, k2tog; rep from * to end.

Row 20: K2tog, rep to end.

Break yarn, leaving a 12" tail. Draw tail through rem sts and secure. Use tail to mattress st seam closed, leaving 1" open. Stuff with polyester filling, adding optional packet of catnip (see below), and finish seam.

Optional:

Fold 2" × 4" piece of muslin in half with right sides tog and sew sides. Turn right side out, fill with catnip, and sew top closed. Machine sewing is recommended to keep the catnip secure. Add to ball before sewing seam, making sure to mold it to round shape, and mattress st seam.

Cord:

With A and dpns, CO 3 sts, leaving a 10" tail.

Alternating 2½" of color A, then B, then C, work in I-cord until piece measures 40" from beg, ending with A.

Leaving a 10" tail, break yarn and draw tail through sts to secure.

FINISHING

Sew cord to balls, using 10" tails to secure. Weave in ends.

About Michelle

I started knitting properly about two years ago, after many years of sporadic, failed attempts. Apparently my mother used to knit many moons ago and, while it's hard to believe, there is one scarf in the family to substantiate that claim. Needless to say, the skill wasn't passed down, and it took awhile before I finally got the hang of it. But I've had projects on the go ever since—way too many scarves, grand plans, and works in progress. The result of my endeavors (sewing, knitting, and otherwise) will be housed at orangeplush.com. I work as a graphic designer in Toronto, Ontario, which, happily, is also home to an active, creative, and inspiring knitting and crafting community.

I'm with the Band

SHOW ME YOUR TIPS!

THINGS TO DO WITH YOUR BALL BAND

*T*he most helpful tip my mom gave me was to use the paper band around the yarn to start winding the ball. That way, when you run out of yarn, you've got the color and dye lot right there to buy more! *Kate Lew, Napa, CA*

● I learned the hard way that when a pattern calls for a particular type of yarn, it makes sense to staple the ball band or write the yardage and weight of the yarn on the pattern. That way, if the yarn is discontinued or if you want to use a different yarn, you've got the info you need to make a good substitution. *Susan Smith Crawson, Tewksbury, MA*

M. K. CARROLL

Mobile Monsters

You might be wondering why I call these Bunny and Piggy cell phone cozies "monsters," but don't be fooled by their squishy fluffiness. These are in fact criminal masterminds, hellbent on taking over the world, which is why they want your mobile phone (and have also been known to snack on PDAs and mp3 players). Don't believe me? You won't see a pattern here for a kitty, because the one I knitted stole my phone and drove off in my car, never to be seen again.

You can get two monsters out of one skein, as I discovered when I showed the first monster to my anime-crazed teenage sister, who immediately claimed it as her own, and the sizes here should accommodate most styles. Piggy can hold most folding phones with slot-shape plug-ins, and Bunny can hold longer phones with pin-shape plug-ins. The pocket is the right size for the hands-free headset and cord that I use, and the openings at the bottom let me plug in the headset and look like I'm talking to a small fluffy toy. Whether you put the pocket on the front or the back of the cozy is up to you; some of us carry our junk in the trunk and some of us keep the junk up front.

Trying to measure a gauge swatch made with this yarn can make you cry, which is why I listed black thread in the notions. Knitted together with the Plush, it makes counting stitches and rows much easier.

Sizes

Finished measurements:

Bunny: 5" high, 2¾" wide, 1" deep

Piggy: 4" high, 3" wide, ½" deep

Materials

Berroco Plush (100% nylon; 50g/90 yds)

BUNNY

1 skein #1934 Black Out or #1924 Jazzy Turquoise

Small piece of white felt

Two ¼" round beads

PIGGY

1 skein #1932 Precious Pink

Small piece of pink felt

Two $7/16$" domed shank buttons

One 1" pink 4-hole coat button

US 5 (3.75mm) straight needles, or size needed to obtain gauge

Stitch markers

Tapestry needle

Sewing needle

Black sewing thread and thread to match yarn

Gauge

20 sts and 19 rows = 4" in garter st

DIRECTIONS

BUNNY BODY

CO 27 sts. Work in garter st until piece measures 5" from beg.

Next row: BO 19, k8.

Work 2 rows in garter st.

Next row: K1, *yo, k2tog; rep from * to last st, k1.

Work 2 rows in garter st.

BO.

Sew base (see diagram) and side seam.

PIGGY BODY

CO 32 sts. Work in garter st until piece measures 4" from beg.

BO and break yarn, leaving a 15" tail.

Use tail to sew side seam. With phone inside, whipstitch bottom seam closed, leaving space open so that slot is accessible.

FACE (FOR BOTH)

Select which side will be the back. Pu 10 sts along the top edge of the back, centered on the body.

Work 5 rows in garter st.

Next row: K1, inc1, k to last 2 sts, inc1, k1.

Next row: K all sts.

Rep these 2 rows twice more—16 sts.

Work 4 rows in garter st.

Next row: K1, skp, k to last 3 sts, k2tog, k1.

Next row: K all sts.

Rep these 2 rows 3 times more.

Next row: K1, skp, k2, k2tog, k1—6 sts.

BO.

BUNNY EAR (MAKE 2)

Pu 5 sts from top edge of face to correspond with picture.

Work 2 rows in garter st.

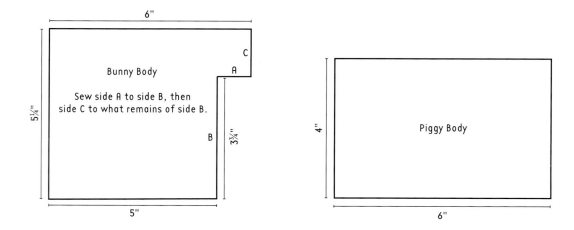

Bunny Body

6"

5¼"

Sew side A to side B, then side C to what remains of side B.

C

A

B

3¾"

5"

Piggy Body

4"

6"

Next row: K1, inc1, k1, inc1, k1

Work in garter st until ear measures 2½" from beg.

Next row: K1, skp, k1, k2tog, k1

Next row: K all sts.

BO.

PIGGY EAR (MAKE 2)

Pick up 5 sts to correspond with picture.

Work 2 rows in garter st.

Next row: Skp, k1, k2tog.

Next row: Skp, k1.

Next row: K2tog.

Break yarn and pull tail through rem st to secure.

POCKET (FOR BOTH)

CO 12 sts.

Work in garter st until piece measures 2½" from beg.

BO, leaving a 20" tail.

FINISHING

Bunny:

Sew on beads for eyes. Cut out felt shapes for teeth and the tongue, using the templates given below, and sew in place. Use very small stitches on the face side. Trim teeth to desired size, if necessary. Sew pocket on desired location. Weave in all ends.

Piggy:

Sew on eye buttons and nose button. Cut out a felt shape for the tongue, using the template given, and sew in place. Use very small stitches on the face side. Sew pocket in desired location. Weave in all ends.

About M.K.

See the Head Huggers pattern, page 59, for M. K.'s bio.

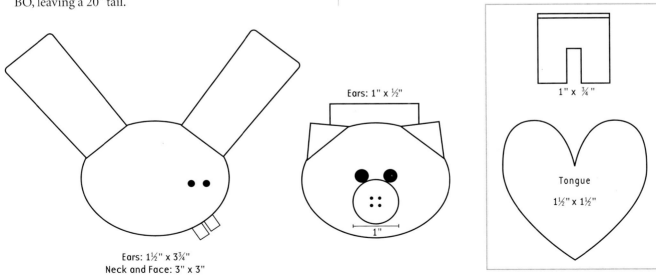

Ears: 1" x ½"

Ears: 1½" x 3¾"
Neck and Face: 3" x 3"

1"

1" x ¾"

Tongue
1½" x 1½"

ANGELA HACKNER

Knit Your Own Rock Star

JOEY RAMONE, HENRY ROLLINS, AND JOAN JETT

A fter abandoning my dream writing project, "Knitting with Rollins," I decided that the world desperately needed a punk rock doll. So with furrowed brow and a tangle of yarn, I set out to knit my own Henry Rollins doll, complete with tattoos and self-deprecating wit. With his angst channeling through me, I began knitting his doll lookalike. I kept clicking away, and next came Joey Ramone, then Joan Jett. Make up your own dolls. Take this pattern and mix it up. Shred it to pieces. Set it on fire. Destroy it. Then start knitting and see who comes screaming off the needles.

DIRECTIONS

UPPER BODY—*JOEY RAMONE AND HENRY ROLLINS DOLLS* (MAKE 2)

With red (black) yarn, CO 22 (24) sts.

For Joey, alt 2 rows of red with 2 rows of blue yarn; for both dolls, work in St st for 30 (20) rows, ending with RS facing.

BO 1 st at beg of next 2 rows.

Size

Finished height: Joey: 16 (Henry: 13, Joan: 13)"

Materials

Tahki Cotton Classic
(100% mercerized cotton; 50g/108 yds)

JOEY RAMONE

1 skein #3001 White

1 skein #3002 Black

1 skein #3003 Off White

1 skein #3997 True Red

1 skein #3874 Blue

HENRY ROLLINS

1 skein #3001 White

1 skein #3002 Black

1 skein #3003 Off White

1 skein #3336 Dark Brown

JOAN JETT

1 skein #3001 White

1 skein #3002 Black

1 skein #3003 Off White

1 skein #3997 True Red

Note: *Main pattern instructions are written for the Joey Ramone doll. Any specific changes for the other dolls are in parentheses (Henry Rollins followed by Joan Jett).*

(continued)

*Next row (RS): K1, sl1, k1, psso, k to last 3 sts, k2tog, k1.

Work 1 row even.*

Rep from * to * 5 times more.

BO.

UPPER BODY FRONT: JOAN JETT
With black yarn, CO 21 sts.

Work even in St st for 10 rows.

*Next row: K1, sl1, k1, psso, k to last 3 sts, k2tog, k1.

Work 1 row even.*

Rep from * to * 1 time.

Work even in St st for 4 rows.

Next row: K2, m1, k to last 2 stitches, m1, k2.

Work 1 row even.

Work even in St st for 2 rows.**

Next row: K1, sl1, k1, psso, k6, work 7 chart sts, k6, k2tog, k1.

Work 1 row even.

Cont as est, working 1 less st before and after chart on RS rows for 6 rows.

BO.

UPPER BODY BACK: JOAN JETT
Work as for front to **.

*Next row: K1, sl1, k1, psso, k to last 3 sts, k2tog, k1.

Work 1 row even.*

Rep from * to * twice.

Work even in St st for 2 rows.

BO.

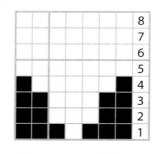

								8
								7
								6
								5

☐ Off White   ◼ Black

Materials (continued)
Fonty Serpentine
(100% polyamide; 50g/145 yds)

JOEY RAMONE
1 skein #825 Black (for optional jacket)

Katia Danubio
(76% wool, 24% nylon; 50g/100 yds),
1 skein #2 Black (for hair)

US 6 (4mm) straight needles,
or size needed to obtain gauge

US 6 (4mm) double-pointed needles
(set of 5)

Tapestry needle

Fiber fill

Gauge
20 sts and 28 rows = 4" in St st with
Tahki Cotton Classic

ARM (MAKE 2 EACH)

With off-white yarn, CO 10 (10, 7) sts.

Working in St st, inc 1 st at each edge of EOR 2 (2, 4) times, then every foll 4th row 3 (3, 0) times.

Work even in St st for 13 (15, 16) rows.

Change to blue (black) yarn.

Work even in St st for 2 rows.

For Joey Ramone:

Change to red yarn and work in St st for 2 rows. Alternating 2 rows blue and 2 rows red, cont as follows:

BO 1 st at beg of next 2 rows.

For Joey Ramone and Joan Jett:

*Next row: K1, sl1, k1, psso, k to last 3 sts, k2tog, k1.

Work 1 row even.*

Rep from * to * 5 (3) times.

For all dolls:

BO.

LEG (MAKE 2 EACH)

With black (brown, black) yarn, CO 18 (20, 18) sts.

*Work even in St st for 16 (14, 14) rows.

Next (dec) row: K1, sl1, k1, psso, k to last 3 sts, k2tog, k1.

Work 1 row even.*

For Joey Ramone and Henry Rollins:

Rep from * to * once more, changing to off-white yarn on row 17 for Henry.

Work even in St st for 8 (8, 10) rows.

For Joan Jett:

Change to white yarn and work 1 row even.

Change to red yarn and work 1 row even.

Enough Is Enough

THE RIGHT YARN LENGTH FOR COLOR WORK AND TO FINISH A ROW

*W*hen working intarsia, I like to pull out a strand of color the length of my extended arms (from palm to palm, about 3 feet). I can always undo the tangles in that length or a bit shorter. *Skippy Kaufman, N. Versailles, PA*

● When you're nearing the end of a ball of yarn, fold the tail in half and tie a loose slip knot at the center point. If you come to the halfway knot while knitting the next row, you don't have enough yarn to complete another row. *Nikki Myers, New York, NY*

Rep dec row.

Work even in St st for 5 rows.

Change to white yarn and *rep dec row.

Work 1 row even.*

Rep from * to * once.

For Joey Ramone:

Change to white yarn and work in St st for 2 rows.

Change to black yarn.

Rep dec row.

Work even in St st for 6 rows.

Change to white yarn and *work 1 row even.

Rep dec row.*

Rep from * to * once

For Henry Rollins:

Rep dec row.

For all dolls:

Break yarn and draw tail through rem sts, pull tight, and secure.

FINISHING BODY
Mattress st sleeve edges to front and back armholes. Seam sleeves and side seams.

HEADS
With off-white yarn and dpns, pick up 24 (24, 32) sts around neck opening.

Work 5 (5, 1) rnds in St st.

For Joey Ramone and Henry Rollins :

*Next rnd: Inc 2 sts evenly around.

Work 2 rnds even.*

Rep from * to * 3 times.

Work 2 rnds even.

Joey's face

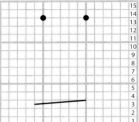

Joan's face

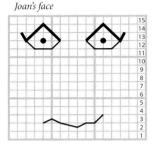

Henry's face

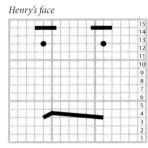

Henry's tattoos

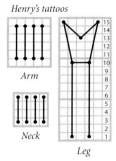

Arm

Neck

Leg

━━ *Cotton Classic*

▅▅ *Cotton Classic, go over the same stitches 3 times*

●   *French knots*

── *Cotton Classic, split*

For all dolls:

Next rnd: *K6, k2tog*; rep from * to * to end of rnd.

Work 1 rnd even.

Rep last 2 rows, working 1 less st between decs on every other rnd, to 16 (16, 20) sts.

Work 1 (1, 3) rnd even in St st.

For Joan Jett:

Work 2 rnds in St st, increasing 2 sts evenly on each rnd.

*Work 1 rnd even.

Work 1 rnd, increasing 2 sts evenly around.*

Rep from * to * once.

Work 4 rnds even.

Next rnd: K5, k2tog.

Work 1 rnd even.

Rep last 2 rnds, working 1 less st between decs on every other rnd, to 16 sts.

For all dolls:

*K2tog; rep from * to end of rnd.

Break yarn and draw tail through rem sts. Pull tight and secure.

FINISHING DOLLS

Seam back of legs.

Embroider facial features and tattoos on dolls to correspond with templates given.

Stitch laces onto Joey's and Joan's sneakers. For Joey's hair, attach strands of Katia Danubio to head. For Henry, duplicate stitch hair onto head. For Joan's hair, attach strands of black yarn to head and cut into a mullet.

Stuff all body parts with fiber fill and mattress st rem seams. Sew upper body to lower body.

About Angela

For me, knitting was an acquired taste. After learning the basics from my mom, I crept along for six months on my first project—a potholder that I gave to my boyfriend. Luckily, I was ignorant of the boyfriend potholder curse (and its variations); otherwise he and I might not be married today. The experience underwhelmed me, but after I moved from dusty Texas to sunny Los Angeles, where all knitters are beautiful, I gave it another chance. This time something was different, and I dove right in and knit my way through a novelty scarf and a baby hat that, upon completion, resembled a giant square of Shredded Wheat cereal. I spend my sunshiny days tangled in a mess of audio wires, making sound for film and television. I spend each night at home tangled in a mess of yarn, knitting punk rock dolls and chronicling my crafting adventures at www.yarngirls.com.

The Binds that Tie

BEEFING UP THE LAST BOUND-OFF STITCH

Here's a trick to neaten the last stitch of a bind-off: Cast off your row until only one stitch remains on the left needle and one on the right. Slip the stitch from the left needle onto the right so there are now two loops on the right needle. With the tip of the left needle pick up the left side of the loop of the stitch *below* the slipped stitch from front to back. Slip the slipped stitch back onto the left needle (there are now two loops on the left needle) and knit both loops together. Slip the next-to-last stitch over this knitted stitch, and then pull yarn through last remaining stitch. Altogether tidier! *Susan Hoover, Mount Vernon, NY*

REBECCA DEWEY

Knit My Ride

FUZZY DICE & STEERING WHEEL COVER

Size

Finished measurements:
Dice: $3\frac{1}{2}$" × $3\frac{1}{2}$" × $3\frac{1}{2}$"

Finished measurements:
Steering wheel cover: to fit

Materials

DICE

MC: Paton's Allure (100% nylon; 50g/
47 yds), 2 skeins #4532 Garnet

Embroidery floss to match MC

CC: 2 yds black scrap yarn

Two 3" foam cubes

42 black felt dots with sticky backing

STEERING WHEEL COVER

Paton's Allure (100% nylon; 50g/
47 yds), 2 skeins #4532 Garnet

Nonslip drawer padding OR glue gun

BOTH

US 8 (5mm) straight needles,
or size needed to obtain gauge

DMC rayon floss in Red

Sewing needle

Gauge

16 sts and 20 rows = 4" in garter st

his dice pattern came about as a joke for a friend. I had recently gotten back into knitting and kept saying that I would knit her seat covers for her new car. That never happened, but one day I thought, What about fuzzy dice? And they came about by themselves. As for why the steering wheel cover, I live in Arizona, where it can get to 125 degrees in the summer, and you need something to protect your hands from getting scalded on the steering wheel. A matching steering wheel cover just seemed like a perfect fit for the fuzzy dice.

DIRECTIONS

DICE (MAKE 2)

With MC, CO 12 sts.

Work in garter st until piece measures 3" from beg.

CO 12 sts at beg of next 2 rows—36 sts.

Work in garter st until piece measures 6" from beg.

BO 12 sts at beg of next 2 rows—12 sts.

Work in garter st until piece measures 12" from beg.

BO.

CORD

With CC, CO 40 sts.

BO.

FINISHING

With red floss, seam adjoining sides A, B, C, and D to form a cube shape, leaving 2 sides of the top flap open. Place foam cube inside and sew one side shut. Place one end of the cord into the corner and continue the seam through both the fabric and the cord. Rep for second die using the other end of the cord.

Stick felt dots on the dice to correspond with a real die.

STEERING WHEEL COVER

To determine the number of sts to CO (X), measure around the outside of the wheel and add ½". Multiply this number by 4 and round off to the closest whole number, if necessary.

To determine the length you should knit to (Y"), measure the diameter of your steering wheel (from edge to edge across the center). Multiply this number by 3.14. Then subtract 6 and round off to the closest whole or half number, if necessary.

CO X sts.

Work in garter st until piece measures Y" from beg.

BO.

FINISHING

Either cut 7 pieces of nonslip drawer padding 3" × 2" and sew them to WS of fabric with red DMC floss every six inches *or* use a hot glue gun to evenly space rows of glue every 6" on WS of fabric and allow to cool. This will help keep the cover from slipping off.

Sew CO row to BO row, turn RS out, and pull it onto steering wheel.

About Becky

I am a twenty-four-year-old hair stylist and Arizona native. My mom taught me to knit and would always cast on and bind off for me. I did about five scarves and left it at that. I got back into knitting about three years ago, I guess as a way to stay connected with my mom after her death. I took a class at my LYS to relearn the basics and have kept on knitting since then. When I'm not knitting, I spend time playing with my cats, Pepper Ann and Moose, and my Chihuahua, Maggie, and learning to spin with a drop spindle.

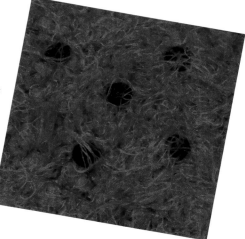

STITCH 'N BITCH GROUPS
Beyond the Borders

Aberdeen, Scotland

Taiwan, as close as Ireland and England, and include a resident Scottish "pit-knitter" (aye, many lasses in Scotland do knit with a needle in their armpit!). Our knitting styles are as unique and interesting as the members. Somehow, nobody ever looks as if we are doing the same thing, and yet we are all knitting.

Helen Ralph

BRISTOL, ENGLAND, SnB

Stitch 'n Bitch Bristol arose when a gang from Ladyfest Bristol took a trip to offer support, sell 'zines, and have fun

ABERDEEN, SCOTLAND, SnB

While knitting in a pub during the local playgroup's "mums' night out," I met a few fellow knitting moms who fancied having a real Stitch 'n Bitch session. As a Cincinnati expat, I used just the initials "SnB," fearing British knitters might hesitate to join a "Bitch" group, but this was completely unnecessary, as all the knitters have enthusiastically embraced the name. In February 2003, the Aberdeen Stitch 'n Bitch was formed, and it became the first UK group to be listed on the SnB Web site.

Since then, things have really taken off, and the group's gotten media coverage from *The Sunday Times*, *The Sun*, and BBC Radio Scotland. We meet at a cafe that's inside a movie theater. It's got good lighting, it's comfortable, and it's not too smoky. It's the ideal place to knit, chat, and drink vodka and tonic.

Our two dozen members hail from as far away as Canada, Germany, Estonia, and

Bristol, England

with the kids from Ladyfest Devon. But when we arrived at the venue, we discovered that nearly every person in the building was knitting. At first we were totally put off by this, but slowly we got drawn into the knitting frenzy and by the end of the night many of us were totally hooked—although our first stumbling knitting efforts were done under the influence of girl bands and too much booze.

Cardiff, Wales

Upon our return home, we were determined to continue to knit together, so in November 2003 we held our first official Stitch 'n Bitch at our organization's Here shop and gallery. We meet online under the banner "the post-ironic spinsterhood" and gather at the shop for stitchin' 'n bitchin', sewing, crocheting, puppet making, storytelling, and drawing. I'm not sure any of us are what you would call accomplished knitters—it's all about getting together, reviving an old craft, and sharing skills and passing on knowledge. And it's more than just knitting; it's networking for women who have skills and talents and don't know where to go with them. It's a safe space to try stuff out.

Camilla Stacey

CARDIFF, WALES, SNB

I started knitting in 2001 and used to feel so jealous when I read about the exciting Stitch 'n Bitch groups springing up all over the U.S. I wanted a group like that near me! So I found A Shot in the Dark, a good café with organic, fair-trade coffee and tea, comfy seats, and nice big tables where people could spread out their projects.

A few of my friends attended the first meeting, and since then we've met up every month at the coffee shop and sometimes we have special sessions at one another's homes. Among those who've joined is one member who got *Stitch 'n Bitch* as a Christmas present, went to stitchnbitch.org like the book advises to see if there were any meetings near her, and found us. She couldn't believe there was a group in Cardiff.

We usually meet on a Saturday afternoon. We used to joke that one end of the table was for stitching, the other for bitching, but even the nonknitters have been inspired to pick up needles. Cardiff SnB is the only chapter in Wales and one of only four in the United Kingdom. We hope that will soon change.

Marie Irshad

MELBOURNE, AUSTRALIA, SNB

Despite not having knit since age five, when I was thirty six I decided that I could make my own lace sweaters. I began devouring knitting books and while scouring the Internet for inspiration discovered the phenomenon of Stitch 'n Bitch groups. Stitch 'n Bitch Melbourne held its first official meeting in January

Melbourne, Australia

2003 in a coffee shop on trendy Chapel Street, and since then the group has expanded to more than one hundred. Thirty regulars begin meetings by showing off knit projects to rounds of applause, and then quickly mess up the café tables with vintage patterns, the latest books, and yarn. We've even pulled out ball winders and swifts and set up a whole production number in the window, becoming quite the spectacle and attracting new members in the process. Online we share Web links and book titles, give technical assistance and advice on pattern choices, and arrange ad hoc SEX (stash-enhancing excursions) and trips to yarn events.

The group remains united through the simplicity of yarn, needles, conversation, and real friendships that feed the soul. When one member's father died in April, the group rallied 'round, and knitting became a way to pick up the pieces and knit herself back together.

Sharon Steer-Courtenay

MONTREAL, CANADA, KNITTING BEE

When the Montreal Knitting Bee members became the Revolutionary Knitting Circle and held a knit-in at a tent city to highlight a housing crisis, some of our supplies and projects were confiscated by riot police. It's not always this political for the group, who formed in the fall of 2002 as part of the Montreal Church of

Craft. About ten of us (out of eighty) meet once a week in a member's home to knit or create other fiber arts, chat, and sample homemade vegan deserts. There are a few male members, and all ages from two on up are represented. Projects in the works include a knitting sound art project with a record label and a knitting fashion show. We've been the subject of a documentary and an anthropological study and are looking for more opportunities to go out into the community and spread the word.

Alanna Lynch

Montreal, Canada

TOKYO, JAPAN, SnB

I started the Tokyo Stitch 'n Bitch with American expat Jennifer Okano in January 2004. It wasn't very hard to drum up interest. Unlike in the U.S., there have always been books and magazines in Japan

that cater to the younger knitter. It is really common for teenage girls and young women to knit a scarf or sweater for their boyfriend; it is a sign of love. The magazines geared to them focus on the bulkier yarns and on patterns for small accessory items in fun colors, and they're big on layering.

Several members of Tokyo SnB are bilingual, so our meetings are carried out in a mixture of Japanese and English. We find that our love for all things crafty helps us overcome any language barriers.

The big differences between American and Japanese knitters are that most Japanese work in Continental style and Japanese patterns consist mostly of diagrams, rather than words and abbreviations. It really helps the knitter visualize the project, rather than just following directions and knitting blindly. We also have access to local Avril yarns, which are gaining notoriety Stateside.

Tokyo can sometimes be a big, faceless city, but our Stitch 'n Bitch has provided many of us with a warm, cozy environment where we can talk about the latest in knitting magazines and craft ideas, as well as the problems and joys of living in a foreign city.

Kat Mok

KAREN BAUMER

Chill Pillows

the design of these pillows was inspired by the groovy 1970s-era house my friends bought on the side of a hill near Los Angeles. They built a cushioned sofalike platform along two sides of their living room, and suddenly they needed pillows—lots of pillows—to pad the "back" of the sofa, which was simply a wall. This was just the excuse I needed to play with some funky stitch patterns (loop and nubble) that would mesh well with the overall look of the house.

Tip: If you prefer, you can use fabric for the backs of the pillows instead of knitting them. This is especially handy if you want to use up leftover yarn and don't have enough to make both a front and a back panel.

STITCH PATTERN
LOOP STITCH
Row 1 (WS): K.

Row 2 (RS): K1, *ML; rep from * to last st, k1.

Note: *Directions for nubbly pillow on page 249.*

Size
14" square

Materials
LOOP PILLOW
Brown Sheep Lamb's Pride Worsted (85% wool, 15% mohair; 113g/190 yds), 3 skeins #78 Aztec Turquoise

US 8 (5mm) straight needles, or size needed to obtain gauge

Tapestry needle

14" square pillow form

Gauge
12 sts and 16 rows = 4" in loop st

16 sts and 32 rows = 4" in garter st

Abbreviations
ML (MAKE LOOP)
K1 without slipping st off left needle. Bring yarn to front between needles. Wrap yarn around left thumb to form a loop. Bring yarn to back, between the needles, and k the same st again, this time slipping to right needle (2 sts now on right needle). Lift first st over second st and drop it off the needle.

DIRECTIONS

LOOPY PILLOW

Front:

CO 42 sts.

Work in loop st patt until piece measures 14" from beg, ending with RS facing.

BO.

Back:

CO 2 sts.

Next row: Inc1, k to end.

Rep inc row until the side measures 14".

Next row: Skp, k to end.

Rep dec row until 2 stitches rem.

BO.

FINISHING

Mattress st back to front along 3 sides, being careful not to catch loops into seam. Insert pillow form and seam last side closed.

Show me your tips!! Wrap Star

A NEW WAY TO HOLD YOUR YARN

I've been knitting for about five years, but only recently started knitting like a madwoman. The reason? I finally found a comfortable way to hold the yarn. When I began experimenting, I found that I knit best when I wrap the yarn twice around both my middle and ring fingers held together. It helps me maintain an even tension, feels more secure on my fingers yet is easy to take off, and I can just slide my fingers down the yarn to adjust the amount I need without having to drop it off my fingers and pick it up again. *Amanda Schehr, St. Louis, MO*

STITCH PATTERN
NUBBLE

Row 1 (WS): K.

Row 2 (RS): K1, *MN, k1; rep from * to end.

Row 3: K1, *p1, k1; rep from * to end.

Rows 4 and 5: K.

Row 6: K1, *k1, MN; rep from * to last 2 sts, k2.

Row 7: K2, *p1, k1; rep from * to last st, k1.

Row 8: K.

DIRECTIONS
NUBBLY PILLOW

CO 55 sts.

Work in nubble patt until piece measures 14" from beg, ending with a row 3 or row 7. Change to garter st and work even until piece measures 28" from beg.

BO.

FINISHING

Fold piece in half with wrong sides tog. Mattress st back to front along 2 sides. Turn RS out. Insert pillow form and seam last side closed.

Size
14" square

Materials
NUBBLY PILLOW
Brown Sheep Lamb's Pride Worsted (85% wool, 15% mohair; 113g/190yds)

3 skeins #140 Aran

US 8 (5mm) straight needles, or size needed to obtain gauge

Tapestry needle

14" square pillow form

Gauge
16 sts and 24 rows = 4" in nubble st

16 sts and 32 rows = 4" in garter st

Abbreviation
MN (MAKE NUBBLE)
Pull loop through next st as if to k, then place this loop on left needle next to original st—2 sts. Pull new loop through second st as if to k, then place loop on left needle next to second st—3 sts. Repeat twice—5 sts. BO 4 kwise. The fifth stitch is now on the right needle.

AMY BARKER

Two for Tea

Size

Fits a classic 4-cup teapot

Finished width: 7½"

Finished height: 7½"

Materials

Brown Sheep Nature Spun Worsted
(100% wool, 100g/245 yds)

8 BALL
MC: 1 skein #601 Pepper

CC: 1 skein #740 Snow

COFFEE, TEA, OR ME? (CTOM)
MC: 1 skein #115 Bit of Blue

CC1: 1 skein #N54 Orange You Glad

CC2: 1 skein #108 Cherry Delight

US 6 (4mm) straight needles,
or size needed to obtain gauge

US G/6 (4mm) crochet hook

Tapestry needle

Safety pins

Gauge

17 sts and 26 rows = 4" in St st

Special Skills

INTARSIA/DUPLICATE STITCH

there was a time when no self-respecting hostess would serve her guests from a (gasp!) naked teapot. Today we are a little more open-minded about these matters, but maybe those ladies were on to something—a knitted cozy does keep your brew toasty warm.

I'm a three-cup-a-day tea drinker (Earl Grey, black, two sugars) and a knitter as well, so putting together a tea cozy seemed logical. But the frilly patterns out there left me cold. I wanted something with a sense of humor to fit in with my retro kitchen (emphasis on kitsch), and this is the result. These 8-ball and Coffee, Tea, or Me? cozies fit a classic four-cup teapot and will keep your tea hot, hot, hot!

DIRECTIONS
BACK
(Instructions are for 8-ball, with CTOM directions in parentheses.)

With MC (CC2), CO 44 sts.

Work 8 rows (2 rows of MC and 2 rows of CC) in 1 × 1 ribbing.

With MC, work in St st for 24 rows.

**Next row: K2tog, k to last 2 sts, k2tog.

P 1 row.**

Rep from ** to ** to 36 sts.

Next row: K2tog, k8, k2tog, pm, k10, k2tog, pm, k10, k2tog.

P 1 row.

Next row: K2tog, *k to 2 sts before marker, k2tog, sm; rep from * once, k to last 2 sts, k2tog.

P 1 row.

Rep last 2 rows to 16 sts.

Next row: K2tog across row.

BO.

FRONT

Work as for back, beg chart on 5th row of St st as foll:

K14 (6), k16 (32) sts from chart, k14 (6). Cont shaping as for back and working chart at the same time.

Optional: The "8" of the 8-ball cozy can be knit when working from the chart or those sts can be worked in CC and embroidered on with MC and duplicate st.

FINISHING

Duplicate st "8" on 8-ball cozy motif if necessary.

With RS tog, use safety pins to temporarily join, marking openings for spout and handle. Turn cozy RS out before you seam to make sure the design is on the side that will be seen while the tea is being poured (you may want to make one of these for a left-handed tea drinker). Turn wrong side out and use MC and crocheted slip st to join.

About Amy

I am an American expat living in Sydney, Australia, with my husband and one very spoiled cat. My mother-in-law taught me to knit a few years ago while we were visiting her in Florida, and I've been hooked ever since. I consider myself a "short attention span knitter" and favor projects that can be completed in a sitting or two. Of course, in that warm Sydney sun we can only use so many hats and scarves, so I knit lots of cat toys and home accessories. A few years ago I was a featured knitter in the Australian book *It's My Party and I'll Knit if I Want To,* by Sharon Aris. Sharon and I met at a local SnB while dropping stitches over beer.

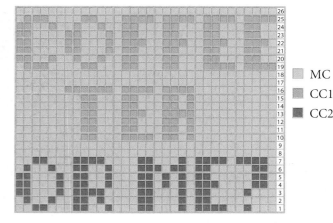

- ☐ MC
- ▨ CC1
- ■ CC2

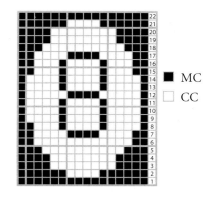

- ■ MC
- ☐ CC

The Knitty-Gritty

A REFRESHER COURSE

Slip Knot

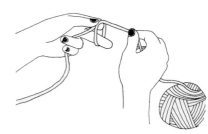 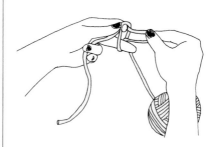 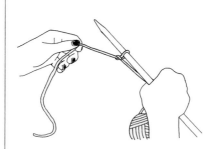

1 Wrap the ball end of the yarn clockwise around your forefinger and middle finger, with your fingers spread approximately 1 inch apart.

2 Pull a loop of the ball end of the yarn through the loop of yarn around your fingers.

3 Slide that loop onto a knitting needle, and pull on the tail and ball ends to tighten it.

Double Cast-on (CO)

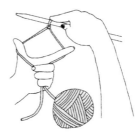   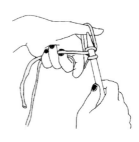

1 Make a slip knot, leaving a tail that's at least three times the width of the piece you want to knit. Hold the needle with your right hand, with the long tail end hanging to the left and the ball end hanging to the right. Close the bottom three fingers of your left hand

around the yarn and, with your thumb and forefinger, spread apart the two strands of yarn.

2 Scoop up the strand of yarn that runs across your palm to the bottom of your thumb.

3 Wrap the yarn on your left forefinger around the front of your knitting needle, counter-clockwise.

4 Bring the loop of yarn that's on your left thumb over the tip of your knitting needle. Pull your thumb outta there and

tighten the cast-on stitch, returning your left hand to the same position as in step 1. Continue steps 2–4 until you've cast on the desired number of stitches.

Single Cast-on (CO)

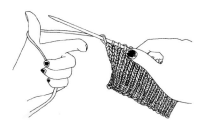
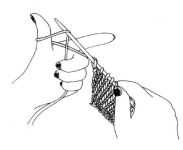
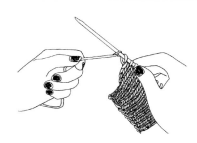

1 Take the needle with the stitches on it in your *right hand,* and close the bottom three fingers of your left hand around the ball end of the yarn. Then, let the yarn run across your palm and over your thumb.

2 Scoop up the yarn strand that runs from your three fingers to the base of your thumb from underneath.

3 Drop that loop off your thumb, and tighten the stitch.

Cable Cast-on (CO)

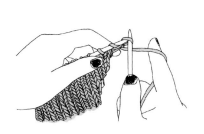
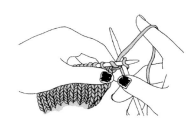

1 Knit a stitch, but do not drop the old stitch off the left needle.

2 Transfer the new stitch to the left-hand needle by inserting the left needle into the front leg of this loop from *right to left* (and from front to back) and pulling it off the right needle.

3 To continue casting on, stick your right needle *in between* the first two stitches on the left needle and knit a stitch (wrap the yarn around the needle, and pull it through to the front), but do not drop the old stitch off the left needle. Transfer the new stitch to the left needle in the same manner as you did in step 2.

Knit Stitch (K)

THE ENGLISH (RIGHT-HAND) WAY

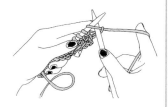 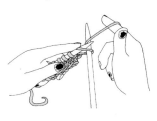 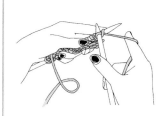 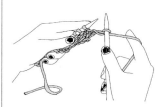

1 Take the needle with the stitches on it in your left hand. Hold the yarn in your right hand, over your right forefinger. Slide the point of the right needle through the first loop on the left needle from front to

back so that the two needles make an X.

2 With your right hand, wrap the yarn around the tip of the right needle counterclockwise (from back to front).

3 Pull the yarn taut (not tight!) with your forefinger, and slide the point of your right needle down and back out of the loop the opposite of the way you came in: *from the back to the front.* Make sure you bring the new loop along!

4 Once you're back out, slide the right needle up again so that the new loop is about 1½ inches from the tip, and push the old loop off the tip of the left needle.

THE CONTINENTAL (LEFT-HAND) WAY

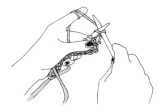  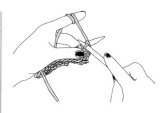 

1 Hold the yarn with your left hand, with the yarn wrapped around your left forefinger, and use your bottom two fingers to hold the needle. Slide the point of the right needle through the first loop on the left needle

from front to back so that the two needles make an X.

2 With the tip of the right needle, grab that strand of yarn that's coming from your forefinger so that it wraps counterclockwise around the right needle.

3 Pull this new loop back out the loop you came in from.

4 Once you're back out, slide the right needle up again so that the new loop is about 1½ inches from the tip, and push the old loop off the left needle.

Purl Stitch (P)

THE ENGLISH (RIGHT-HAND) WAY

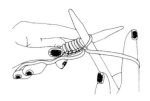   

1 Hold your yarn and needles the same way you would to make a knit stitch, but bring the yarn between the tips of your needles so that it is *in front* of your right needle. Insert the right needle from

back to front through the first stitch on the left needle. Your needles are now in an X shape.

2 Take the yarn in your right hand, and loop it around the point of your right needle counterclockwise.

3 Carefully slide your right needle down along the base of the left needle, pushing the point of the right needle—and your new loop—out through the back of the stitch you came in through.

4 Push the right needle back up again and slide the old loop up and off the left needle.

THE CONTINENTAL (LEFT-HAND) WAY

1 Hold your yarn and needles the same way you would to make a knit stitch, but bring the yarn between the tips of your needles so that it is *in front* of your left needle. Insert your right needle from back to front through the loop on the first stitch on the left needle.

Your needles are now in an X shape.

2 Bring the yarn in your left hand around the point of your right needle counterclockwise, then bring your left pointer finger (the one with the yarn around it), down below the center of the X.

3 Carefully slide your right needle down along the base of the left needle, pushing the point of the right needle out through the back of the stitch you came in through.

4 Slide the right needle back up again and push the old loop up and off the left needle.

Binding Off (BO)

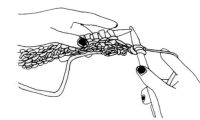

1 Starting at the beginning of a row, knit two stitches.

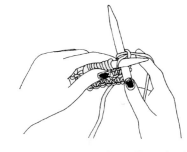

2 Slide the tip of the left needle under the front leg of the first stitch you knit.

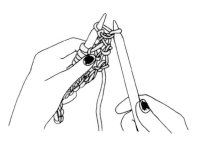

3 Then lift that stitch up and over the second stitch and let it drop off the tip of the right needle.

Binding Off (continued)

4 Repeat until all of your stitches have been bound off, and you're left with only one stitch. Cut the yarn about 6 inches from the end and pull it through that last stitch, tightening gently.

Bar Increase (INC 1)

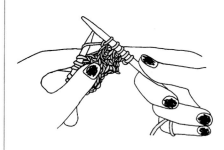

1 Knit into the next stitch on the needle, *but don't drop it off the left needle.*

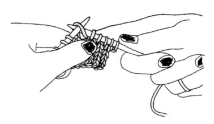

2 Now, knit into the *back leg* of that same stitch. This time drop it off the needle; you should now have an extra stitch on your right needle.

Make One Increase (M1)

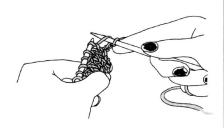

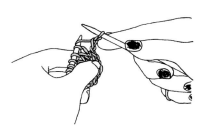

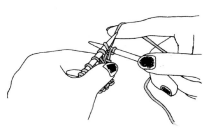

1 With the right needle, pick up the strand of yarn that lies between the stitch you just knit and the next stitch on the needle. Pick up this strand by inserting the needle under it *from front to back.*

2 Lift this strand off the right needle and onto the left by inserting the left needle under it *from front to back* and dropping it off the right needle.

3 Knit into the *back* of this stitch.

Yarn Over (YO)

Knit Two Together (K2TOG)

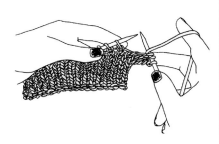

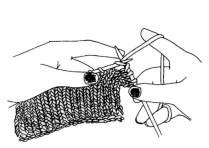

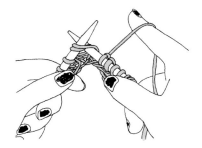

1 Knit the first stitch, then bring your yarn to the front between the two points of your needles.

2 With the yarn still in front, knit the next stitch. Knitting a stitch this way will leave an extra strand of yarn lying across your needle.

1 Stick the right needle into the next two stitches on the left needle knitwise. Knit these stitches together as one.

Piece of cake, right? And, just as you can knit two knit stitches together, you can also purl two purl stitches together.

Slip. Slip. Knit (SSK)

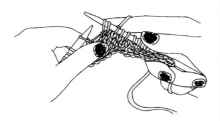 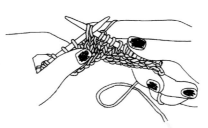 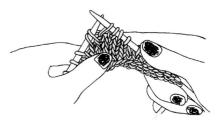

1 Stick your right needle into the next stitch as if you were going to knit it, but then slide it off the left needle and onto the right. Slip the next stitch knitwise too.

2 Take your left needle and slip it through the front legs of those two stitches, from left to right.

3 With the needles in that position, make a knit stitch by wrapping the yarn around, pulling the loop through to the front, then dropping the old loops off the left-hand needle.

Slip. Knit. Pass Slipped Stitch Over (SKP)

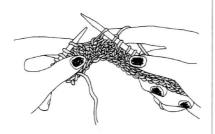 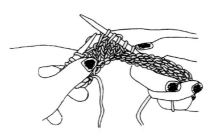 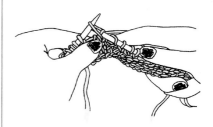

1 Slip one stitch knitwise.

2 Knit the next stitch.

3 Insert the left needle into the front leg of the slipped stitch and lift it over the stitch you just knit and off the needle—just like when you're binding off.

Sewing Side Seams

1. Before sewing two knit pieces together, you'll need to tack the yarn in place. Begin by threading a yarn needle with a length of yarn long enough to sew the entire seam, and at least another 12" left over. Then tack the yarn in place by pulling the needle up through the rightmost corner stitch at the bottom of the left-hand piece.

2. Secure the yarn by inserting the needle back up through the same hole.

3. Now bring the needle up through the leftmost corner stitch at the bottom of the right-hand piece, and then up through the same hole in the left-hand piece. Pull taut. You've made a little figure eight, and the two corners of your fabric should be right up close together. Continue with the mattress stitch, below.

Mattress Stitch

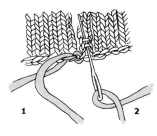

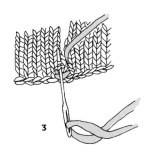

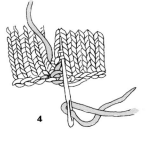

1 Take a close look at the side edge of a piece of stockinette fabric. If you carefully pull apart the edge stitch and the first real row of knit V stitches, you will see the running bars, something like a ladder of yarn. You'll be sewing the two sides together by stitching around these bars. Start by pinning your pieces together, right sides up, and tacking the yarn in place.

2 Pass the needle under the first two running bars of the right-hand piece of fabric, from the bottom to the top.

3 Now pass the needle under the first two running bars of the left-hand piece of fabric the same way.

4 Insert the needle down into the same point where it came out on the right-hand piece of fabric, and carry it under the next two running bars.

5 Insert the needle back into the same point where it came out on the left-hand piece of fabric, and come up two bars later. Repeat those last two steps until you have 2 or 3 inches done, then pull the yarn taut so that the seam becomes invisible.

Two Ways to Sew Tops of Pieces Together

FAKE GRAFTING

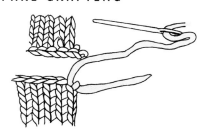

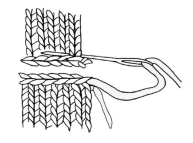

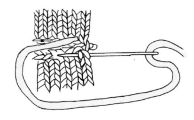

1 Tack a length of yarn to your work by bringing your needle up through the center of the right-most V on the bottom piece, just below the bound-off edge (leave a 6-inch tail). Now come back up through

the center of this V again (the yarn can go around the outside edge of the piece).

2 Bring your yarn down to the right of the bottom of the right-most V on the top piece, and back up to the left of that V.

3 Insert the needle back down into the center of the same V in the bottom piece of fabric where your yarn originated, and come up in the center of the next V to the left. Repeat across.

KITCHENER STITCH

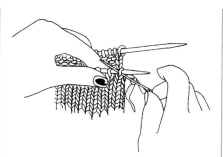

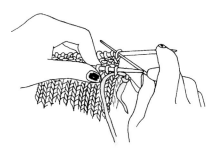

1 Slide the yarn needle through the first stitch on the front needle *as if to knit*. Pull the yarn through and drop that stitch off the needle.

2 Pass the yarn needle through the second stitch on the front needle as if to purl. Don't drop the stitch off the needle.

3 Pass the yarn needle through the first stitch on the back needle *as if to purl*. Drop the stitch off the needle.

Picking Up Stitches

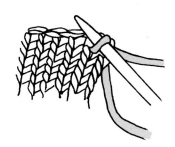

1 With the front of the piece facing you, insert your knitting needle through the center of a stitch.

2 Wrap your yarn around it.

3 Draw this new loop from the back of the fabric to the front.

Three-Needle Bind-off

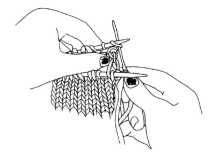

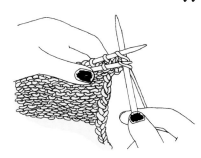

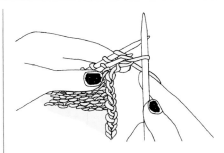

4 Pass the needle through the second stitch on the back needle *as if to knit.* Leave that stitch on the needle. Repeat steps 1–4 until all the stitches are grafted together.

1 With the right sides of your work facing each other, hold the two knitting needles in your left hand with their points facing to the right. Then, take a third needle and insert it, knitwise, through the first stitch on the front needle and knitwise through the first stitch on the back needle.

2 Knit the two stitches together. Do the same on the next stitch, then leapfrog the first stitch over this second one. Repeat to the end.

Fringe

1 Wrap yarn around a sturdy rectangular thing that's a bit longer than the length you want your fringe to be, then cut it at one end.

2 Grab a few strands and fold them in half. Stick a crochet hook *from back to front* through the space in your knitting where you want to add fringe. Hang your folded yarn over the hook and pull it through to the back of the fabric. With a crochet hook or with your fingers, pull the tails of the yarn through the loop.

3 Keep hanging fringe until your piece is all fringed up. Then trim the bottoms so they line up like little toy soldiers.

I-Cord

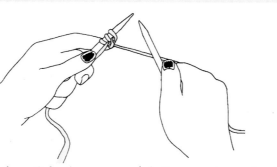

Start by casting three stitches (or as many as your knitting pattern tells you to) onto a double-pointed needle. Knit those stitches. Switch the needles in your hands without turning your work, and slide the stitches to the other side of the needle. With the yarn still hanging from the left, knit across using another double-pointed needle. Be sure to pull the yarn tight when you make your first stitch so that the fabric rolls in on itself.

Blanket Stitch

Tack the yarn at the left-hand edge of fabric. Insert the needle into the fabric about ½" to the right of this, and ½" above the edge. Hold the yarn tail down and slip the point of the needle over it. Pull through. Continue around the edge of your work.

Pom-Poms

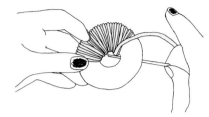 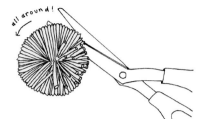 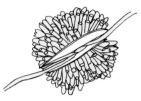

1 First, create a little pom-pom maker with two doughnut-shaped pieces of cardboard or plastic. The hole in the center should be about half the size of the circle itself. Then take your yarn, either threaded on a needle or with your fingers, and wind it around the two stacked doughnut shapes, until the center hole is filled with yarn.

2 Cut through the loops all the way around the outside of the dough-nut.

3 Pull a length of yarn up between the two halves of the pom-pom, wrap it tightly around the core of the pom-pom, and make a sturdy square knot to hold it together. Cut out the cardboard rings, fluff up your pom-pom, and trim it as necessary to even up the ends.

Duplicate Stitch

 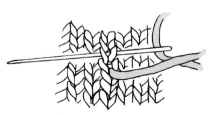 

1 Thread a length of yarn through a yarn needle, and come up from the back to the front of your work through the bottom point of one of your knit Vs. Pull the yarn up and through to the right, leaving a nice 6-inch tail at the back that you can work away later.

2 Now pass the needle under the bottom two legs of the stitch above the one you are duplicating, from *right to left*. Pull the yarn through, gently.

3 Insert the needle back down into the first hole you came up through. Come back up at the base of the next stitch you need to duplicate. Continue to do this with all the stitches you want to color in, pulling the yarn through so that the new stitch just sits on top of the original stitch.

Cables

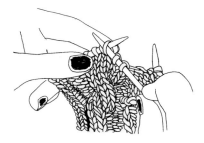

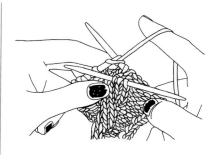

1 To make a cable, slip the required number of stitches purlwise onto a cable needle. For a front-crossed cable, let the cable needle with the stitches dangle to the front of your work. For a back-crossed cable, hang the stitches to the back of your work.

2 Knit the next stitch on the needle, pull the yarn tight, and knit the remaining number of required stitches.

3 Now knit the first stitch off the cable needle, pull the yarn tight, and knit the remaining stitches.

Fair Isle

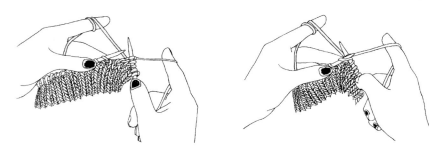

1 Take the main color of yarn in your right hand and hold it as you would for English knitting (see page 256). Take the other color in your left hand and hold it as you would for Continental knitting (see page 256).

2 As each color is needed, knit it with the hand that is holding that color yarn. Be careful not to pull the yarn too tightly. It is very important, when carrying yarn at the back of your work, that you leave enough

of it between stitches so that it lies flat but still allows the fabric to stretch.

Intarsia

TO ADD A SECOND COLOR OF YARN IN A ROW:

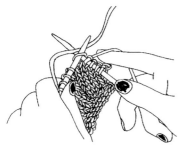 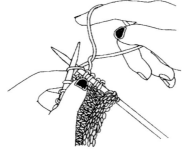

1 Slide your right needle into the first stitch as if to knit (or purl if that's what you're doing), but don't make the new stitch. Instead, lay the *new* color of yarn across the tip of the needle, leaving about a 6-inch tail hanging to the left and the ball end of the yarn to the right.

2 Bring the ball end of the yarn *around and underneath* the old color, then wrap it around the needle to make a knit (or purl) stitch. Finish the stitch in the usual way, dropping both the old loop and the tail of the new yarn over the newly formed stitch.

TO CHANGE FROM ONE COLOR TO THE NEXT IN A ROW:

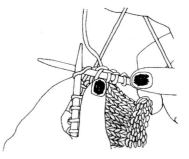

1 Bring the old color up and to the left, then bring the new color up *from under* the old color, and make the new stitch, linking the two stitches together.

Chain Stitch

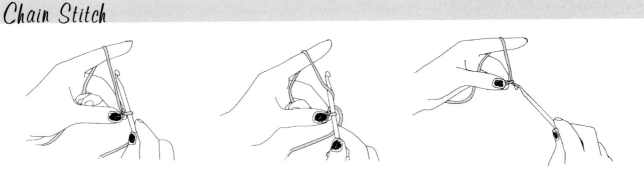

1 Make a slip knot about 6 inches from the end of your yarn and tighten it at the neck of the crochet hook. Hold the crochet hook in your right hand and the ball end of the yarn in your left.

2 With the hook facing up, wrap the yarn over the front of the needle clockwise, from right to left.

3 Twist the crochet hook so that the hook faces down and toward the knot, and pull the yarn through the loop.

4 Twist the hook so that the hook part is facing up again, wrap the yarn as in step 2, and pull another loop through.

Crab Stitch

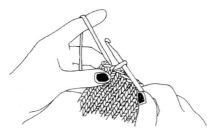
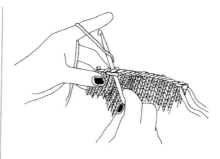
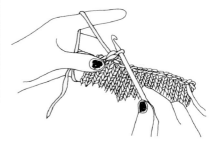

1 Insert a crochet hook into the edge of your knitting. Wrap the yarn around your hook clockwise, and pull a loop through.

2 Slide your crochet hook back into the fabric, in a space to the right of your last crab stitch. Wrap the ball end of the yarn clockwise around your crochet hook.

3 Pull the yarn through, so that you now have two loops on your crochet hook. Wrap your yarn one last time around the crochet hook, clockwise, then pull it through both loops.

Single Crochet (sc)

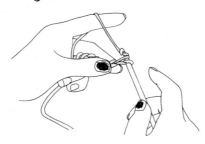
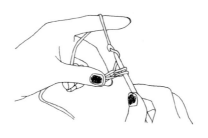

1 Slip your crochet hook through the second chain stitch from the hook, wrap the yarn around it clockwise, from right to left, and pull the loop through one loop. You now have two loops on your crochet hook.

2 Wrap the yarn around the crochet hook again, and this time pull it through *both* the loops on the hook.

Reminder:

Crocheting requires you to constantly pull loops of yarn through your previously formed loops. So you want to leave enough space in those loops to pass a crochet hook through. You might even try leaving them purposely loose until you get the hang of how small they can go and still allow your hook to fit.

Also, when you make a chain stitch or a single crochet, you are always working from right to left—like reading Hebrew. The crab stitch is the exception: It is made from left to right.

Resources

YARN STORE NATION
270

YARN SUPPLIERS
282

INDEX
283

KNITTING NOTES
290

Yarn Store Nation

A STITCH 'N BITCH GUIDE TO LOCAL YARN STORES

Arizona

MESA

Fiber Factory
150 West Main Street
Mesa, AZ 85201
480-969-4346
888-969-9276
www.fiberfactory.com
I always make a point to visit
the Fiber Factory when I'm in
town. The employees are very
helpful to beginners. They also
teach kids and offer a wealth
of classes in spinning, socks,
crochet, tatting and bobbin
lace, and dying and weaving.
Sandra Harper

SCOTTSDALE

Knitting in Scottsdale
7116 East Mercer Lane
Scottsdale, AZ 85254
480-951-9942
The owner, Roberta, carries
mostly natural fibers, including a number of good ole standards. She really takes time to
work with you on projects and
provides a fun atmosphere for
knitting. Every time I drop in,
I feel like I'm catching up with
an old friend.   *Onida Perkel*

California

LONG BEACH

Alamitos Bay Yarn Company
174 Marina Drive
Long Beach, CA 90803
562-799-8484
www.yarncompany.com
This store has a very helpful
staff, a beautiful selection,
and even a birthday club.
Tina Paredes

LOS ANGELES AREA

Jennifer Knits
108 Barrington Walk
Los Angeles, CA 90049
310-471-8733
www.jenniferknits.com
Jennifer is awesome. She creates custom designs and helps
everyone pick out the perfect
yarn for their project. Many
west side knitters consider this
small Brentwood haven their
home away from home.
Faith Landsman

Knit Cafe
8441 Melrose Avenue
Los Angeles, CA 90069
323-658-5648
www.knitcafe.com
If you're looking for a cute chick
with cat-eye glasses to teach
you to purl, Mary Heather's
your girl. They have inspiring

and original knit and crocheted
artwork throughout, including
Ellen Bloom's famous (and oft
stolen) crocheted Oreo cookies.
Faith Landsman

Stitch Cafe
12443 Magnolia Boulevard
Valley Village, CA 91607
818-980-1234
www.stitchcafe.com
Not content to have wonderful
staffers, serve yummy sand-
wiches, and offer comfy
couches, they sometimes
stay open until midnight.
Who could ask for more?
Faith Landsman

Stitches from the Heart
3306 West Pico Boulevard
Santa Monica, CA 90405
310-452-5151
www.stitchesfromtheheart.org
This shop has high-end and
lower-end yarn, classes, and a
cheerful volunteer staff. Pur-
chases are tax-deductible donations to the Stitches from the
Heart nonprofit organization,
which donates knitted and
crocheted items to premature
babies at hospitals.
Ellen Bloom

Suss Design
7350 Beverly Boulevard
Los Angeles, CA 90036
323-954-9637
www.sussdesign.com
Their selection is yummy and
still competitively priced, and
all the yarns are swatched
(which really gives you a taste
of what these yarns will do).
The finished articles around
the store are incredibly inspiring. Suss also has her own line
of easy and hip patterns.
Hilda Erb

Unwind
818 N. Hollywood Way
Burbank, CA 91505
818-840-0800
www.unwindyarn.com
This centrally located store has
luscious yarns that will make
any knitter drool. Plus, owner
Stephanie Steinhaus holds
Atwater Stitch 'n Bitch meetings at her store.
Karen Cahall

MONTEREY AREA

Monarch Knitting and Quilts
529 Central Avenue, Suite 3
Pacific Grove, CA 93950
888-575-YARN
www.monarchknitting.com
This place exemplifies why the
term "stuffed to the gills" was
invented. You can find sale

yarns in the back, and balls of remnants for 50 cents each, and they frequently have good bag deals. Monarch has a very friendly staff—and a huge white dog. *Gunilla Leavitt*

ORANGE COUNTY AREA
Micki's California Yarn Sales
9542 Hamilton Avenue
Huntington Beach, CA 92646
714-965-0018
This small tucked-away shop is owned by Micki, an amazing Japanese lady who is always helpful with knitting, crochet, and anything to do with yarn. She'll also help match yarns to your specifications and quickly order whatever you need.
Diana Camden

Strands and Stitches
1516 South Coast Highway
Laguna Beach, CA 92651
949-497-5648
Strands and Stitches is great, and, unlike another area store that pulled the first *Stitch 'n Bitch* book from the shelves because of "vulgar" language, they sell it and recommend it!
Melissa Sheppard

PARADISE
Knitwits
6433 Skyway
Paradise, CA 95969
530-877-YARN
My knitting group meets here weekly, and Devvy has been great at finding any yarn we request. *Heatherly Walker*

SAN FRANCISCO AREA
Artfibers
124 Sutter Street
San Francisco, CA 94104
415-956-6319
888-326-1112
www.artfibers.com
Hidden away on the second floor of a small building in San Francisco's financial district, Artfibers might seem to be an intimidating lair, but beginning knitters are most welcome. They sell only their own brand of yarn, which is created especially for them all over the world, and knitted samples hang by the shelves of lustrous yarns with informational cards describing the yarns in detail, from content to gauge to suggested quantities for various types of projects. The store has a circle of comfortable chairs, all sizes of needles, and, amazingly, balls of sample yarns so any interested buyer can knit a swatch for him- or herself before buying.
Karen Hudson

Article Pract
5010 Telegraph Avenue
Oakland, CA 94609
510-652-7435
This is the coolest, hippest, most happening yarn store in the East Bay. Everything about it inspires creativity and gets the juices flowing—from the always encouraging owner, Christina, to the yarns, which are luscious, vibrant, and begging to be fondled, to the supportive clientele, from whom I have received many a tip as well as hands-on help. The store itself, located in a bustling Oakland neighborhood, calls you in with the ever-changing window displays. If someone asked me where to go for knitting and crafty adventure and fun, I'd send them straight to Article Pract. *Lucretia Ausse*

ImagiKnit
3897 18th Street
San Francisco, CA 94114
415-621-6642
www.imagiknit.com
A cozy, well-stocked, and very inviting shop, ImagiKnit is the kind of place that you want to visit just because the atmosphere is so nice. One can get lost just handling the yarns, flipping through the books and patterns, or sitting in the back and working out the latest trouble spot with a friendly staff member. *Michael Cooper*

Knitting Arts
14554 Big Basin Way
Saratoga, CA 95070
408-867-5010
www.goknit.com
This shop's energetic and knowledgeable employees won't leave you high and dry. They carry most of the higher-end yarns, as well as Brown Sheep and Sirdar yarns for budget-minded knitters. Having a computerized inventory means they can tell you exactly how many balls in each color are in stock, and they also offer dozens of classes and free in-house patterns. *Mary Wisnewski*

Lacis
3163 Adeline Street
Berkeley, CA 94703
tel: 510-843-7178
fax: 510-843-5018
www.lacis.com
This shop is a lacemaker's dream. In their huge space, they carry supplies for making crocheted, tatted, and knitted lace, lace panels, and a wide variety of old and out-of-print books on all sorts of needlecrafts. They also have a large amount of vintage and antique lace for sale, as well as antique clothing on display. It's really more than a store—it's almost a museum. After five minutes in there I understood why my pen pal in Germany orders all of her supplies from Lacis.
Marizel Pelayo

Urban Knitting Studio
320 Fell Street
San Francisco, CA 94102
415-552-5333
www.urbanknitting.com
Urban Knitting Studio is airy and modern, with a lounge in the front next to large windows, so it's perfect for my two favorite activities: knitting and people-watching. They have a great selection and a friendly, helpful staff that doesn't watch

you like a hawk when you're using their skein winder in the back of the store. *Jen Tanner*

SAN JOSÉ AREA
The Golden Fleece
303 Potrero Street
Number 29-101
Santa Cruz, CA 95060
831-426-1425
www.thegoldenfleece.com
This beautiful store has wonderful yarns (some on the expensive side), a friendly, helpful staff, and a very nice classroom. Sale yarns (30 percent off) are out front in baskets.
Gunilla Leavitt

The Rug and Yarn Hut
350 East Campbell Avenue
Campbell, CA 95008
408-871-0411
www.rughut.com
This yarn store has comfy chairs to just sit and knit in. They offer classes and instruction and are right across the street from the San Jose Stitch 'n Bitch site. In the back is an inflatable kiddie pool full of sale yarns, and they're not kidding, either—"sale" here means 50 percent off!
Gunilla Leavitt

The Yarn Place
625 Capitola Avenue
Capitola, CA 95010
831-476-6480
www.theyarnplace.com
This is a smallish three-room store with a huge selection of

yarns; make sure you go over each room thoroughly at least twice. Their prices are reasonable (I've seen the same yarns in other places for more money) and there's a sale nook in the back room. *Gunilla Leavitt*

Colorado

BOULDER
Shuttles, Spindles, and Skeins
635 South Broadway, Unit E
Boulder, CO 80305
303-494-1071
800-283-4163
www.shuttlesspindlesand
    skeins.com
They have a terrific selection of classic and trendy yarns, patterns, and other essentials for knitting, weaving, and spinning. Their classes are known throughout the area. One of the owners has a bearded collie who is as much a fixture in the store as the yarn is!
Karen Scappini

COLORADO SPRINGS
Green Valley Weavers & Knitters Supply
2115 West Colorado Avenue
Colorado Springs, CO 80904
719-448-9963
800-457-8559
This store is absolutely fabulous! It's not big, but very cozy. The class schedule is excellent, and the owners are kind and down-to-earth. They even have a shop dog and shop-dog-in-training. *Melanie Wallace*

DENVER AREA
A Knitted Peace
5654-C South Prince Street
Littleton, CO 80120
303-730-0366
www.aknittedpeace.com
You'll find plenty of Brown Sheep, Rowan, Interlacements, Mission Falls, and Noro yarns, alongside books, kits, and needles. Owner Peggy Anderson has been known to set up one-of-a-kind private classes for small groups. Although this store is not as fully stocked as some of the other well-known Colorado shops, they more than make up for it in ambiance and friendliness. *Amanda Berka*

Lambspun of Colorado
1101 East Lincoln Avenue
Fort Collins, CO 80524
970-484-1998
800-558-5262
www.lambspun.com
Family owned for more than a decade, this is a shop with a very sweet staff. They have classes, selection, and prices. They're the leading source for fine fiber arts and are committed to finding the best yarns nature has to offer in to-die-for colors. *Amber Bell*

La Ti Da
1551 South Pearl Street
Denver, CO 80210
303-715-1414
www.latidadenver.com
La Ti Da is the best yarn store in Denver! Rita and Zack are

always generous with tips and suggestions. Their Pajama midnight sale is an event not to be missed. The store has a coffee shop complete with treats from a local bakery, a gift shop, and a live music series in the spring and summer months.
Amber Bell

LAKEWOOD
The Recycled Lamb
2010 Youngfield Street
Lakewood, CO 80215
303-234-9337
www.recycledlamb.com
The staff couldn't be friendlier or more helpful, and they offer great classes in knitting, crocheting, spinning, and weaving. Their outstanding newsletter celebrates the joy of knitting in light of holidays and seasonal weather changes.
Danielle Fay

Connecticut

DEEP RIVER
Yarns Down Under
37C Hillside Terrace
Deep River, CT 06417
860-526-9986
www.yarnsdownunder.com
This peaceful and welcoming shop is on a golf course near a pond. They recently put in an addition that is now chock-full of yarn. The combination of helpful owners, atmosphere, and surroundings make it a nice place to spend a few hours. *Suzanne Barnes*

TORRINGTON
Hither and Yarn
835 New Harwinton Road
Torrington, CT 06790
860-489-9276
Hither and Yarn's owner is a prolific designer and a very sweet woman. She stocks a bounty of rare treasures, including unusual choices from Europe and hand-painted yarns produced by local farmers. You can even pick up fabric for lining your latest knitted handbag. When you're here, be sure to say hi to Phoebe, the poodle, who is always dressed to the nines.
Rebecca Lovelace

District of Columbia

WASHINGTON AREA
Knit and Stitch = Bliss
4706 Bethesda Avenue
Bethesda, MD 20814
301-652-7194
866-5NEEDLE
www.knitandstitch.com
Just when you think you'll never fall in love with another yarn, you discover ten more at this store! This place has the widest variety of yarns in the area and stocks everything from the finest hand-dyed fibers from New Adirondack to those irresistible novelty scarf yarns. The staff is new-and-improved and they all know and love the craft of knitting. *Ricki Seidman*

Springwater Fiber Workshop
808 North Fairfax Street
Alexandria, VA 22314
703-549-3634
www.springwaterfiber.org
Springwater Fiber has a wide range of yarns, from exotic handspun and dyed yarns to easy-care, less expensive yarns (perfect for knitting baby clothes that can be worn for more than just a studio picture). They carry a lot of knitting notions and offer a very wide range of fiber art classes.
Tina Hsu

Stitch DC
731 8th Street SE
Washington, DC 20003
202-544-8900
www.stitchdc.com
The shop just opened this summer and is shaping up to be pretty great. There's a good selection of yarn and more arriving every day. The owner, Marie Connolly, is super nice and friendly, very helpful, and loves to let you browse. She has an outdoor courtyard in the middle of the shop, with a few tables and chairs for people to sit and knit with friends, as well as a couch and couple of chairs inside for those muggy D.C. summer days. She also has a back room with a large table for classes. She's happy to host Stitch 'n Bitch groups and is also happy to let random knitters hang out and knit away.
Anna Pohl

Woolwinders
404 King Farm Boulevard
Rockville, MD 20850
240-632-YARN
www.woolwinders.com
I go to the suburbs only for necessities, and Woolwinders is tops on my list of must visits. You can find what you need for projects at any price or skill level, and their excellent return policy allows you to buy that one skein extra so you won't have to finish with the wrong dye lot. *Ricki Seidman*

Yarns International
5110 Ridgefield Road
Suite 200
Bethesda, MD 20816
301-913-2980
www.yarnsinternational.com
With high-quality natural fibers at the right price and an inspirational staff, you'll probably find exactly what you're looking for at Yarns International. It's a paradise for Fair Isle knitters; they've even developed their own line of yarn.
Ricki Seidman

Georgia

ATLANTA
Neases Needlework
345 West Ponce de Leon Avenue
Decatur, GA 30030
404-377-6875
www.neasesneedlework.com
The woman who owns and runs Neases will sit down and help anyone with his or her knitting needs, and she carries a great selection of yarn including Manos del Uruguay (my favorite), which is made by a collective of women abroad. Neases also holds silent auctions to raise money for charity.
Mahsa Yazdy

Illinois

CHICAGO AREA
Arcadia Knitting
1211 Balmoral
Chicago, IL 60640
773-293-1211
www.arcadiaknitting.com
Two stylin' sisters take the fear out of knitting in their North Chicago store. Featuring shelves full of yarn in glorious textures and colors, this small store has every kind of yarn you never knew you wanted—and best of all, it's organized by color! The always welcoming Arcadia gals are ready to help you check your gauge, figure out the Greek that is your pattern, or just let you sit on one of the front sofas and knit. Their classes offer something for every level of knitter, and their passion for passing on the knitting bug abounds. *Sarah Stray*

CloseKnit, Inc.
622 Grove Street
Evanston, IL 60201
847-328-6760
A cozy yarn shop near the campus of Northwestern University, CloseKnit offers

an assortment of designer yarns, lots of patterns, buttons, and handmade gifts.

Claire Buenaflor

Have Ewe Any Wool
120 North York Road, Suite 220
Elmhurst, IL 60126
630-941-YARN
www.haveeweanywool.com
This shop's staff is helpful without being pushy, and classes are wonderfully instructive and full of interesting people. The yarn is of the highest quality, some with prices to match. Saturday mornings can be hectic, with several classes going on at the same time, but Peggy keeps things fun by serenading everyone with tunes on her Barbie karaoke machine.

Kerri Skrudland

Knitters Niche
3206 North Southport Avenue
Chicago, IL 60657
773-472-9276
Lots of people are afraid of this yarn shop, but I think it's the best one in Chicago. The owner, MaryAnn, is kind of gruff and doesn't like dealing with people who want her to cast on for them, but she has a heart of gold. Her classes are awesome, and they're much cheaper and longer than others in the city.

Lena Parsons

Knitting Etc., Inc.
9980 West 151st Street
Orland Park, IL 60462
708-349-7941
This store, converted from a big, old home, is my favorite in the area. The ladies who work here are extremely knowledgeable and helped me go from fledgling knitter to designer. And unlike some craft stores, the yarn here is displayed neatly according to yarn type and color in the front room.

Kim Fermoyle

Knitting Workshop
2218 North Lincoln Avenue
Chicago, IL 60614
773-929-5776
www.knittingworkshop.com
Knitting Workshop carries lots of designer yarns as well as good old standards. This shop has more books than other city shops and displays projects that inspire you to knit. Shop owner Mary offers classes as well as a weekly knit night.

Michele Cullom

Mosaic Yarn Studio, Ltd.
1585 Ellinwood Street #101
Des Plaines, IL 60016
847-390-1013
www.mosaicyarnstudio.com
Mosaic Yarn Studio carries many designer yarns, books, and a full supply of knitting needles and notions. The staff is extremely helpful, and the store is roomy, so you don't

feel crowded while browsing. They also offer classes and a frequent buyer card.

Claire Buenaflor

Pearl Art & Craft Supplies
225 West Chicago Avenue
Chicago, IL 60610
312-915-0200
Pearl sells some knitting supplies, such as needles and yarns from Lion Brand. They don't have much of a selection, but their prices are great!

Cindy Iglesias

We'll Keep You in Stitches
67 East Oak Street, 4th Floor
Chicago, IL 60611
312-642-2540
This shop, located just off of the Magnificent Mile, stocks an assortment of designer yarns and some knitting needles and accessories in a small space. The staff is knowledgeable and helpful. It's a nice change of pace if you feel the yarn yen while shopping in downtown Chicago.

Claire Buenaflor

Indiana

BOONVILLE
The Village Knitter
8A West Jennings
Newburgh, IN 47630
812-842-2360
www.thevillageknitter.com
Docia, the owner, is very knowledgeable, is always willing to help, will order anything

she can get from suppliers, and will even carry lines that you suggest.

Chris Behme

Iowa

MUSCATINE
Crazy Girl Yarn Shop
208 West 2nd Street
Muscatine, IA 52761
563-263-YARN
www.crazygirlyarnshop.com
This oasis for knitters from eastern Iowa and western Illinois is set in the corner of a refurbished button factory overlooking the Mississippi. With unique displays (bamboo knitting needles stuck into a vat of popcorn kernels), the shop sells well-known yarns, including Brown Sheep and Mission Falls, as well as locally produced yarns. The Crazy Girls hand-dye yarn, hold regular Knit and Whine nights, and have a growing button line.

Ann Rushton

Kansas

LAWRENCE
Yarn Barn
930 Massachusetts
Lawrence, KS 66044
785-842-4333
www.yarnbarn-ks.com
Yarn Barn has a great selection, and the staff are quick to adopt new things. They also stock weaving yarns, fleece, looms, and spinning wheels. I am

glad it's such a ways away from me, or I'd be spending more money there than I already do. *Roberta Bragg*

Maryland

BALTIMORE
A Good Yarn
1738 Aliceanna Street
Baltimore, MD 21231
410-327-3884
www.agoodyarn.com
A Good Yarn is located on a tree-lined street in the historic Fell's Point neighborhood and has become a warm and welcoming meeting point for the local knitting community. The store carries mostly natural fibers, including some hand-spun yarns. Owner Lorraine Gaudet invites you to come in to drink a cup of tea, chat a while, and get inspired!
Beth Demko

FUNKSTOWN
Y2Knit
100 East Baltimore Street
Funkstown, MD 21734
301-766-4543
www.y2knit.net
Located in a building that's more than two hundred years old, in the lovely village of Funkstown, Y2Knit has character to spare. The staffers at Y2Knit are friendly and helpful, and the yarn is carefully laid out in colorful displays.
Emma K. Williams

Massachusetts

BOSTON AREA
A Good Yarn
4 Station Street
Brookline, MA 02445
617-731-4900
www.agoodyarn.biz
A colorful shop with reasonably priced yarns and a welcoming feel. The owner, Beverly, really takes the time to help you with projects and has a big table where people are always working on things. *Amy Corveleyn*

Black Sheep Knitting Co.
1500 Highland Avenue
Needham, MA 02492
781-444-0694
The Black Sheep Knitting Co. is an unpretentious, bright, and very well organized store with a fabulous selection of yarns. The staff is always helpful without being pushy. It has a very friendly and relaxing atmosphere, complete with classical music and M&Ms.
Hannah Loughlin

Circles: A Knitting Salon
555 Amory Street
Jamaica Plain, MA 02130
617-524-5500
www.circles-salon.com
Circles's knowledgeable and kind owner Allison will help you with any problem and has an uncanny knack for locating patterns based on almost no description. She selects her spectacular yarns

with supporting artists and sustainability in mind. The store has a knitting room and a children's playroom.
Karen Noyes

The Knitting Room
2 Lake Street
Arlington, MA 02474
781-483-3442
www.knitroomboston.com
The very helpful staff of the Knitting Room is always willing to take time out to answer your questions. They offer a wide selection of yarns and a great variety of courses on knitting and crocheting. *Crystal Smith*

Mind's Eye Yarns
22 White Street
Cambridge, MA 02140
617-354-7253
www.mindseyeyarns.com
The owner, Lucy, carries mostly natural-fiber yarns. She even stocks some of her own hand-spun yarns, and she spins in the store. The atmosphere is cozy, and even though the shop is small, it never feels overcrowded. Lucy's a good teacher and a fabulous enabler!
Dyana Fine

Putting on the Knitz
1282 Washington Street
West Newton, MA 02465
617-969-8070
Although there are no official classes here, newbies and experienced knitters alike are welcome to—and do!—stop by at

any time and get help with their projects free of charge. The store's friendly owners stock a wide variety of imported and domestic yarns and patterns and more than twenty major brands for one-stop stash enrichment at its best.
Beth Demko

Wild & Woolly Studio
7A Meriam Street
Lexington, MA 02420
781-861-7717
I like this suburban store because it is a good size with a correspondingly large selection of yarns. I also like the selection of books, which seems larger than what most other stores offer. *Martha Spizziri*

Windsor Button
35 Temple Place
Boston, MA 02111
617-482-4969
www.windsorbutton.com
Charming in a quirky, anti-yuppie way, Windsor Button has an interesting vibe, and it's located right off the Common in a forgotten block near wig shops and an antique bookseller. It's an old button and sewing shop that has expanded its yarn selection by leaps and bounds. *Aimee Dawson*

Woolcott and Company
61 JFK Street
Cambridge, MA 02138
617-547-2837
www.woolcottandco.com

Next door to the Redline Bar (where a Stitch 'n Bitch is held weekly), Woolcott and Company focuses on natural fibers but also carries some novelty yarns. The people who work there are obsessive about knitting, and the wool overflows from the shelves. Knitters like to stop by and show off what they've made.

Jessica Marcus

LENOX
Colorful Stitches
48 Main Street
Lenox, MA 01240
413-637-8206
www.colorful-stitches.com
This store is well worth a visit if you're in western Massachusetts. They have two floors full of mostly high-end yarns, patterns, and notions, and a sitting area where you can look at patterns or knit. You can also shop on-line.

Martha Spizziri

Minnesota

TWIN CITIES
Borealis Yarns
1340 Thomas Avenue
St. Paul, MN 55104
651-646-2488
www.borealisyarns.com
The Twin Cities' newest yarn store has a great mixture of the fancy and the classic. There's a big table up in front by the windows where knitters are always

welcome to sit and chat or ask questions. The store hosts a weekly community and charity knitting group in addition to its weekly knit night.   *Chris Silker*

Crafty Planet
2318 Lowry Avenue NE
Minneapolis, MN 55418
612-788-1180
www.craftyplanet.com
Crafty Planet is the place for the renegade crafter, with ever expanding hours and selection and unique classes. They are always on the lookout for new knitting, crocheting, sewing, and needlework supplies, so bring suggestions. Don't miss CCCP (Craft 'n Chat @ Crafty Planet), and look for owners Matt and Trish's vintage Vespas outside.   *Meghan McInerny*

Depth of Field Yarn
405 Cedar Avenue
Minneapolis, MN 55454
612-340-0529 x3
www.depthoffieldyarn.com
You can't go wrong with this store; it has classes in the basement, an amazing array of yarns on the main floor, and a great sale loft. There is so much yarn, it's astounding!

Chris Silker

Needlework Unlimited
4420 Drew Avenue South
Minneapolis, MN 55410
612-925-2454
888-925-2454
www.needleworkunlimited.com

Needlework Unlimited recently became more working-girl friendly with the addition of later weeknight hours. They offer a variety of classes, books, and patterns, and the staff has rescued me from disaster on more than one occasion with patience and good humor. Their monthly Karen's Knit Knite is a fun way to socialize and compare projects with knitters of all levels.

Meghan McInerny

Missouri

ROLLA
Uniquely Yours
404 East Highway 72
Rolla, MO 65401
573-364-2070
www.rollanet.org/~uniquely
Uniquely Yours is a fiber and quilt shop that carries crafting supplies and yarn and also offers classes. They offer a nice range of mid-priced yarns in a fabulous selection of colors and weights. Other perks are the monthly potluck and the cozy back room for classes and gatherings.

Catherine Popalisky

ST. LOUIS AREA
Weaving Department
The Historic Myers House
180 West Dunn Road
Florissant, MO 63031
314-921-7800
Located on the second floor of a historic building (above a

quilting store), this shop is set up in several yarn-filled rooms. Owner Nancy Quade offers classes in knitting, weaving, spinning, and machine knitting. This fantastic find draws customers from other states.

Sharron Miller

New Jersey

PRINCETON
Glenmarle Woolworks
301 North Harrison Street
Princeton, NJ 08559
609-921-3022
www.glenmarlewoolworks.com
The entire Rowan line, Koigu, and Manos del Uruguay are only part of the yummy natural-fiber feast available at Glenmarle. A separate section of the store is devoted to novelty yarns, another to felting. Hand-sewn and hand-blown glass buttons and hand-painted needles round out the selection at this upscale shop.   *Beth Demko*

New York

IRVINGTON
Flying Fingers Yarn Shop
19 Main Street
Irvington, NY 10533
914-591-4113
www.flyingfingersyarnshop.com
Elise, the friendly owner, offers innovative classes—"Beyond Scarves," for instance—to calm first-sweater fears and a seasonal introductory course for

college students on winter break. "Fine and unusual yarns from unique sources" is more than just a motto—Elise will honor special orders to far-away lands such as Australia.
Jane Murray-Stringer

NEW YORK CITY
Brooklyn General
135 Union Street
Brooklyn, NY 11231
718-855-8885
I'm really lucky that Brooklyn has so many cool stores, like the fairly new Brooklyn General. It's a very cute store with a small selection of high-quality, interesting stuff, and the staff gives lessons. *Dalton Rooney*

Downtown Yarns
45 Avenue A
New York, NY 10009
212-995-5991
This shop is like a little piece of western Massachusetts snuggled up in the East Village. They don't have a compost heap out back, but they do have a terrific selection of yarns in different price ranges and an adorable dog who will wag his tail for free. *Susanna Goldfinger*

Knit-A-Way
398 Atlantic Avenue
Brooklyn, NY 11217
718-797-3305
This place rocks! It's one of the many reasons to go to Brooklyn. They have both high-

and low-end yarns—and good karma. *Kathleen Woodberry*

Knit New York
307 East 14th Street
New York, NY 10003
212-387-0707
www.knitnewyork.com
When I first started knitting, Jill at Knit New York set me straight with advice on yarn, needles, reading patterns, and general techniques. The store has very snazzy yarns and delicious teas, too. It might be a bit pricey, but I like supporting independents, and everyone is so darn nice there. Plus they're open later than most stores in the city. *Lynn Andriani*

P&S Fabrics
355 Broadway
New York, NY 10013
212-226-1534
www.psfabrics.com
Not just a knitting store, but a cheap-yarn bonanza. Lots of Lion Brand (some of the best prices around), Red Heart, and other brands. They also stock Patons booklets, books, needles, and supplies.
Olugbemisola Amusashonubi-Perkovich

Purl
137 Sullivan Street
New York, NY 10012
212-420-8796
www.purlsoho.com
The walls are painted a soothing mint green and the floor-

to-ceiling shelves hold a rainbow assortment of mostly luxury yarns. Purl's SoHo location makes it the prime destination for crafty fashionistas, and the women who work there are hip and friendly. *Susanna Goldfinger*

School Products Co., Inc.
1201 Broadway
New York, NY 10001
212-679-3516
www.schoolproducts.com
If you're from out of town, this should be the first yarn store you visit in NYC. In addition to some of the usual suspects, you'll find cheap cones of mohair, angora, cashmere, and other specialty yarns left over from designer knitwear factories. Only in New York, kids, only in New York.
DS

Seaport Yarn
135 William Street,
near Fulton, 5th floor
New York, NY 10038
212-608-3100
www.seaportyarn.com
It might not look like much from the outside, but once inside the store, you won't be disappointed. There are several rooms of yarn, everything from Artful Yarns to Adrienne Vittadini, and the prices are the lowest in the city.
Elaine Hamilton

The Yarn Company
2274 Broadway, 2nd floor
New York, NY 10024
212-787-7878
888-YARNCO1
www.theyarnco.com
The Yarn Company carries a wide selection of imported and hand-dyed yarns and a large variety of patterns. The staff are very helpful and welcome you to come in, take a seat, and knit, knit, knit.
Kathleen Woodberry

Unique Knitkraft
257 West 39th Street
New York, NY 10018
212-840-6950
www.uniqueknitkraft.com
Unique Knitkraft carries lots of European and Asian yarns and some Patons at great prices. You'll be able to pick up a nice surprise every time you visit.
Olugbemisola Amusashonubi-Perkovich

PELHAM
Wool Works
214 Fifth Avenue
Pelham, NY 10803
914-738-0104
Situated in the center of Pelham, Wool Works has a small but very nice selection of yarn, groovy patterns, a mellow vibe, and two cordial owners. They gave me a free tape measure, which makes me a fan for life!
Neela Banerjee

North Carolina

HILLSBOROUGH

Wal-Mart Supercenter
501 Hampton Pointe
Boulevard
Hillsborough, NC 27278
919-732-9172
I have been to plenty of knitting boutiques and online stores, as well as many Wal-Marts, but Store #1191 is a standout! They have an awesome stock of Red Heart, Caron, and Bernat, and a selection of eyelash and boa yarns. If you are in the area, be sure to stop by and stock up.
Samantha List

Ohio

COLUMBUS

Wolfe Fiber Arts
1188 West 5th Avenue
Columbus, OH 43212
614-487-9980
www.wolfefiberarts.com
Wolfe Fiber Arts is a cool store with an independent spirit. They offer plenty of unusual classes, including courses in dying, spinning, and Japanese braiding. Best of all, they have a trunk that's full of chocolate—perfect for convincing spouses and children to be patient while you browse! *Rebecca Pavia*

WOODMERE

The Knitting Room
28450 Chagrin Boulevard
Woodmere, OH 44122
216-464-8450

The selection here is fabulous; you can find delicious yarn at any price, the women are wonderful and helpful, and the samples on display make you want to knit. *Marne Loveman*

Oregon

EUGENE

dyelots!
676 Polk Street
Eugene, OR 97402
541-485-1880
This downtown cottage is chock-full of hand-painted yarns (some from local shepherdesses), loose fiber for spinning and felting, soy silk yarns, and hand-painted alpaca yarn. It's a riot of color in yarn, fiber, and accessories for knitters, spinners, weavers, felters, and surface design junkies. There's even a dye kitchen on site for those who are daring enough to color their own.
Janis Thompson

PORTLAND

Yarn Garden
1413 SE Hawthorne Boulevard
Portland, OR 97214
503-239-7950
www.yarngarden.net
My favorite of Portland's many yarn emporiums is the comfy and often charmingly jumbled Yarn Garden. The wacky chicks and fellas who work there are hilarious, helpful, and willing to correct your mistakes so that you can get your WIP under

control. Despite the siren song of some of the newer boutiquey yarn shops, this place keeps me coming back. *Amanda Valley*

Pennsylvania

PHILADELPHIA

Sophie's Yarns
918 Pine Street
Philadelphia, PA 19107
215-925-KNIT
www.sophiesyarns.com
Sophie's Yarns recently moved to a sunny, roomy shop with gorgeous yarns and books, all beautifully displayed. They host regular classes and knitting circles. I always feel welcome, even if I'm just browsing.
Kitty Schmidt

Rhode Island

MIDDLETOWN

Knitting Traditions and More
1077 Aquidneck Avenue
Middletown, RI 02842
401-847-2373
Recently redesigned, with a big sign boasting "the largest scarf bar in New England," this yarn and bead shop is owned by a handful of women who really love to knit. They encourage you to come in and touch everything. *Rubi McGrory*

PROVIDENCE

Bella Yarns
508 Main Street
Warren, RI 02885
401-247-7243

What Bella Yarns lacks in size, it makes up for in character. Owner Kim Conterio will order whatever you desire, be it felting, eyelash, or a rare sweater yarn. *Dana Eltringham*

WICKFORD

And the Beadz Go On
1 West Main Stret
Wickford, RI 02852
401-268-3899
Set in an older storefront on the main street of a charming old port town, this store is expensive but on the cutting edge of yarn trends.
Lindsay Woodel

Texas

AUSTIN

Hill Country Weavers
1701 South Congress
Austin, TX 78704
512-707-7396
www.hillcountryweavers.com
Don't let the country-folk-sounding name scare you off. This is actually a fairly hip little cottage with a decent variety of yarns. I'm from L.A., where there tends to be a little bit of knitting snobbery in some of the shops. You won't find that here! *Vickie Howell*

DALLAS AREA

The Woolie Ewe
1301 Custer Road #328
Plano, TX 75075
972-424-3163
800-460-YARN

www.woolieewe.com
This inviting store is owned and run by a sweet and helpful mother-daughter team. They stock mostly high-end yarns, but offer a little something for every price range. There are always people knitting away at a table with one of the owners helping them out. It's like a slice of heaven in there!
Adelle Locatelli

HOUSTON
Yarns 2 Ewe, Inc.
603 West 19th Street
Houston, TX 77008
713-880-KNIT
This store is a great asset to the Houston knitting scene. Owner Wendy Moses learns every customer's name immediately. She has a great selection of yarns, several class offerings, and even throws a pizza-and-knitting party every Friday night. The shop has a little living room area where you can always find several knitters enjoying one another's company.
Sharron Miller

Vermont

BURLINGTON
Kaleidoscope Yarns
15 Pearl Street
Essex Junction, VT 05452
802-288-9200
www.kaleidoscopeyarns.com
www.kyarns.com
Just outside Burlington, this store is an embarrassment of

riches. Beautiful custom yarns and a huge selection of knitting supplies make this a favorite in the area.
Rebecca Schiff

Virginia

ALEXANDRIA
Knit Happens
127A North Washington Street
Alexandria, VA 22314
703-836-0039
Knit Happens is a lovely pink store with huge armchairs, lots of fun novelty yarns, and an excellent selection of mainstream yarns. Liz and Kristine are really helpful—they even got down on their hands and knees to help me find the pattern I was looking for.
Amelia Jones

RICHMOND AREA
Got Yarn
13211 Midlothian Turnpike
Midlothian, VA 23113
804-594-0323
www.gotyarn.com
Got Yarn has a full supply of novelty and sock yarns. The staff is attentive without being overbearing. It's close to three different interstates, making it easily accessible.
Evelyn Rowe

Washington

BAINBRIDGE ISLAND
Churchmouse Yarns & Teas
118 Madrone Lane
Bainbridge Island, WA 98110
206-780-2686

www.churchmouseyarns.com
Churchmouse, located a ferry ride away from Seattle, is a delightful find! It's adorable and a knitter's dream. They offer a beautiful selection of fiber, a charming staff, and tea.
Jill Woolcock

KENT
Pastimes Yarn & Sitting Room
321 West Smith Street
Kent, WA 98032
877-520-YARN
253-520-YARN
www.pastimesyarn.com
Beautiful fiber is everywhere you look at Pastimes: displayed in gorgeous wooden cabinets, stacked up along the walls, or hanging just so. The shop is bright and welcoming, and the staffers are all excellent knitters. It's worth the drive south of the city.
Jill Woolcock

SEATTLE
Acorn Street Shop
2818 NE 55th Street
Seattle, WA. 98105
206-525-1726
www.acornstreet.com
Acorn Street Shop is one of those little treasures that lure lifelong knitters time and again through the front door into a welcoming librarylike maze of floor-to-ceiling shelves jammed with rich and vibrant yarns. Textured swatches and handmade garments sporting a mix of domestic and international yarns and an entire wall of

pattern books and magazines complete a cozy and inviting atmosphere that will delight both the novice and seasoned knitter. This shop is not to be missed!
Sharon Holt Gann

Hilltop Yarn and Needlepoint
2224 Queen Anne Avenue North
Seattle, WA 98109
206-282-1332
www.hilltopyarn.com
Beautiful yarn, personal service, and expert instruction and advice can be found in this warm, elegantly restored Craftsman-style home in the Queen Anne shopping district.
Jennifer Hill

Wisconsin

DELAVAN
Needles 'n Pins Yarn Shoppe
W9034 County Road A
Delavan, WI 53115
608-883-9922
www.needlesnpinsyarnshoppe.com
Needles 'n Pins is the largest knitter's and crocheter's shop in the area, with a lot of high-quality yarns, books, patterns, and needles. It's well organized, bright, and spacious. Funny and always willing to help, owner Doreen makes you feel right at home.
Cinda Collins

EAU CLAIRE

Yellow Dog Knitting

420 South Barstow Street

Eau Claire, WI 54701

715-839-7272

www.yellowdogknitting.com

This is a great little knitting shop with a huge selection of interesting yarns of all sorts. Another perk is the friendly staffers who will gladly help you out. If stopping in small towns to hunt for yarn while road tripping through the Midwest is your thing, this is one place not to miss.

Jessica Brooke Rodenwald

AUSTRALIA

Victoria

MELBOURNE AREA

AK Traditions

524 Malvern Road

Prahan VIC 3181

03-9533-7576

www.aktraditions.com

AK supports a community in Kirgizstan who make felt and felted products for the store (not slave-labor style), have their own doll designs that you can get kits and patterns to knit clothes for, and also stock Rowan, Jo Sharp, and a few knitting accessories.

Sharon Steer-Courtenay

Craftee Cottage

Shop 40-41

Oakleigh Central Shopping Centre

Portman Street

Oakleigh VIC 3166

03-9567-0311

www.crafteecottage.com.au

Craftee Cottage carries a wide range of (Australian) Patons yarns, along with Cleckheaton, Heirloom, JJ's hand-dyed mohair, Panda yarns, Shepherd, Sirdar, and Wendy, plus patterns. They also do mail orders.

Lynne Shandley

Knit 'n Purl

179 Lonsdale Street

Dandenong VIC 3175

03-9793-3530

Knit 'n Purl has the best range of eight-ply (DK or worsted weight) yarns that I have ever seen. They also carry a range of Anny Blatt yarns and Italian novelty yarns. *Lynne Shandley*

Mansfield Craft Den

21 High Street

Mansfield VIC 3724

03-5775-2044

www.craftden.com.au

Gina carries a range of Naturally NZ wools, plus Heirloom and Noro, Opal sock yarns, Cleckheaton and Paton's wools, alpaca blends, and a few U.S. imports. It's always worth popping in.

Lynne Shandley

Marta's Yarns

33 Waverley Road

East Malvern VIC 3145

03-9572-0319

www.martasyarns.com

Marta's Yarns is just gobsmacking. Marta hand dyes her rainbow of mohair and wool yarns. There are walls full of beautiful colors, including a wide range of mostly novelty yarns, including yarns from On Line. This is glitzy knitting in spades!

Lynne Shandley

Sunspun

185 Canterbury Road

Canterbury VIC 3126

03-9830-1609

www.sunspun.com.au

Sunspun is an "olde worlde-style" shop stuffed to the brim with yummy European yarns and inspirational contemporary and traditional samples. I got addicted to Rowan yarns here, but they run a discount program and are happy to hold yarns if you are on a budget.

Sharon Steer-Courtenay

Wool Baa

124 Bridport Street

Albert Park VIC 3206

03-9690-6633

www.woolbaa.com.au

Owner Leonie has used her keen eye and attention to detail to create a light and bright shop with carefully displayed pattern books along the wall, pattern leaflets arranged in plastic sleeves in categorized folders, and interesting buttons in natty little jars.   *Trish Blackman*

Wool Village

Brandon Park Shopping Centre

Springvale Road

Mulgrave VIC 3170

03-9560-5869

The Wool Village's amazing range of new and old yarns attests to their many years in business. Most of the yarns are packed in boxes and bags, and it is preferred that you don't paw them before taking them to the counter. *Lynne Shandley*

Queensland

Threads and More

141 Boundary Road

Bardon QLD 4065

www.threadsandmore.com.au

Sue and her team carry a range of totally droolsome European and American yarns like Debbie Bliss, Jo Sharp, Noro, On Line, Touch, and Trendsetter. They also have an on-site cafe and run regular classes.

Lynne Shandley

CANADA
Alberta

EDMONTON
Knit & Purl
10412 124th Street
Edmonton, Alberta T5N 1R5
780-482-2150
Knit & Purl carries a wide variety of domestic and international yarns in all price ranges and has great novelty yarns. The staff will help you customize your garment so that it is a "one-of-a-kind" piece. Or if a pattern doesn't fit, they will adjust it for your body type.
Penny Erickson

Manitoba

WINNIPEG
Camille's Elegant Yarn
935 Nairn Avenue
Winnipeg, Manitoba R3T 5A1
204-667-6265

Camille carries an assortment of yarns that ranges from utilitarian to exotic, and her prices are often lower than other stores'. She also carries an excellent array of buttons and closures as well as patterns (commercial and her own creations).
Leslie Hancock

Ontario

OTTAWA
Yarn Forward and Sew On
581 Bank Street
Glebe, Ottawa
Ontario K1S 3T4
613-237-8008
www.yarnforward.com
Yarn Forward has a good selection of kits and needles and different kinds of yarn from the exotic to the everyday. They offer lots of great advice for a seminovice like me, like telling me to use smaller-size needles for socks when I would have bought the size listed on the yarn label.
Jennifer Amey

TORONTO
Lettuce Knit
66½ Nassau Street
Kensington Market
Toronto, Ontario M5T 1M5
416-203-9970
www.lettuceknit.com
Located in vibrant Kensington Market, Lettuce Knit's shelves burst with hand-picked yarn. The shop is home to weekly Stitch 'n Bitch meetings and at least one Church of Craft craft-on. Owner Meagan is helpful with those pesky knitting questions and offers great workshops and one-on-one lessons. She even served champagne and cupcakes on Valentine's Day!
Carla Agnesi

UNIONVILLE
Mary's Yarns
136 Main Street
Unionville, Ontario L3R 2G5
905-479-7833
Mary and her associate, Christine, made me feel completely at home when I was a shy new knitter. Now they know me and ask about my projects, and I always appreciate feeling part of a friendly community. Oh, and they have a great selection of yarns, too.
Maggie Simser

Quebec

MONTREAL
Magasin de Fibre L. B. Inc.
La Bobineuse de Laine
2270 Mont-Royal East
Montreal, Quebec H2H 1K6
514-521-9000
Here they sell yarn by the pound and they'll spool together a selection of different fibers from their vast assortment for you. The staff is really warm and the prices are super-cheap.
Alanna Lynch

Yarn Suppliers

ANNY BLATT
Rue de la Concorde
84107 ORANGE
Cedex FRANCE
+33 4 90 11 80 88
www.annyblatt.com

AUSTERMANN VERTRIEBS-GMBH
(Distributes Austermann)
Bühlstrasse 14
D-73079 Süssen
Germany
Tel: +49 7162 9603 0
Fax: +49 7162 9603 10
www.austermann-wolle.de

BERROCO, INC.
P.O. Box 367
14 Elmdale Road
Uxbridge, MA 01569-0367
508-278-2527
www.berroco.com

BLUE SKY ALPACAS, INC.
P.O. Box 387
St. Francis, MN 55070
888-460-8862
www.blueskyalpacas.com

BROWN SHEEP YARN COMPANY
100662 County Road 16
Mitchell, NE 69357
www.brownsheep.com

CARON INTERNATIONAL
P.O. Box 222
Washington, NC 27889
www.caron.com

CASCADE
P.O. Box 58168
Tukwila, WA 98138
800-548-1048
www.cascadeyarns.com

COATS & CLARK
(Distributes Red Heart)
P.O. Box 12229
Greenville, SC 29612-0229
800-648-1479
www.coatsandclark.com

CRYSTAL PALACE
2320 Bissell Avenue
Richmond, CA 94804
510-237-9988

HARRISVILLE DESIGNS
Center Village
P.O. Box 806
Harrisville, NH 03450
603-827-3333
800-338-9415
www.harrisville.com

KARABELLA YARNS
1201 Broadway
New York, NY 10001
800-550-0898
www.karabellayarns.com

KNITTING FEVER, INC.
(Distributes Katia, Noro, Debbie Bliss)
35 Debevoise Avenue
Roosevelt, NY 11575
www.knittingfever.com

LION BRAND YARN
34 West 15th Street
New York, NY 10011
800-258-YARN
www.lionbrand.com

MUENCH YARNS, INC.
(Distributes GGH)
285 Bel Marin Keys
Boulevard #8
Novato, CA 94949
www.muenchyarns.com

PATONS
P.O. Box 40
Listowel, ON N4W 3H3
Canada
www.patonsyarns.com

TAHKI STACY CHARLES, INC.
8000 Cooper Avenue
Building 1
Glendale, NY 11385
800-338-YARN

TRENDSETTER YARNS
16745 Saticoy Street #101
Van Nuys, CA 91406
818-780-5497

UNIQUE KOLOURS
(Distributes Colinette)
1428 Oak Lane
Downington, PA 19335
800-25-2DYE4

WESTMINSTER FIBERS
(Distributes Rowan)
4 Townsend West, Unit 8
Nashua, NH 03063
www.knitrowan.com

NOTIONS, ETC.

BEAD DINER
www.beaddiner.com

INCOMPARABLE BUTTONS
1307 Commonwealth
Avenue, #8
Allston, MA 02134
617-787-6099
www.buttonmad.com

M & J TRIMMING AND M & J BUTTONS
1000 and 1008 Avenue of
the Americas
New York, NY 10018
1-800-9MJ-TRIM
www.mjtrim.com

Index

A

Abbreviations used in knitting patterns, 14–15

Accessories
The Bead Goes On wrist cuffs, 182–184
Belt de Jour, 200–202
Felted Furry Footwarmers, 192–195
Hurry Up Spring Armwarmers, 196–199
Later 'Gator Mitts, 71–73
Mobile Monsters cell phone, 230–233
Quick and Dirty fishnet stockings, 136–138
Roller Girl Legwarmers, 186–188
Valentine's Hat and Mittens, 54–57
see also automobile accessories; bags and totes; hats; home accessories; pet accessories; scarves

Accidentally on Purpose: Drop Stitch Vest, 144–147

Adorno, Jenna, 122–125, 132–135, 221

Airplanes, knitting tools on, 181

Alexander, Adina, 40–43

Alphabet letter charts, 161–163

Ameron, Michelle, 226–229

Arizona knitting group, 131

Armwarmers, Hurry Up Spring, 196–199

Australia knitting group, 244–245

Automobile accessories, fuzzy dice and steering wheel cover, 240–242

B

Babies, knits for
Bunny Hat, 212–215
Li'l Devil Pants, 204–207
One-Hour Baby Booties, 216–218

Baby's First Tattoo sweater, 208–211

Bags and totes
Candy Stripers: Messenger and Laptop Bags, 152–156
Going Out with a Bag, 178–180
Letter Have It, 158–163
Om Yoga Mat Bag, 168–170
Poster Boy bag, 164–167
Saucy Tote, 174–177

Bag sealers, as yarn holders, 57

Bam 13 sweater, 118–121

Barbazette, Leslie, 174–177

Bar increase (inc1), 258

Barker, Amy, 250–252

Basic Cable hat, 74–76

Bateman, Kathy, 51–53

Baumer, Karen, 246–249

The Bead Goes On wrist cuffs, 182–184

Beads, knitting with, 178, 179, 182, 184

Belt de Jour, 200–202

Binding off (BO), 258
with crochet hook, 113
with larger needle, 113
three needle bind-off, 263
tidier last stitch, 239

Black Licorice Hat, 74–76

Blanket stitch, 264

Blocker for socks, 138

Body measurements, 20, 23

Boob tube or miniskirt, 148–151

Booties, One-Hour Baby, 216–218

Bunny Hat, 212–215

Butterflies Are Free scarf, 40–43

Bzzz Hat for Queen Bees, 44–46

C

Cable cast-on (CO), 255

Cabled Newsboy Cap, 66–69

Cables, 66, 201, 266
basic, 74–75
vines and leaves, 198

California knitting groups, 189–191

Canada knitting group, 245

Candy Stripers: Messenger and Laptop Bags, 152–156

Capelet, Spiderweb, 110–112

Caratzas, Nicholas, 37–38

Carroll, M. K., 59–62, 230–233

Casey's Coat, 222–225

Casting on (CO)
cable cast-on, 255
double cast-on, 254
with larger needle, 113
single cast-on, 255

Catwarming Set, 226–229

Cell phone cozies, 230–233

Chain stitch, 267

Chicago knitting group, 172

Chill Pillows, 246–249

Chopsticks, making knitting needles from, 203

Chupick, Jamie, 144–147

Circular needles
accurate gauge for, 124

Circular needles (*continued*)
  changing patterns to, 101
  labeling, 43
  making I-cord on, 161
  tips for working with, 150
  using as stitch holder, 188
Clover Lace Wrap sweater, 102–106
Coleman, Georgia A., 158–163
Collins, Carrie, 200–202
Colorado knitting groups, 130–131
Color changes in ribbing, 215
Color charts
  coffee, tea, or me, 252
  8-ball, 252
  Fair Isle, 84
  flames, 80–81
  heart, 56
  initials, 161–163
  mud flap girl, 134
  polka dots, 143
  poster boy, 167
  skull, 211
  star, 211
  swallow, 211
  United Kingdom flag, 95
Connecticut knitting groups, 47–48
Continental (left-hand) method
  knit stitch, 256
  purl stitch, 257
Crab stitch, 268
Craft Yarn Council, 11, 19
Crew necks, 26–27
Crochet hook, binding off with, 113
Crochet stitches, 267–268

D

Decreases
  adapting patterns and, 7–10, 18

knit two together (k2tog), 259
slip, knit, pass slipped stitch over (skp), 260
slip, slip, knit (ssk), 260
  tip for ssk decrease, 135
  see also binding off (BO)
Depue, Peggy, 222–225
Dewey, Rebecca, 240–242
Diagonal lace stitch, 169
Dixon, Heather, 54–57, 152–156
Dog sweater, Casey's Coat, 222–225
Dolls, Knit Your Own Rock Star, 234–239
Double cast-on, 254
Double-pointed needles, as stitch holder, 188
Drop shoulder sweaters, 22
Drop stitch, 34, 36, 144–146
Duplicate stitch, 265
Dyeing yarn with Kool-Aid, 219

E

Earwarmers, 59–62
Ease, 19–20
Edges, altering, 28–29
Embellishments
  beads, 178, 179, 182, 184
  butterflies, 40–43
  devil's tail, 206
  felted flower, 99–100
  flowers and leaves, 61–62
England knitting group, 243–244
English (right-hand) method
  knit stitch, 256
  purl stitch, 257
Excel, making knitting graph paper in, 30

F

Fairchild, Kimberly, 126–129
Fair Isle, 266

adding or changing designs, 29
  Fairly Easy Fair Isle cardigan, 82–85
  Poster Boy bag, 164–167
Fairly Easy Fair Isle cardigan, 82–85
Fake grafting, 262
Felted Furry Footwarmers, 192–195
Felted projects
  Candy Stripers: Messenger and Laptop Bags, 152–156
  Felted Furry Footwarmers, 192–195
  Flower Power sweater, 99
  Letter Have It bag, 158–163
Felting instructions, 99, 157
Fischer, April, 78–81
Fitted sleeves, 22
Flower Power sweater, 96–100
Fringes, 264
Fuzzy dice and steering wheel cover, 240–242

G

Gauge, 6–7
  circular knitting and, 124
  substituting yarns and, 10–18
Going Out with a Bag, 178–180
Grutzeck, Laura, 71–73

H

Hackner, Angela, 234–239
Halter top, 126–129
Hats
  Basic Cable, 74–76
  Black Licorice Hat, 74–76
  Bunny Hat, 212–215
  Bzzz Hat for Queen Bees, 44–46
  Cabled Newsboy Cap, 66–69
  Head Hugger earwarmer, 59–62
  Jellybean Hat, 74–76

knitted liner for, 46
Russian Winter, 51–53
Valentine's Hat and Mittens, 54–57
Head Huggers: Neckwarmer and
 Earwarmer, 59–62
Hemmed edges, 28–29
Henry Rollins doll, 234–239
Home accessories
 Chill Pillows, 246–249
 Two for Tea teapot cozy, 250–252
Howard, Hannah, 92–95
Hurry Up Spring Armwarmers, 196–199

I

I-cord, 161, 264
Illinois knitting group, 172
Increases
 adapting patterns and, 7–10, 18
 bar increase (inc1), 258
 make one increase (m1), 259
 yarn over (yo), 259
Initial charts, 161–163
Intarsia
 adding or changing designs, 29
 Baby's First Tattoo sweater, 208–211
 changing colors, 267
 Itsy-Bitsy Teeny-Weeny Purple Polka-Dot
  Tankini, 140–143
 Jesse's Flames sweater, 78–81
 Letter Have It bag, 158–163
 London Calling sweater, 92–95
 Mud Flap Girl Tank Top, 132–135
 Two for Tea teapot cozy, 250–252
 yarn handling tip, 237
Iowa knitting group, 171–172
Itchy yarn, 46
Itsy-Bitsy Teeny-Weeny Purple Polka-Dot
 Tankini, 140–143

J

Japan knitting group, 245
Japel, Stefanie, 148–151
Jellybean Hat, 74–76
Jesse's Flames sweater, 78–81
Joan Jett doll, 234–239
Joey Ramone doll, 234–239
Joining yarn with spit-splice method, 199

K

Kentucky knitting group, 108–109
Kitchener stitch, 262
Knit My Ride fuzzy dice and steering wheel
 cover, 240–242
Knit stitch (k), 256
Knitting graph paper, 29, 30
Knitting groups, 33
 beyond the borders, 243–245
 California, 189–191
 Mid-Atlantic, 89–91
 Midwest, 171–173
 New England, 47–49
 New York, 63–65
 Northwest, 220–221
 South, 107–109
 Southwest, 130–131
Knitting two pieces at the same time, 85
Knit two together (k2tog), 259
Knit Your Own Rock Star, 234–239
Kool-Aid, dyeing yarn with, 219

L

Lace
 Clover Lace Wrap sweater, 102–106
 Om Yoga Mat Bag, 168–170
 Razor's Edge poncho, 86–88
 Spiderweb Capelet, 110–112
 tips, 112
 Totally Tubular miniskirt or boob tube,
  148–151
Ladd, Renee, 182–184
Lam, Delia, 208–211
Laptop bag, 152–156
Later 'Gator Mitts, 71–73
Laura-Jean, the Knitting Queen, 96–100
Left-hand (Continental) method
 knit stitch, 256
 purl stitch, 257
Legwarmers, Roller Girl, 186–188
Letter Have It bag, 158–163
Li'l Devil Pants, 204–207
London Calling sweater, 92–95
Loop stitch, 246
Love sweaters, curse of, 120

M

Magic Formula to space increases and
 decreases evenly along a diagonal, 18
Maine knitting groups, 48–49
Make one increase (m1), 259
Margulies, Ellen R., 34–36
Maryland knitting groups, 89–90
Massachusetts knitting group, 47
Mattress stitch, 261
McGowan-Michael, Joan, 136–138
Mesa, Nilda, 86–88
Messenger bag, 152–156
Miniskirt or boob tube, 148–151
Mistakes
 lace unraveling tip, 112
 learning from, 29–30
 tips for, 129
Mittens
 Later 'Gator Mitts, 71–73
 Valentine's Hat and Mittens, 54–57

Mobile Monsters, 230–233
Mom's Sophisticated Scarf, 37–38
Mouse toys, 226–229
Mrse, Stephanie, 168–170
Mud Flap Girl Tank Top, 132–135
Muller, Trinity, 178–180

N

Necklines, 26–28
Neckwarmer, 59–62
Needles
    on airplanes, 181
    different colors of, for right and wrong
        side of work, 170
    keeping stitches on, 224
    making from chopsticks, 203
    organizing, 43
    as stitch holders, 188
    tips for working with circular, 150
Neth, Marcy, 204–207
Neurauter, Heidi, 216–218
New Jersey knitting group, 90–91
New York knitting groups, 63–65
North Carolina knitting groups, 107–108,
    109
Nostepinnes, 77
Nubble stitch, 249

O

Ohio knitting groups, 171, 173
Om Yoga Mat Bag, 168–170
One-Hour Baby Booties, 216–218
Oregon knitting group, 220–221

P

Patterns
    altering for circular needles, 101

altering to fit, 18–29
calculating gauge, 6–7
following, 33
importance of understanding, 5–6
increases and decreases, 7–10, 18
organizing, 43
repeats in, 14–15, 33
sizes, 18–20, 33
substituting different gauge yarns, 13–17
substituting same gauge yarns, 10–13
    see also accessories; automobile acces-
        sories; baby stuff; bags and totes; hats;
        home accessories; scarves; summer
        stuff; sweater patterns
Pennsylvania knitting group, 91
Pet accessories
    Casey's Coat, 222–225
    Catwarming Set, 226–229
Picking up stitches, 263
Picot edge, 29
Pillows, Chill, 246–249
Planes, knitting tools on, 181
Pom-poms, 265
Ponchos. *See* shawls and ponchos
Poster Boy bag, 164–167
Pre-knitual agreement, 120
Purl stitch (p), 257

Q

Quick and Dirty fishnet stockings,
    136–138
Quirion, Christine, 74–76

R

Raglan sweaters, 22
Razor's Edge poncho, 86–88
Repeats, 14–15, 33

Ribbing
    bottom and sleeve edges, 28
    color changes in, 215
    sweater waistline shaping, 27
Rigdon, Renee, 196–199
Right-hand (English) method
    knit stitch, 256
    purl stitch, 257
Rolled edge, 28
Roller Girl Legwarmers, 186–188
Roll necks, 27
Ross, Share, 118–121
Rows per inch, 6–7
Rulers, impromptu, 117
Russ, Rachael, 36–37
Russian Winter hats, 51–53

S

Sample cards, 177
Sargent, Zoe, 140–143
Saucy Tote, 174–177
Scarves
    Mom's Sophisticated Scarf, 37–38
    Warm Fuzzies, 39
    Wavy Gravy, 36–37
    Yo, Drop It!, 34–36
Scoles, Melanie, 114–117
Scoop necks, 27
Scotland knitting group, 243
Seams
    sewing, 261–262
    tip for perfect, 105
Sexie halter top, 126–129
Shawls and ponchos
    Razor's Edge, 86–88
    Spiderweb Capelet, 110–112
    That Seventies Poncho, 114–117

Single cast-on (CO), 255
Single crochet (sc), 268
Size standards, 18–19, 20
Sleeves
    altering patterns for different gauge yarn, 17–18
    changing length of, 24, 26
    edges, 28–29
    spacing increases and decreases, 18
    types of, 21–22
Slip, knit, pass slipped stitch over (skp), 260
Slip, slip, knit (ssk), 260
Slip knot, 254
Slippers, Felted Furry Footwarmers, 192–195
Socks
    blocker for, 138
    Quick and Dirty fishnet stockings, 136–138
Spiderweb Capelet, 110–112
Spit-splice method of joining yarn, 199
Standard body measurements, 20
Standard Yarn Weight System, 12
Stash sample cards, 177
Steering wheel cover, 240–242
Stitches
    blanket stitch, 264
    cable, 66, 74–75, 198, 201, 266
    cable cast-on (CO), 255
    chain stitch, 267
    clover lace, 103
    Continental (left-hand) knit stitch, 256
    Continental (left-hand) purl stitch, 257
    crab stitch, 268
    crochet stitches, 267–268
    diagonal lace stitch, 169
    double cast-on (CO), 254
    drop stitch, 34, 36, 144–146

duplicate stitch, 265
English (right-hand) knit stitch, 256
English (right-hand) purl stitch, 257
Fair Isle, 266
fake grafting, 262
horizontal herringbone stitch, 152
I-cord, 161, 264
intarsia, 267
Kitchener stitch, 262
knit stitch (k), 256
knitting with beads, 182, 184
knit two together (k2tog), 259
lace, 86, 103, 110–112, 148, 169
loop stitch, 246
make one increase (m1), 259
mattress stitch, 261
nubble, 249
picking up stitches, 263
picot edge, 29
purl stitch (p), 69, 257
Razor's Edge lace, 86
single cast-on (CO), 255
single crochet (sc), 268
slip, knit, pass slipped stitch over (skp), 260
slip, slip, knit (ssk), 260
slip knot, 254
spiderweb lace, 110–112
three-needle bind-off, 263
tips for counting, 53
windowpane stitch, 137
Wrap and turn (W&T), 118, 193, 212
yarn over (yo), 259
Stitches per inch, 6–7
Stitch holders, double-pointed and circular needles as, 188
Stitch markers, tips for improvising, 146
Stitch 'n Bitch groups. See knitting groups

Stoller, Debbie, 164–167
Storage tips, 43
String toy, 226–229
Summer knits
    Accidentally on Purpose: Drop Stitch Vest, 144–147
    Itsy-Bitsy Teeny-Weeny Purple Polka-Dot Tankini, 140–143
    Mud Flap Girl Tank Top, 132–135
    Quick and Dirty fishnet stockings, 136–138
    Sexie halter top, 126–129
    Totally Tubular miniskirt or boob tube, 148–151
    Ultra Femme sweater, 122–125
Swatches, 12–13, 33, 124
Sweater patterns
    Baby's First Tattoo, 208–211
    Bam 13, 118–121
    Clover Lace Wrap, 102–106
    Fairly Easy Fair Isle, 82–85
    Flower Power, 96–100
    Jesse's Flames, 78–81
    London Calling, 92–95
    Ultra Femme, 122–125
Sweaters, knitting and fitting basic shapes, 21–22
    bottom and sleeve edges, 28–29
    changing length of, 24
    curse of the love sweater, 120
    ease dimensions, 19–20
    neckline changes, 26–28
    recycling yarn from, 185
    size standards, 18–19, 20
    sleeve length alteration, 24, 26
    substituting yarns of different gauge, 13–18
    substituting yarns of same gauge, 10–13

Sweaters, knitting and fitting basic shapes (*continued*)
understanding patterns, 7–10
using measurements from favorite, 20–21
waist shaping, 25, 27
Swenson, Amy, 192–195
Swimsuit, Itsy-Bitsy Teeny-Weeny Purple Polka-Dot Tankini, 140–143

T

Tankini, 140–143
Tank top, 132–135
Tape measures, impromptu, 117
Tea cozy, 250–252
Texas knitting groups, 107, 108
That Seventies Poncho, 114–117
Three-needle bind-off, 263
Totally Tubular miniskirt or boob tube, 148–151
Totes. *See* bags and totes
Truesdale, Traci, 186–188
Turtlenecks, 27
Two for Tea teapot cozy, 250–252

U

Ultra Femme sweater, 122–125
Unraveled yarn, removing kinks from, 155
Utah knitting group, 131

V

Valentine's Hat and Mittens, 54–57
Vest, 144–147
Virginia knitting group, 89
V-necks, 27–28

W

Waist shaping, 25, 27
Wales knitting group, 244
Warm Fuzzies scarf, 39
Washington, D. C., knitting group, 91
Washington knitting groups, 220, 221
Watson, Kate, 82–85
Wavy Gravy scarf, 36–37
Weckerle, Erin, 110–112
Wherle, Melissa, 102–106
Williams-Alleyne, Shannita, 66–69
Windowpane stitch, 137
Wire hanger sock blocker, 138
Wolfe, Anne, 44–46
Wrap and turn (W&T) stitch, 118, 193, 212
Wrist cuffs, The Bead Goes On, 182–184
W&T (wrap and turn), 118, 193, 212

Y

Yarn
calculating amount needed, 13
determining length to finish another row, 237
dyeing with Kool-Aid, 219
evaluating personality of, 13
joining with spit-splice method, 199
keeping balls and cones under control, 225
method of holding to maintain even tension, 248
natural fibers, understanding behavior of, 94
organizing, 43
recycling thrift-store sweaters, 185
removing kinks from unraveled, 155
saving ball bands from, 229
standard weight system, 12
stash sample cards, 177
substituting different gauge, 13–17
substituting same gauge, 10–13
test for itchiness, 46
winding tip, 194
Yarn bras, making your own, 73
Yarn holder, bag sealers used for, 57
Yarn over (yo), 259
Yarn stores, 270–281
Yarn suppliers, 282
Yarn winding tool (nostepinne), 77
Yo, Drop It! scarf, 34–36
Yoga Mat Bag, 168–170

Credits

Fashion photography: Karen Pearson

Styling: Ellen Silverstein

Hair and makeup: Amy Schiappa

Cover photograph: Karen Pearson

Cowgirl cover art: Enoch Bolles

Miscellaneous spot photography: Michael Fusco

Additional photos, pages 209, 217: Dietrich Gehring

FASHION CREDITS Page 40: dress and jacket—Screaming Mimi's; pages 50 and 52: jackets—Free People; pages 55 and 56: jacket—Paul & Joe for Simon; pages 58–60: dresses—courtesy Victoria Escalle; page 74: sweater—courtesy Victoria Escalle; pages 87 and 88: turtleneck—Twinkle for Steven Alan; page 102: hat— Lola, skirt—courtesy Victoria Escalle, tank top—Free People; page 106: skirt—Free People; page 148: left, socks—Ralph Lauren, right, skirt and tank top—Free People; page 150: skirt and tank top—Free People; page 160: chevron sweater—Twinkle for Steven Alan; page 164: suit—Free People, shoes—courtesy Victoria Escalle; page 174: dress—courtesy Victoria Escalle; pages 179 and 180: left, dress—Twinkle for Steven Alan; pages 186–188: dress and shoes—courtesy Victoria Escalle; page 192: pajamas—Tepper Johnson; page 197: shirt—Free People; pages 200 and 202: green sweater—Paul & Joe for Simon, green plaid skirt—Free People, multicolored striped skirts—Screaming Mimi's; pages 204–205: shirt—Space kiddets; page 215: jacket and sweater—Natalie & Friends; page 232: dresses—courtesy Victoria Escalle.

Author's Note

Each of the patterns in *Stitch 'n Bitch Nation* has been checked by not one but two technical editors. However, despite our best efforts, sometimes errors will occur. Please check my Web site, www.knithappens.com, for the most current list of corrections. Should you have a question about a pattern or discover a mistake, please e-mail me at stitchnbitch@bust.com, and let me know.

Knitting Notes

Knitting Notes

Knitting Notes

Knitting Notes

Knitting Notes

About the Author

ebbie Stoller was born in Brooklyn, New York, to an American father and a Dutch mother. She spent many summers in Holland, surrounded by knitters, including her mother, her aunt, her grandmother, and many great-aunts. In high school, Debbie was the geek who sewed all the costumes for the school play, and secretly enjoyed an even geekier hobby: counted cross-stitch. But knitting was not a passion—in fact, for many years she pretty much hated it. Following two and a half miserable years at a state college that shall remain unnamed, Debbie lived in Holland for six months, then started graduate school at Yale University, where she spent the next six years studying the psychology of women, earning her Ph.D., and not knitting at all. Upon graduation she did what many Ph.D.s do—she became a secretary, and after a number of directionless years as a low-level cubicle slave, Debbie started the third-wave feminist 'zine *BUST* with a couple of girlfriends. Soon the magazine grew and spawned a book: *The BUST Guide to the New Girl Order* (1999, Penguin), of which she is co-editor. It was while promoting this book that Debbie tried knitting again, and actually ended up liking it. Today Debbie is the co-publisher of *BUST,* together with Laurie Henzel, and serves as its editor-in-chief. She is also the author of *Stitch 'n Bitch: The Knitter's Handbook* (2003, Workman Publishing). She lives in Brooklyn with her dog, Shadow, and a giant yarn collection. In addition to knitting and publishing her magazine, she enjoys bird-watching, gardening, and other nerdy pastimes.